Weeknights with Alice

For Nick, who makes weeknights,
weekdays and weekends wonderful.
And always does the washing up.

Smart, speedy dinners,
starting with the veg

Weeknights with Alice

Alice Zaslavsky

murdoch books
Sydney | London

Orange

Red

Purple

Brown

Dark Green

Light Green

Yellow

White

From Scratch

Well, hello there!

What do weeknights look like at your place?

This question is a common ice-breaker for me ... except it's often met with some version of 'harumph' – not exactly the kind of sparky response that inspires confidence. But fear not: THIS is the book to help you find that spark. To inspire you to try something new for dinner tonight that might just become a go-to at your place forever.

Go-to meals are always a moveable feast. As I write more books, I realise that each volume is a time capsule, not only of how my baby's hands have expanded but also of where my attention lies, who I'm spending my time with and what I'm focusing on. These days, life is quite terrestrial, and I spend most mornings and afternoons at school drop-off and pick-up. And while we stand huddled together, the conversation invariably turns to what's for tea (or dinner, depending who I'm asking!). Which is how I've noticed that the instinct for most people when that question is asked is to grimace or groan or shrug. Whether it's time-pressures, finicky tastes, competing dietaries, or a general lack of inspiration, this persistent pinch-point proves a right old pain in the tuchus for many. Let me get that for you.

All cooking, particularly midweek, is based on a hierarchy of needs – and each household's hierarchy hinges on their priorities. Some need more accessibility of ingredients, others have mobility needs, others want to save on washing up, others don't care because someone's doing the washing up for them ... and if you're beyond all of that, time is a big priority for all.

That's why you'll find handy timing guides included with each recipe: **chop + stir**, which refers to the active time each recipe requires at the chopping board and the stove, along with **set + forget**, where you can set a timer and get on with other weeknight jobs, or even get a headstart on tomorrow's dinner by sweating some onions, picking herbs, spinning greens, or flipping through the book to work out which page to dog-ear next (lived-in copies, along with annotations and passata spatters, are always my favourite).

For busy heads and hands, I've broken the recipes up into steps with sticky, punny subheadings to help you pick up where you left off more quickly, and absorb your favourites onto autopilot too.

Double duty tips abound, to give you clever twists on what's left over and speed up tomorrow's lunch or dinner too.

Maybe you're just not sure what you're in the mood for? Well, have I got something to show you on page 24!

Every recipe starts with the veg, so you can follow the seasons and/or use up what's in your crisper, mine the surplus-laden bins at the shops for what's tasting – and nourishing – best when Mother Nature has it in abundance, and support your local growers and grocers. Because the veg forms the bulk of these recipes, with the animal (or plant) protein as the cherry on top instead of the main event, you'll find they're hip-pocket friendly too.

If you've ever felt overwhelmed by nutritional advice, here is an easy message to digest: make the focus loading up your diet with colour and variety.

We continue to discover more about the phytonutrients and bioactives contained within each unique hue. And it's an easy remit for me to deliver on because more veg always means more colour!

On the protein front, I've prioritised a lot of mince (whether that's meat, tofu or even mushroom), along with sustainably caught fish and seafood that's quick to cook or even comes out of a tin. If it's a recipe of the flexitarian variety, I'll provide you with planty substitutions.

I've also suggested seasonal subs for the veg where appropriate, but you're welcome to try your hand at switcheroo, swapping in other veg with similar characteristics such as fibrousness or cooking time. These recipes are designed to be as easy and intuitive as possible, with smart twists and hacks that simplify processes (and lean on processors!) and save on washing up as well.

I've tried to stick to **staple ingredients and condiments** you probably already have in your pantry and fridge (see pages 15–21), with full permission to use shop-bought pastes and sauces (or **foolproof 'make your own' options** on pages 211–29), along with prompts to use gadgets and cookware that help speed things along without stacking up the space by your sink. Speaking of space! On pages 9–13, you'll find what's worth yours for weeknight wonders.

The wonder of weeknights, ultimately, is that you have five or so nights a week to switch off from the day, to tune out of the hustle and bustle, and tune in instead to the sizzle and pop in the pan. You can fall for the foamy butter, relax with the onions as they sweat, deepen your breath as the garlic releases its aroma.

Creativity is a muscle, and flexing it, unconditionally, with such low stakes as dinner for four (or less, or more), is a handy way of building on what you've already got. Learning to go with the flow, to take shortcuts, to lean in to the imperfections of a rough chop – they're the kinds of lessons you can subconsciously store away and share with anyone who's up for helping in the kitchen.

And on that, if you're reading this in the throes of a family food journey, or with an averse adult eater or two in your midst, allow me to share some advice, as someone who's just made it to triple digits of a telly program designed to encourage people to try new ingredients, or learn to love those they've resented before: their help matters most! Touching the food before they eat it will lead to a higher likelihood of trying (unprompted is important!) – and serving meals 'family style' means they feel a sense of agency for what they choose to try. You'll notice that many of the dishes in this book are made in this style, for this very reason – and because it means the cook gets to sit down faster too.

Finding your midweek mojo won't happen overnight. I will be the first to tell you that there are weeknights where I experience foodtigue and our day ends with hot chook and roasted veg tossed through leafy greens, or steamed frozen dumplings in shop-bought broth with blanched greens. But really it's no biggie – because there's always tomorrow night to find a new lease on life, with this book on your kitchen bench beckoning our next adventure.

Cheerio!

Go-to Gadgets for Midweek Magic

When expediency is essential, gadgets and tools are your friends. But time and space are both considerations in a modern kitchen. So, if you'll allow me my own theory of relativity (I hope Einstein, who was enough of a foodie to joke that adding an egg to soup was his second greatest idea, won't mind either), your gadget-drawer contents should be relative *to what you cook the most.*

Since this is a book for veg-cooks, not bakers, I've included my go-to gadgets for a veg-forward kitchen here – and you're welcome to crib from the glorious pic of very well-loved tools over the page.

Before I get into the fidgety bits, let's talk about appliances.

Oven → I've tested the recipes in this book across multiple ovens, all using the fan-forced setting. If yours is a conventional oven, increase the temperature by 10–20°C (50–70°F), depending on how hot your oven runs. For midweek, I'd suggest you go up the full 20°C (70°F), but check on your veg 10 minutes early. My oven is 60 cm (24 inches) wide, and the oven trays (sometimes referred to as baking trays) I use are the ones that come with the oven, so they're as wide as the racks will allow. If your oven or trays are narrower, you may need to use two trays.

Microwave → Once the domain of dreary diet cookery, the microwave is back, baby! Modern micros are multicookers, which means I can also incorporate an air-fry component into this conversation to satisfy the evangelists without endorsing a piece of tech I'm yet to personally embrace. Microwaves make fast work of veg, tenderising eggplant (aubergines) and sweet potatoes, steaming corn and softening breads – let alone reheating last night's dinner into tonight's. Combi settings help to keep things moist while crisping the outside. It's a brave new world for faster midweek cookery and I'm trés here for it.

Rice cooker → It may seem like one of those appliances that's going to take up valuable cupboard or bench space, but once you've tried the tender fluffiness of rice-cooker rice, it's much easier to justify the real estate. Look for bonus features like steaming inserts to do your veg at the same time, and don't forget that these machines are designed to cook any grain – whether that's buckwheat or barley – to perfection too.

Food processor → For speedy blitzing and grating, a food processor is a big plus. For a mid-sized household, a two-to-three bowl processor is a good option, so you can do everything from pesto to a full slaw. Choose machines with long warranties and not too many niggly parts. If you're picking between a processor and a blender, I'd say a processor and a stick blender are the best bang for buck.

Stick blender → Otherwise known as an immersion blender, this is your quickest pathway to smooth veg soups and purées. It pays to invest in one with a metal wand rather than a plastic one, so you don't have to wait for the pot to cool down before blitzing.

SOFFRITTO

Now to plug some tools that don't need plugging in ...

Scales (ideally digital) → When it comes to speedy measuring, a set of digital scales is ace. They're relatively inexpensive these days, and will earn their keep when you're making up spice mixes and pastes, measuring stocks and condiments and, less relevant to our application but no less relevant to ROI, baking!

Timer → If time management gets you in a tizz, make like a *MasterChef* contestant and get around the kitchen timer! Now, you've probably already got one in the back of the cutlery drawer, but if *that's* not forthcoming, you're probably already staring at one without even realising it ... your smartphone! Make a habit of setting the timer before you step away from the cooktop or oven, whether it's manually tapping into the clock app and scrolling across, or asking Siri to do it for you. Try it now: 'Hey Siri, set a timer for 4 minutes' (about the time it'll take to finish reading this section). Magic!

The biggest bowl you can find → All of my stuff fits inside this one bowl, which is a catering size from a local hospitality shop. The largest size that will fit into your deepest drawer or cabinet is what you're looking for, to see you through tossing big portions of veg for roasting, dressing salads properly, and one-tray marinating.

Salad spinner → At the risk of sounding like a broken record, get thee a thpinnery! A salad spinner living in your giant mixing bowl can and *will* prompt you to turn over a new leaf when it comes to living the salad life. I'd recommend buying one that can fit in your cupboard and your fridge so you can soak, chill, then spin as you need. You'll notice I pick herbs into a spinner, tear lettuce straight in. Even leeks and choys (pak, bok, etc) benefit from soaking and spinning before cooking. If you're *still* unconvinced, soak your veg in a bowl, then use a tea towel (dish towel) spun above the head outside. A few months of this will hopefully tip you over.

Chef's knife → A chef's knife with a 20–24 cm (8–9½ in) long blade will make swift work of most kitchen jobs. You can buy a quality chef's knife at kitchenware shops, or splash out in a specialty knife shop if you're ready to invest. These knives tend to fall into two categories: German-style (single sheet of metal, heavier blade) or Japanese style (layers of metal, finer blade). German knives are sturdy but heavy, and those who do a lot of meat-work (big cuts of beef and the like) stick with the German-style brands like Wusthof and Zwilling. The Japanese knives are pricier, but I prefer them because I do a lot of finicky veg work and use them to fillet my fish too.

Regardless of how much yours cost, or where it's from, the most important thing is that it's sharp! Before you fork out for a new chef's knife, check whether yours could just use a good sharpen. Even if you've got a knife sharpener at home, a professional sharpen once a year (or, let's face it, once in a blue moon!) will make your slicing experience much more enjoyable and LESS likely to result in injury. If you've been keeping your knife blunt to prevent cutting yourself, remember that blunt knife blades can bounce off an ingredient, while sharp knife blades actually *slice* – so a sharp knife is always safer than a blunt one! You can drop your knives off to some kitchenware shops or locksmiths – or, type your suburb and 'knife sharpening' into a search engine and you could even find a local mobile one that comes to you.

Serrated (bread) knife → Soft things like bread and roasted things like pumpkin chunks are best sliced with a serrated knife to ensure even cutting (rather than squashing). There's no need to go all-out on these, and their irregular use means they won't need sharpening as often either. I've had the same Shun serrated bread knife for 15-odd years, and it's still doing its thing. Serrated knives are NOT to be used for hard things – they're more 'bitey' than chef's knives, so proceed with caution when there's any chance of slippage.

Paring knife (or two) → These are my favourite little worker bees in the kitchen, and they should only set you back a few bucks. Victorinox and Opinel are the brands to go for. I have flat-bladed ones with a pointy end for fine carving, and small serrated ones for slicing up cherry tomatoes and the like.

Julienne peeler → If you want to circumvent fine knifework midweek, a julienne peeler or slicer is a terrific hack. Savannah is a brand I've found to be very reliable, whether I'm grating carrots for a slaw, or zipping strips off my zucchini (courgettes) for zoodling. You'll find great julienne slicers at East Asian grocers and specialty stores, and they'll set you back less than 10 smackaroos, so it pays to grab both a finer and coarser blade if you can.

Mandoline/V-slicer → PROCEED WITH CAUTION! But it would be remiss of me not to include a mandoline, considering how swiftly you can slice through a cabbage or an onion with one of these vegetable guillotines. Pick a V-slicer with a stainless steel blade and a guard – and now I'm gonna go all Yoda on you for a second ... USE THE GUARD, LUKE!

Microplane → For zesting citrus and grating hard cheeses, a super-fine grater like a Microplane can't be beat. The one you really need is the fine grater, ideally stainless steel with a wooden handle, which will last you much longer than a plastic one. Because it's stainless, you can use the same tool for savouries and sweets, so nutmeg, garlic and even chocolate can all end up on the same fine grate.

Box grater → Any quality box grater (with as few separate fiddly parts as possible) is very useful. Even pulling your old one out of the cupboard and towards the front to remind you to use it might be the difference between dinner made and dinner ordered in.

Teaspoons + tablespoons → It's worth noting that I use Australian tablespoon measures, which are 20 ml (¾ fl oz), rather than the 15 ml (½ fl oz) tablespoons used elsewhere. Check yours and add an extra teaspoon (5 ml) per tablespoon if need be.

Garlic crusher → I'm not one of those purists who'll tell you not to use a garlic crusher. In fact, if it's what's standing between you and using that pongy stuff from a jar, crush away! A stainless steel crusher is what you want, both for ease of washing and because it won't corrode; a Dreamfarm 'Garject' is my pick. Be sure to wash your garlic crusher straight away after using – it's the sticky stuff in garlic that makes your crusher blocked up and harder to wash. When my recipe tells you to mince garlic, you can totally use the garlic crusher or a fine Microplane, or use the salt and knife rolling method. Even if a recipe says 'sliced garlic', I'd be cool with you mincing too.

Bench scraper → If I had a buck for every time someone asked me about the fancy paddle I use to sweep things off my chopping board and into bowls and pots, I'd have enough dollars to buy another board scraper! You can find them as pastry scrapers or even as wide paint scrapers at hardware shops, but you're really looking for one that's not got too sharp an edge. I bought mine as reclaimed wood and steel from MD Knives, and I can't see myself replacing it any time soon.

Wooden spatula/turner → A quality spatula with a flat edge is the safest and most reliable tool for stirring and flipping. I have many on rotation, but return to those with a flat, slightly tapered bottom because they're just so comfortable in the hand – like it's your fingers scooping the ingredients directly.

Pots → A set of stainless-steel pots with heavy bases in three different sizes are worth snapping up when they're on sale, along with a nice deep pasta pot.

Cast-iron pots are terrific for oven-to-table and can be bought second-hand and brought back to life with bicarbonate of soda (baking soda) and vinegar. I have a 28 cm (11¼ in) wide shallow casserole, and a deep soup pot measuring 26 cm (10½ in) across.

Pans → Look for pans with heavy bases for even heat distribution. You can turn any surface non-stick by lining it with baking paper once the pan is hot – you'll notice I do this for frying throughout the book, as it helps use less oil and doesn't leave half your golden crust on the bottom of the pan.

I use a 32 cm (12¾ in) wide shallow pan with high sides and a lid instead of a wok on my induction cooktop, and it works a treat.

P. Net: 50g
Net Wt.: 1.8 oz
P. Esc.:
P. Égoutté: 30g
Drained Wt. 1.1 oz
ANXOVES DE L'ESCALA S.A.
M. SUREDA
FILETS D'ANXOVA EN OLI D'OLIVA
FILETS D'ANCHOIS À L'HUILE D'OLIVE
ANCHOVY FILLETS IN OLIVE OIL
FILETS D'ANXOVA EN OLI D'OLIVA
FILETS D'ANCHOIS À L'HUILE D'OLIVE
ARMELIN
FAGIOLI ROSSI
400 g

Pantry Picks for Weeknight Wins

Here you'll find a list of everything you'll need to make the recipes in this book – and riff on a heck of a lot more. A pantry is a lot like a wardrobe – you tend to use the stuff at the front much more than the stuff that wallows at the back. This list is intentionally light-on, as I'd rather you load up on the staples you'll use all the time midweek, and work towards trying new things. That doesn't mean there isn't a place for that bottle of pomegranate molasses or baharat spice or furikake – which is why I've included the odd recipe in this book using these ingredients (in case you've been looking for a reason to use them up). But I always include substitutions so you don't have to head out for them if they're not already in your pantry.

You'll notice that some of the items below are fridge jobs, not pantry ones, but I hope you won't mind their inclusion – they're important! The non-negotiables are **underlined***, and the rest are 'nice to haves'.*

Fats + oils

Olive oil → For cooking, I buy a cheaper local olive oil in a drum and then decant into dark glass.

Extra virgin olive oil → I keep a smaller bottle of the good stuff for dressing and finishing (which is a fancy way of saying, 'flick some olive oil over the dish so it looks lush!).

Neutral oil → This is an oil with a high smoke point, meaning it can be heated to high temps without burning. It's good for frying with but doesn't have much flavour. I like grapeseed, rice bran and peanut oils.

Coconut oil → If you're using coconut milk or cream in a curry, coconut oil is always welcome. I prefer the oil that's solid at room temperature, then melts as soon as it hits the pan because it has a sweeter, richer flavour.

Roasted sesame oil → Some sesame oils can be quite bland, which is why I always seek out 'roasted' or 'toasted' on the label. The roasting process brings out a lovely nutty toastiness that rounds out dishes beautifully.

Butter → I keep a cheaper block of local butter in the fridge for cooking, then a higher-fat French butter in a butter bell at room temp for spreading on crusty bread. You're welcome to use the one type for both applications, of course.

Ghee → Otherwise known as clarified butter. You can buy ghee in a jar, or make your own by slowly melting a block of butter, then allowing it to set hard in the pot, turning it out and wiping off the milk solids (which will, ironically, remain liquid). The absence of milk solids means ghee can also be heated to a higher temperature than regular butter, but you can fake the effect by foaming butter together with oil to raise its smoke point while infusing extra flavour and richness into the dish.

Sour cream/crème fraiche → I use a lot of both for adding richness and tang to dishes. Sour cream is lighter than crème fraiche, and tends to have a more consistent texture, while crème fraiche is richer and more decadent. They can be used interchangeably here.

Acids + vinegars

White wine vinegar → Chardonnay vinegar is my holy grail for dressings. The brand I buy is Forum, which is sweeter than many on the market, but any quality white wine vin is a winner. Taste and add a pinch of sugar if you feel it needs it.

Red wine vinegar → This is great for adding zip to Mediterranean/Middle Eastern sauces and dressings ... but at a pinch you could use lemon juice instead.

Balsamic vinegar → A good balsamic will last you ages, and can be used for dressing and splashing. An aged balsamic for finishing and dipping is also a 'nice to have', of course, but you can fake the effect by reducing some cheaper balsamic with maple syrup or sugar until thickened.

Sherry vinegar → For Spanish dishes, for dressing and for glazing. PX is my fave. It's definitely a 'nice to have', as is **malt vinegar**, which is great for tomatoes on toast with a good crack of pepper.

Apple cider vinegar → This is a nice mid-strength vinegar for light dressing, and for sipping diluted as an elixir or a shrub.

Rice wine vinegar → This is the acid I'd use for any East Asian and South-East Asian dressings. If you're making a lot of Japanese dishes, **mirin** (sweet rice wine) is also very worthwhile.

Black vinegar → A Chinese vinegar for saucing and balancing. If you like steaming dumplings at home, the easiest sauce is one made with black vinegar and freshly grated ginger.

Shaoxing rice wine → This Chinese cooking wine adds sour–savoury depth to stir-fry sauces.

Lemons + limes → These always live in my fruit bowl. Of course, depending on the time of year, these can be so expensive at the shops ... plant a tree if you can, or make friends with green-thumbed neighbours.

Pickles + preserves

Dill pickles → Different to sour pickles, with more of a briney-herbaceous finish. My favourite brands are tinned and can be found in the kosher section at the supermarket.

Cornichons → Tiny pickles with a very tangy flavour. I like cutting them up finely for potato salads and serving on cheese boards. Also, standing by the fridge eating them straight from the jar.

Kimchi → Some kind of kimchi is always in my fridge, featuring in breakfast spreads, salad toppings and fried rice fillings.

Sauerkraut → Fresh kraut from the fridge section is much funkier than the shelf-stable kind, and it's my preference for flavour and gut-loving goodness.

Pickled ginger → Perfect for poke bowls and anytime you want to add pops of warmth and colour. The pickling liquor is terrific in dressings too.

Capers → These vary in size from lilliput to caperberry and provide pops of briny flavour and crunch. Fried capers become crispy and savoury, like vegan anchovies. A tops topping for pasta and salads.

Olives → Black kalamata and green Sicilian are my faves. I buy them locally grown, with the pit still in for structural integrity, then squash and pop the pips before roughly chopping or keeping whole for chunky sauces.

Narcissus
Rice Vinegar
OIL 180g
Best Before 11.01.2026
Premium
TUNA FILLETS
PINALER
ALCAPARRAS
PINALER
ふりかけ
MADE IN JAPAN
NUTRITION INFORMATION

25014A
SAN REMO
RICURIGATI No. 3
Made in Australia from 100% Australian ingredients
BAKE

Tomato paste (concentrated purée) → The most concentrated of the tomato preserves. To bring out its best, be sure to cook out the rawness for a minute or so when adding it to your sauces. Once opened, keep in the fridge lid-side down, or freeze in ice cube trays for longer storage.

Passata/polpa → Passata (puréed tomatoes) is the smoother, creamier cousin to chunky polpa, where the skin and seeds are kept in. I have both in the pantry, and use them interchangeably.

Tinned whole tomatoes → My favourite kind are tinned cherry toms, which give you sweet little pops of freshness through a sauce.

Jarred peppers → An easy shortcut to extra veg that'll save you 40 minutes of roasting. Piquillo peppers are the most flavoursome, but the long red type are still very tasty and great bang for buck.

Jarred artichokes → I'm a big fan of these for adding to pasta dishes, or blitzing with cream cheese and parmesan as a dip.

Coconut cream/coconut milk → The richer the better. If you don't use the whole tin, decant into a jar and store in the fridge, or freeze in ice cube trays.

Tinned tuna/sardines/anchovies → This is one ingredient group that definitely benefits from spending a little more for better quality fishies – especially if they're the primary protein or flavour base in a dish. They're still great bang for buck.

Preserved lemon → A very unique flavour, where less is more. Scoop as much of the pith off as you can before using, as this is where the bitterness lives.

Jam → For glazing ... as well as grazing. Mum adds a tablespoon of jam into borsch for sweetness, too (plum works best because it's tangy and sweet).

Seasonings

Salt flakes → I use Murray River pink salt flakes for seasoning and finishing. It's a salt with a lighter level of salinity, so it reads sweeter for me. If you're using a different flaky salt, remember to add less to begin with, then taste and season to your liking. You can always add more, but you can't take it away. Salt flakes twinkle like glitter on the top of dishes and melt on the tongue for a more effective interplay of ingredient and seasoning. Well worth investing in!

Fine sea salt → For a well-seasoned pasta pot, there's no point using the good stuff, so have a fine salt handy for this. One that doesn't contain anti-caking agents would be ideal. Nothing a good shake every now and then can't fix. Olsson's is my pick.

Sugar → You'll notice I suggest a pinch of sugar here and there, for highlighting a veg's natural sweetness. You can use white or brown sugar, or leave it out if you'd prefer.

Maple syrup → A bottle of North American maple syrup is always in our fridge. For pancakes, of course, but also as an unrefined sugar source with complexity that's fab on orange veg such as pumpkin (squash) and sweet potato. It's also a terrific substitute for honey if you're keeping things planty.

Honey → When a recipe calls for honey, unless specified otherwise, you're after a mild-flavoured one, from flowers such as yellowbox or meadow flowers. If your honey doesn't specify which flowers the bees have foraged upon or where it's from, you might like to seek one out that does – the flavour and aroma difference is remarkable.

Spices

Black pepper → Almost every dish in this book contains some freshly ground black pepper (pep!). Pepper is almost as important as salt to me because of the way it opens up the olfactory system and finishes a dish. Grinding peppercorns fresh will give you the most complexity, as the oils have a short shelf life ... nothing worse than just sprinkling dust on a dish. There's no need to splash out on a fancy grinder, though – just buy a small grinder filled with peppercorns from the shops to start with.

White pepper → Like black pepper, white pepper is always best when freshly ground, but pre-ground white pepper is better than none. It's used in Cantonese and French cookery – anywhere you don't want to see specks of black pepper. I will say, I'd much rather finish a dish with black pepper than white because it has quite a barnyard aroma, but the flavour is fantastically floral.

Mild madras curry powder → The spices will vary from maker to maker but, broadly, they'll give your subcontinental dishes a rounded, grounded depth. A nice **garam masala** mix is always worth keeping on the shelf too.

Khmeli suneli → Georgia's version of garam masala, this is a mix of spices that brings a uniquely piquant and savoury combination to Georgian dishes. You can use a shop-bought blend, or make your own (see page 211). If you're in a bind, use curry powder and add some extra ground coriander to fake suneli.

Baharat spice mix → A seven-spice mix that I like to use for rice dishes and tagines. You can make it at home by adding ground cumin, paprika and coriander to a garam masala.

Chinese five-spice → Gorgeous added to broths, rice dishes and anything fried. Containing cinnamon and star anise, it's also a lovely addition in desserts like panna cotta.

Ground coriander → If I had to pick one ground spice, it'd be ground coriander because I've grown up with Mum saying everything 'needs more coriander'. Any dish you use fresh coriander (cilantro) in, you could add ground coriander to. It's surprisingly zesty, and acts as a natural preservative too.

Cumin → This would be my second most used spice, especially on orange veg. If I had to choose between ground cumin and seeds to use whole or to grind, I'd choose the seeds, as they make nice nutty surprises on sweet potato and pumpkin (squash) pieces. But if you can't grind at home, buy smaller quantities of ground cumin and use within 6 months if possible.

Ground turmeric → This lasts for ages in the pantry, and always adds a lovely warm grounding element and sunshiny colour.

Fenugreek → Depending where you are in the world, fenugreek will vary in intensity. Georgian fenugreek is a 'blue' variety, which is milder and more floral. Taste yours and if it's quite bitter, use half the measure. If grinding from seed, halve also!

Paprika → Ground paprika is smoky-sweet through a dish, and speckled blush on top. Sweet and smoky are the types I most commonly use. If you have to pick one, I'd pick sweet! A little tin goes a long way.

Garlic powder → My favourite is Simply Organic. If yours hardens, give it a scratch about and a shake, and you should be right – better than going with a chunkier mix, flavourwise.

Dried chillies → There's all manner of dried chillies to choose from, but dried chilli flakes are a great place to start. Mild chilli flakes, or Aleppo pepper, are my pick.

Carby things

Basmati rice → A longer-grain rice that I like to buy aged, if I can find it. The nutty flavour of a good basmati is so delish. You can read more about riffs and how to cook it on page 227.

Jasmine rice → A fragrant, floral rice, which is a go-to midweek carb for our weeknights. You can read more about riffs and how to cook it on page 228.

Rice paper + dumpling wrappers → These store terrifically well – rice paper in the pantry, and dumpling wrappers in the freezer, ready for thawing overnight. They're a brilliant shortcut for stuffing, or leaving unwrapped too – whether boiled or fried!

Pasta + noodles → I use a lot of quick-cook dried pasta and noodles throughout the book, along with fresh pasta and noodles, which cook even faster. Look at the ingredients list and ensure it's as close to (and as short as) the list for a home-made version – and when in doubt, cook them for less time than you think. In recipes where I suggest a pasta shape, you're welcome to use a similarly sized shape of your choice – same with the strandy stuff.

Couscous → Instant couscous is a midweek dream. Toast it first for extra nuttiness, and spike it with spices, nuts and dried fruit.

Condiments

Chilli oil → This is always on our table, whether it's chilli crisp oil or Italian-style. I use it for seasoning, adding heat, interest, colour. You can MYO on page 221, or choose your fave local version.

Kewpie mayo → Otherwise known as Japanese mayo, with the red lid and the kewpie doll on the front, this stuff is packed with umami and gives savoury dishes a boost in satisfying depth.

Dijon/wholegrain mustard → The milder of the mustards, elegant and floral. I use dijon for emulsifying (thickening) dressings, but seeded is fun if you want a bit more texture.

Hot English mustard → For a hit of heat, this mustard lives up to the label. It's especially delish with anything cabbage-y. It can also live in your fridge for yonks.

Wasabi → It's one of the food world's worst-kept secrets that most wasabi tubes are basically hot English mustard with green food colouring, so if you don't have one or the other, you can always sub. But wasabi tubes last forever and are fab with cucumbers and avocado – and sushi, of course.

Light soy sauce → I prefer a light soy sauce for cooking because of its more delicate colour and flavour. Kikkoman Premium is my pick these days.

Oyster sauce → Sweet, savoury and funky. My favourite brand is Megachef, which also does a mushroom sauce if you're looking for a planty alternative.

Miso paste → A quick flavour shortcut, which you can buy in a jar. You could also dip a toe in by turning a sachet of miso soup into a paste with a splash of water.

When You Feel Like ...

Something playful + picky-pickable

Something hearty + comforting

Something fun + adventurous

Something fresh + bright

Something set + forget

The great thing about beluga lentils – the black ones that look like giant beads of black caviar, hence the name – is that unlike their brown or yellow cousins, they hold their shape beautifully when simmered, yielding creamy flavour and texture. You'll notice I don't soak the beluga lentils here, as I know this'll be a barrier when you're trying to get dinner on the table quickly, but you're welcome to soak them overnight in cold water if you remember. If you can't find beluga, you can use lentils du puy (small grey-green lentils).

If you're in a hurry, you can use tinned lentils, and serve the dish over a shop-bought carrot or capsicum dip.

Roasted Gochujang-Glazed Carrots + Beluga Lentils + Orange on Orange Dip

Serves → 4

Chop + stir → 20 MINUTES

Set + forget → 30 MINUTES

1 cup (200 g) dried beluga lentils, rinsed
2¼ cups (100 g) baby spinach
1 tablespoon extra virgin olive oil
1 teaspoon salt flakes

Gochujang-glazed carrots

5–6 carrots (about 700 g/1 lb 9 oz), sliced into 1 cm (½ in) thick coins
1 tablespoon gochujang (Korean chilli paste)
⅓ cup (80 ml) olive oil
¼ cup (60 ml) orange juice
2 tablespoons pomegranate molasses
1 teaspoon salt flakes

Orange on orange dip

2 carrots, scrubbed and roughly chopped
2 spring onions (scallions), whites only (reserve the greens for garnishing)
1 garlic clove, peeled
¼ cup (40 g) roasted smoked almonds
¼ cup (60 ml) orange juice
2 tablespoons olive oil
1 tablespoon red wine vinegar
½ teaspoon ground cumin

Home stretch

finely sliced spring onion (scallion) greens
½ cup (80 g) roasted smoked almonds, roughly chopped

Fire up the oven → Preheat your oven to 200°C (400°F), with a baking tray inside to heat up as well.

Lentil as anything → Rinse and drain the lentils. Place in a large pot, pour in 1 litre (4 cups) cold water and bring to the boil. Leave to boil for 5 minutes, then drop the heat and simmer for 25 minutes, until the lentils are softened but still toothsome. Drain, then toss with the spinach, olive oil, salt flakes and a good crack of black pepper. (Avoid seasoning the lentils until they're cooked, as this helps the insides cook through without toughening the exterior too much – you want toothsome, not chewy.)

Glaze the carrots → Toss the carrot coins in a large mixing bowl with the gochujang, olive oil, orange juice and pomegranate molasses, coating well. Sprinkle in the salt flakes and taste for seasoning. Carefully line the preheated baking tray with baking paper, then tumble the carrots over the top, arranging them so that there's room for the air to circulate. Roast the carrots for 25–30 minutes, until burnished and starting to wrinkle up.

Dip in → While the glazed carrots are roasting, make the orange on orange dip. Place all the ingredients in a blender, add ¼ cup (60 ml) water and blitz for a minute to a fluffy texture, scraping down the sides halfway through. Taste for seasoning and set aside until ready to serve.

Bring it home → Smear the dip around a serving bowl or platter, then layer with the lentils and spinach and the glazed carrot coins. Finish with a sprinkling of spring onion greens and almonds.

Double duty → All of these elements can be made a day ahead – the dip a few days ahead! – and assembled when needed. This is a dish you could enjoy warm or cold.

Somewhere between a carrot soup and a split pea dal, the warming spices and vibrant yellow colour emanating from these golden bowls will make you feel like you've let the sunshine in on those nights you need it most. If you have time and would prefer not to get the food processor out, you could roughly dice the veg and cook for an extra 10 minutes to get them fork-tender, then stick-blend or roughly mash them into a chunky stew.

Eagle-eyed readers will notice I'm breaking my 'start from cold' rule for root veg, using just-boiled hot water from a kettle to kick-start the cook because we're working smarter not harder here.

Carrot, Turmeric & Red Lentil Sunset Soup

Serves → 4 (with leftovers)

Chop + stir → 20 MINUTES

Set + forget → 35 MINUTES

1 kg (2 lb 4 oz) medium carrots, scrubbed and topped
1 medium sweet potato (about 400 g/14 oz), peeled and quartered
2 large brown or red onions, peeled and quartered
1 tangy red or yellow apple, cored and quartered
2 tablespoons coconut oil
¼ bunch coriander (cilantro), stems and roots finely chopped (reserve the sprigs for garnishing)
3–4 garlic cloves, minced
2 teaspoons salt flakes
½ teaspoon ground white pepper
1 tablespoon curry powder (mild madras is ideal)
1 teaspoon ground turmeric (or khmeli suneli, page 211)
1 cinnamon quill
2 bay leaves
1 cup (200 g) dried red lentils, rinsed
400 ml (14 fl oz) tin coconut milk
8 cups (2 litres) just-boiled water
2 quality stock cubes (veg/chicken)

Home stretch

2 cm (¾ in) thumb of ginger, peeled and finely grated
coriander (cilantro) sprigs
steamed basmati rice (page 227)
papadums, roti, yoghurt flatbreads (page 226) or other flatbreads

Whiz the veg → Using the coarse grater attachment on your food processor (or a box grater), coarsely grate the carrots, sweet potato, onions and apple.

Make your base → Heat the coconut oil in a large heavy-based pot. Toss in the grated veg and apple mix, along with the coriander stems (and roots, if you've got them), garlic, salt and white pepper. Put the lid on and leave to sweat over medium-low heat for 10 minutes, until the onion is translucent.

Spice it up → Add the curry powder, turmeric, cinnamon quill and bay leaves and stir about for a couple of minutes, until fragrant. Add the lentils. Shake up the coconut milk, then reserve 2 tablespoons before adding the rest to the pan. Stir to deglaze.

Simmertime → Pour in the boiling water, crumble in the stock cubes, give the lot a good stir and bring back to the boil. Cook on a rolling boil, with the lid tipping its hat, for about 20 minutes, until the carrots are soft enough to squish and the lentils have broken down. Remove the cinnamon quill and bay leaves.

Bring it home → Blend the soup to your desired consistency; I like mine with chunks of veg and a bit of texture, but you're welcome to blend yours smooth. Season to taste and stir the ginger through to add some fresh bite. Garnish with coriander and the reserved coconut milk, and serve with rice and your choice of flatbread.

Double duty → The soup will keep in the fridge for up to a week (!) for reheating, or portion and freeze for up to 3 months.

Butter has always been a happy feature of my cooking, but even more so since spending quality time with Asako Yuzuki, author of the smash-hit Japanese novel Butter. *I took Asako on a whirlwind tour of Melbourne and, in a case of life imitating art, she became as obsessed with the butter I introduced her to at my local cheesemonger as her protagonist is in the book. Among the many fancy dishes Asako features in the novel, it's the simple steamed rice with soy sauce and butter that stays with me – particularly since trying it in concert with this dish (pictured overleaf), which really puts the* butter *into butternut squash.*

Dengaku refers to the sweet-savoury miso glaze (often grilled but is roasted here for ease). If you've got any glaze left after brushing it liberally over the pumpkin, use it in the dressing! And if you've got some Soy maple glaze (page 219) in the fridge, use 2 tablespoons as the glaze, along with the miso and garlic powder.

This is a dish that's super comforting – and easy to make ahead and assemble as needed. If you want to speed things along, you could zap the hasselbacked pumpkin circles in the microwave for 10 minutes, then reduce the roasting time to 25 minutes.

Butternut Dengaku Hasselback + Soy Butter Rice + Miso Sesame Slaw

Serves → 4–6

Chop + stir → 10 MINUTES

Set + forget → 45 MINUTES

1 small to medium butternut pumpkin (squash; about 1.2 kg/ 2 lb 10 oz), washed
2 tablespoons sesame seeds

Dengaku glaze

2 tablespoons miso paste (white or red)
2 teaspoons rice wine vinegar
2 teaspoons light soy sauce
1 tablespoon maple syrup
⅛ teaspoon garlic powder (optional but excellent)
2 teaspoons neutral oil
½ teaspoon salt flakes

Miso sesame slaw

2 tablespoons miso paste (white or red)
2 tablespoons rice wine vinegar
1 tablespoon toasted sesame oil
2 teaspoons maple syrup
3 cups (300 g) finely shredded red cabbage (about ¼ small cabbage)
¼ cup coriander (cilantro) leaves

Slice the pumpkin → Preheat your oven to 200°C (400°F) and line a large baking tray with baking paper. Using a large sharp knife, trim the top and bottom ends of the pumpkin. Lay the pumpkin on its side and slice horizontally across the belly, from top to bottom, into 1.5 cm (⅝ in) thick rounds, until you hit the bell with the seed cavity – you should get around six pumpkin rounds. Once you reach the seedy hollow near the base, scoop out the seeds and save them for your stock bag. Cut the hollow bell-shaped end in half lengthways, then again into 1.5 cm (⅝ in) thick arches.

Score the pumpkin → To 'hasselback' the pumpkin, take two chopsticks and place on your bench along each side of a pumpkin round. Use a sharp knife to score a series of lines, about 5 mm (¼ in) apart, cutting only halfway down the pumpkin round; the chopsticks will help stop you cutting all the way through. Repeat with the remaining pumpkin rounds, then place on the lined baking tray. Sprinkle some salt on top and gently rub it in.

Glaze and bake → In a small bowl, combine all the dengaku glaze ingredients, whisking well until smooth. Brush most of the glaze over the pumpkin rounds and arches, ensuring the sides are coated too. Bake for 35 minutes, until the pumpkin is super soft.

Glaze and grill → Pull the tray out of the oven and switch to the grill (broil) setting, or crank the oven up to 240°C (475°F). Brush the rest of the glaze over the slices, coating the sides too, then blast for another 10 minutes, or until the pumpkin is fork-tender and the glaze has caramelised.

Soy butter rice

steamed jasmine rice (page 228)
80 g (2¾ oz) butter
light soy sauce (or soy maple glaze, page 219)

Home stretch

coriander (cilantro) leaves (reserved from the slaw)

Miso slaw → In a large bowl, whisk together the miso paste, vinegar, sesame oil and maple syrup, along with any dengaku glaze dregs. Add the cabbage, along with half the coriander leaves, and toss to combine.

Seeds the day → Heat a small frying pan over medium-high heat. Sprinkle in the sesame seeds and toast for 3–4 minutes, or until golden, switching the heat to low and watching carefully so they don't burn. Sprinkle half the toasted seeds over the miso slaw and save the rest for garnishing.

Bring it home → To make the soy butter rice, simply scoop some steamed rice into your serving bowls, top each with good nub of butter (about a tablespoon), and splash in some light soy sauce - these will get friendly once your eaters start stirring. Top with a few butternut rounds, sprinkle with the remaining coriander and sesame seeds and serve the miso slaw alongside.

Double duty → Just reheat any leftover pumpkin rounds and give the miso slaw a good stir if it's spent time in the fridge overnight.

Butternut dengaku hasselback + soy butter rice + miso sesame slaw → pages 30–1

Here's a lazy person's answer to pumpkin ravioli – all the flavour, none of the folding. I like using fresh pasta sheets here because they cook so quickly, but you could even serve the pumpkin sauce over a nice shop-bought ravioli, finishing with more blobs of ricotta on top. And while we're talking ricotta, I prefer hunks from those hefty wheels you see in the deli counter, rather than the stuff you'll find in a tub. It has a more delicate texture and a tang that's lovely against the sweetness of the sauce.

Smashed Butternut & Orange No-Roll Ravioli

Serves → 4

Chop + stir → 15 MINUTES

Set + forget → 25 MINUTES

½ butternut pumpkin (squash; about 700 g/1 lb 9 oz), washed and cut into 3 cm (1¼ in) chunks (skin on is fine)
2 carrots, roughly chopped
1 large brown onion, peeled and halved
4 garlic cloves, peeled
¼ cup (60 ml) olive oil
50 g (1¾ oz) butter
1 stock cube (veg/chicken), or 1 cup (250 ml) stock
a good scrape of fresh nutmeg
350–400 g (12–14 oz) fresh lasagne sheets
zest and juice of 1 orange
⅓ bunch (about 60 g/2 oz) flat-leaf parsley, finely chopped

Home stretch

250 g (9 oz) fresh ricotta (from the deli section), drained well
50 g (1¾ oz) parmesan or pecorino, finely grated
toasted almonds, hazelnuts or macadamias, roughly chopped
extra virgin olive oil

Blitz the veg → In your food processor, blitz the pumpkin, carrot, onion and garlic cloves to a fine paste.

Bikram butternut → Gently heat the olive oil and butter in a large deep heavy-based pan over medium–low heat. Scoop in the pumpkin and allium mix and swish about to coat in the fats. Crank the heat up to medium–high, listen for a sizzle, toss about, then whack a lid on. Set a timer for 15 minutes and leave to sweat, stirring occasionally, scraping any caramelised bits from the bottom of the pan.

Once the timer goes off and your mix has turned a suitably burnt umber shade and tastes like roasted pumpkin, stir in 1 cup (250 ml) water, along with the stock cube and nutmeg. Tilt the lid halfway off the pan, then cook the lot over medium–high heat, stirring occasionally, for 5–10 minutes, until thick and saucy.

Bubble the pasta → While your sauce is doing its thing, bring a large pot of well-salted water to the boil. Slice the lasagne sheets into raggy, fork-friendly strips, loosen into strands and dump into the water, stirring about for the first minute or so. Cook for 3–4 minutes, depending on how al dente you like your pasta.

Swirl together → When the pasta is cooked to your liking, scoop out using a slotted spoon and stir it through the sauce, over a low heat, adding in a little of the pasta water to loosen the sauce (the water will reabsorb). Stir the orange zest and 2 tablespoons of orange juice through, along with the chopped parsley, allowing the residual heat to soften it. Taste for seasoning, adding salt and pepper to your liking.

Bring it home → Ladle into serving bowls, then use a teaspoon to scoop blobs of ricotta over each bowl. Sprinkle with the grated cheese and nuts, finishing with a lick of olive oil and another crack of pepper.

Double duty → This sauce reheats a treat. You could cook the sauce ahead and stir the freshly cooked pasta and blobs of ricotta through to finish, or just reheat the lot – the ricotta will change texture slightly but it'll still be delish.

For a midweek vego parma, pumpkin really pops! Microwaving it first helps to halve the cooking time, but if you're zap-less, just bake the pumpkin longer until it collapses (another 20 minutes should do it). The breadcrumbs help bulk out the mix and make the top terrifically textural. I prefer panko for their shape and crunch, but if you've got some homemade breadcrumbs handy, use them first!

Basil stems can vary based on variety and season – chop them in only if you can bend them easily. If you've got some PG paste (page 214), you could stir it through instead of – or as well as! – the fresh herbs.

A crisp radicchio salad with a splash of zippy red wine vinegar would be an ideal side here.

One-Pan Pumpkin Parma

Serves → 4–6

Chop + stir → 10 MINUTES

Set + forget → 30 MINUTES

½ kent pumpkin (squash; about 900 g/2 lb), washed and cut into 2 cm (¾ in) cubes (no need to peel)
2 tablespoons olive oil

Herby tomato sauce

1 brown onion, finely diced
3–4 garlic cloves, minced
2 tablespoons olive oil
3 × 400 g (14 oz) tins whole peeled cherry tomatoes
¼ bunch parsley, stems and leaves finely chopped
¼ bunch basil, leaves and softer stems finely chopped
pinch of dried oregano
1 tablespoon red wine vinegar
1 teaspoon salt flakes
¼ teaspoon brown sugar

Cheesy panko topping

2 cups (120 g) panko crumbs
200 g (7 oz) firm mozzarella, coarsely grated
½ cup (50 g) coarsely grated Parmigiano Reggiano
¼ cup (60 ml) olive oil
2 tablespoons finely chopped parsley
2 tablespoons finely chopped basil

Home stretch

extra virgin olive oil

Start the sauce → Toss the onion, garlic and olive oil in a wide shallow casserole dish or large deep baking dish. Whack into your cold oven, then crank the temperature to 200°C (400°F) and leave for about 15 minutes, so the onion can start to soften and caramelise.

Zap the pumpkin → Meanwhile, tumble the pumpkin into a mixing bowl that comfortably fits it all. Sprinkle with a pinch of salt flakes, add the olive oil and toss to coat. Transfer to a microwave-safe container, keeping the schmutzy bowl handy. Cover and microwave for 10 minutes on high. The pumpkin will collapse and let out some sweet liquid.

Cheesy crumbs → In your schmutzy bowl, toss together all the cheesy panko topping ingredients. Set aside.

Finish off the sauce → Once the oven is heated and the onion mix is translucent and starting to caramelise, pour in the tomatoes, sloshing out each tin with a tablespoon or so of water and pouring that in too. Stir in the remaining sauce ingredients, then taste for seasoning. Whack a lid on (or cover with foil) and place back in the oven to heat through.

Put humpty together → When the pumpkin's done its microwave macarena, stir it through your tomato sauce, along with half the cheesy crumbs. Top with the remaining cheesy crumbs. Cover again and bake in the middle of the oven for 20 minutes, until the cheese is golden melty and the dish is bubbling on the edges. Finally, crank the temperature to 240°C (475°F) or flick on the grill (broil) setting for 5 minutes to get some serious bronze on the crumb.

If you can, let the dish sit out of the oven for 10 minutes before serving. This will help the sauce thicken up more ... and your diners will be less likely to burn their mouths!

Bring it home → Serve drizzled with a little of your best extra virgin olive oil and a little salt flake glitter from a height.

Double duty → The parma can be reheated in the microwave with some more zapping, or in the oven, from cold. Once the oven's warm, the dish will be heated through too!

Tagine-style dishes are designed for low and slow cooking, which ain't nobody got time for midweek. But the flavours of a tagine, and the burnished bits, can be achieved in under an hour by cooking the sauce and veg separately and uncovered. Here we're roasting chunky bits of sweet potato in the oven until syrupy, along with a spiced sauce that's laden with kidney beans and chickpeas, making a perfect hero main when vegos are coming around. You can also turn it vegan by switching the yoghurt out for a planty one.

Harissa is a fiery North African paste that can be found in supermarkets these days, and probably also in the back of your cupboard from the last time you made an Ottolenghi anything. If you've bought some, you can also use it instead of gochujang for the glazed carrots on page 26.

To toast the almonds, pop them in a foil pouch and into the oven for 8–10 minutes while the wedgies roast. If you wanted to bulk this meal out, you could also toss some chicken thighs in the harissa-spiked yoghurt marinade to roast along with the beans, cooking until the juices run clear.

This tray bake is pictured overleaf, and on the cover – because it deserves an encore performance.

Tagine-Inspired Tray Bake + Sweet Potato Wedgies

Serves → 4 (with leftovers)

Chop + stir → 10 MINUTES

Set + forget → 45 MINUTES

3 medium sweet potatoes, quartered lengthways

Harissa yoghurt marinade

1½ cups (390 g) natural yoghurt
2 tablespoons harissa paste
1 teaspoon salt flakes
¼ teaspoon freshly ground black pepper

Loaded tray bake

2 tablespoons olive oil
1 red onion, sliced with the grain into 1 cm (½ in) wedges
1 green capsicum (pepper), chopped into 1 cm (½ in) bits
3–4 garlic cloves, roughly chopped
½ bunch coriander (cilantro) stems, finely chopped (reserve the leaves for the couscous)
400 g (14 oz) tin diced tomatoes
400 g (14 oz) tin kidney beans, rinsed and drained
400 g (14 oz) tin chickpeas, rinsed and drained
½ cup (65 g) chopped dried apricots

Rack your sweeties → Cut the sweet potatoes in half lengthways, then in half again lengthways on an angle into thick wedges about 1.5 cm (⅝ in) wide (or into thirds if the sweet potatoes are bigger). Place directly on the top wire rack in the oven, cut side down, with a baking tray directly underneath to catch any caramelly drips. Crank the oven up to 200°C (400°F) and bake for 45 minutes, or until the sweet potatoes are starting to colour on the outside and are squishy to the touch on the inside.

Mix the marinade → As soon as the sweet potatoes go into the oven, place 1 cup (260 g) of the yoghurt in a large mixing bowl. Stir in the harissa paste, salt and pepper, then taste for seasoning. Transfer half the harissa yoghurt to a smaller serving bowl. To the remainder, stir in the final ½ cup (130 g) yoghurt and set aside.

Load your tray → Pour the olive oil into your large mixing bowl with the yoghurt marinade. Dump in the onion, capsicum, garlic and coriander stems. Pour in the tomatoes, half-filling the empty tin with water and sloshing it around to catch the last of the juice – then pour that in too. Add the beans, chickpeas and apricots and toss the lot around until everything is well acquainted and coated.

Pull the preheated baking tray out of the oven and tip the lot onto it, then place in the oven, back underneath the sweet potatoes to catch any drippy juices. Roast together with the sweet potatoes until the liquid evaporates from the sauce, the onion and capsicum have softened, and the tips are burnished.

Cori couscous

1 tablespoon olive oil
1 cup (200 g) instant couscous
1 vegetable stock cube
1 tablespoon crispy fried shallots (or 2 tablespoons MYO, page 225)
½ bunch coriander (cilantro) leaves, finely chopped

Home stretch

pomegranate molasses
extra virgin olive oil
½ cup (40 g) flaked or slivered almonds, toasted
coriander (cilantro) leaves
pomegranate seeds (optional but excellent)

Couscous → About 15 minutes before everything comes out of the oven, boil a kettle of water and heat the olive oil in a saucepan over medium heat. Toast the couscous in the oil for 2–3 minutes, until bits start turning golden and it starts to smell like cookies, then remove from the heat.

Once the kettle is boiling, crumble the stock cube into the pan and carefully stir in 1 cup (250 ml) hot water (the oil might spit a little). Stir about again, bring up to the boil, then switch off the heat, put the lid on and leave to infuse for 10 minutes. Fluff with a fork, stir through the shallots and the chopped coriander leaves and taste for seasoning.

Bring it home → Arrange the sweet potato wedgies on a serving platter. Tip the saucy chickpeas and beans all around. Blob generous dollops of the reserved harissa yoghurt on top, then drizzle with pomegranate molasses and a little olive oil. Finish by sprinkling with the toasted flaked almonds, coriander leaves and some pomegranate seeds, if you have them, and serve with the couscous.

Double duty → This is one of those 'better the next day' dishes! Leftovers can be reheated separately, or chop the wedgies into chunks and stir the couscous through the veg for a chunky jewelled veggie couscous lunch.

Tagine-inspired tray bake + sweet potato wedgies
→ pages 38–9

I love the way emojis, like a modern cuneiform or hieroglyphics, are fluid in both meaning and meme-ing – a study in semiotics. Like the time Mum wrote 'Yum' as 'Yam' in a Renglish (Russian–English) transliteration, and it became just a 'yam' (sweet potato) emoji, and has now become the best way my team and I declare when something's passed the 'Yammy' test. These noodles are both a yammy and Yammy dish.

'Yam Yam' One-Pot Noodles

Serves → 4

Chop + stir → 15 MINUTES

Set + forget → 20 MINUTES

2 bok choy
100 g (3½ oz) dried sweet potato noodles (dangmyeon)

Mushroom 'mince'

200 g (7 oz) button or Swiss brown mushrooms
100 g (3½ oz) fresh shiitake mushrooms
1 medium sweet potato, roughly chopped
½ bunch spring onions (scallions), whites roughly chopped (reserve the greens for garnishing)
4 garlic cloves, peeled
2 cm (¾ in) thumb of ginger, peeled
1–2 long red chillies, sliced (optional)
225 g (8 oz) tin sliced water chestnuts, rinsed and drained
¼ cup (60 ml) neutral oil

Yam yam sauce

4 garlic cloves, finely chopped
2 cups (500 ml) stock (veg/chicken)
⅓ cup (80 ml) light soy sauce
¼ cup (70 g) peanut butter
2 tablespoons honey
2 tablespoons toasted sesame oil
1–2 tablespoons chilli crisp oil (shop-bought or MYO, page 221)
1 tablespoon Chinese black vinegar (or malt vinegar)
1 tablespoon tomato paste (concentrated purée)

Home stretch

sliced spring onion (scallion) greens
¼ bunch coriander (cilantro), finely chopped
chilli crisp oil (store-bought or MYO, page 221)
mushroom XO (shop-bought or MYO, page 220)

Bang on the bok → Slice the bok choy in half lengthways, then finely slice into strips on a slight angle, following its natural shape, so it'll be easy to pick up with a fork and spoon or chopsticks. Bung the lot into a bowl of cold water to refresh the bok choy and also dislodge any grit or bugs between the layers. (I actually don't mind finding bugs – if the veg is good enough for the bugs, it's good enough for us!)

Get noodling → Cook the sweet potato noodles according to the packet instructions in a large deep pan or wok. Place a colander in the sink and drain the bok choy through, then leave it in the colander while you drain the noodles over the top. Rinse the lot with cold water, then set aside to drain.

Magic mushroom 'mince' → Place all the 'mince' ingredients in a food processor and pulse until everything is about 5 mm (¼ in) in size.

Heat your large deep pan or wok over high heat with a splash of water. Once the water has bubbled away and mostly evaporated, add the mushroom mince and stir occasionally for 8–10 minutes, until browned and caramelised in bits. You want all the moisture to dissipate, allowing the mince to stick and brown a little for that extra syrupy, concentrated flavour.

Yam yam time → Mix all the yam yam sauce ingredients together in a pouring jug. Once the mushroom mince has caramelised, pour the yam yam over the mince. Stir together and let it burble away for 5 minutes or so, until slightly thickened and reduced.

Bring it home → Add the bok choy and cooked noodles to the pan, giving everything a stir. Bring back to a simmer, then sprinkle in the spring onion greens. Taste and adjust the seasoning – you want a good balance of sweet, salty and savoury. Ladle into bowls, top with the coriander and serve with chilli crisp oil and mushroom XO.

Of all my favourite modern culinary thinkers, Tony Tan is the one who's inspired me, and countless others, to break through the shackles of 'authenticity' and into a more playful, cross-cultural state of mind. Like this dish, which is a more pared-back version of one he served up for me at his cosy kitchen cooking school in Trentham, mashing together Indian, Middle Eastern, Malay and Thai ingredients into a crazy delicious curried sauce for plump, juicy mussels. Tony steamed his mussels separately, then pulled out the meat and returned it to the sauce, but I like the idea of chucking the mussels in and letting eaters do the fussy work of scooping out the meat as they go.

Mussels are an inexpensive and quick-cook option for midweek, so don't let the shells intimidate you. I estimate 400 g–500 g (14 oz–1 lb 2 oz) of mussels per person, so buy accordingly.

Sunrise Sweet Potato Mussels

Serves → 4

Chop + stir → 15 MINUTES

Set + forget → 10 MINUTES

3 teaspoons green curry paste (or 1 heaped tablespoon MYO, page 212)
¼ cup (60 g) tomato paste (concentrated purée)
400 g (14 oz) tin coconut cream
1 teaspoon ground turmeric
6 makrut lime leaves
1–2 curry leaf stems (about 16 leaves), stripped
2 medium sweet potatoes (about 800 g/1 lb 12 oz), peeled and cut into 1 cm (½ in) cubes
1.6 kg–2 kg (3 lb 8 oz–4 lb 8 oz) mussels
1 cup (140 g) frozen peas, thawed
1–2 tablespoons fish sauce
brown sugar or maple syrup (optional)

Home stretch

1 lime, for squeezing
steamed jasmine rice (page 228)
coriander (cilantro) leaves
1 long red chilli, finely sliced (optional but excellent)

Base to the place → Place a large high-sided pan with a lid over medium heat. Fry off the curry paste and tomato paste in a small scoop of the coconut cream (from the top of the tin) for about 2 minutes, until fragrant.

Bobbing cubes → Pour in the remaining coconut cream, half-filling the tin with water to extract the remnants, then sloshing that in too. Add the turmeric, lime leaves and curry leaves. Drop in the sweet potato cubes, adding a little more water if needed to ensure they're mostly covered. Bring to the boil, then lower the heat to a simmer. Set the timer for 10 minutes, leaving the lid akimbo on top to let some steam out, but trap some moisture in too.

Mussel up → While the pot comes up to the boil and bubble, scrub, wash and debeard the mussels in the sink (most commercially available mussels have already been well scrubbed), rinsing off any gritty bits.

When the timer goes off, check that the sweet potato has softened (but isn't falling apart). Crank the heat up to high, tumble in the mussels and whack the lid back on for 5 minutes.

Open seasoning → Once the mussels have opened, add the peas. Taste for seasoning, splashing in the fish sauce as needed, remembering that the mussels bring their own brininess, and adding a pinch of brown sugar (or a tiny drizzle of maple syrup or squeeze of lime) if need be.

Bring it home → Serve the sunrise mussels over bowls of steamed rice, garnished with coriander leaves and chilli slices if desired.

Double duty → If you have any leftovers, pick the mussel meat into a separate container, then reheat the broth and add the mussels for the last minute of cooking – you'll have a brothy dipper for flatbreads the next day.

Get ready for your new go-to veg curry, which you can easily turn vegan with neutral oil and coconut yoghurt. Instead of using shop-bought parathas (you'll find the best ones in the freezer aisle), you're welcome to MYO flatbreads (page 226) or simply serve the curry with steamed basmati rice (page 227).

Spiced Sweet Potato & Chickpea Curry + Pumped-Up Paratha

Serves → 4

Chop + stir → 10 MINUTES

Set + forget → 25 MINUTES

1 brown onion, roughly chopped
2 garlic cloves, roughly chopped
2 cm (¾ in) thumb of ginger, peeled and roughly chopped
1 long red chilli, halved lengthways and deseeded
½ bunch coriander (cilantro), roots and stems roughly chopped (reserve the leaves for garnishing)
2 tablespoons ghee or butter
1½ tablespoons mild madras curry powder
16 curry leaves, stripped
1 medium sweet potato (about 400 g/14 oz), peeled and cut into 1 cm (½ in) cubes
400 g (14 oz) tin crushed tomatoes (Italian or organic)
400 g (14 oz) tinned chickpeas, rinsed and drained
1 cup (250 ml) vegetable stock
270 ml (9½ fl oz) tin coconut cream
1 teaspoon salt flakes
1 teaspoon sugar (optional)
250 g (9 oz) frozen spinach (no need to thaw)

Pumped-up paratha

2 tablespoons ghee or butter
4 frozen roti paratha
1 teaspoon nigella seeds (optional but excellent)

Home stretch

coriander (cilantro) leaves
natural yoghurt

Build your base → In your food processor or blender, blitz the onion, garlic, ginger, chilli and coriander stems into a paste. Heat the ghee in a large saucepan over medium–high heat, then add the paste. Stir together, cover with the lid and leave to sweat for 5 minutes, until softened. Add the curry powder, curry leaves and sweet potato, stirring for 30 seconds, until aromatic.

Curry up → Pour in the crushed tomatoes, stirring to scrape up any browned bits on the bottom of the pan. Add the chickpeas, stock and coconut cream, ensuring you have enough liquid to just cover the sweet potatoes. Sprinkle in the salt, and the sugar if using. Bring to the boil, then reduce the heat to medium. Cover and cook for 15–20 minutes, stirring occasionally, until the sweet potato is tender.

Roughly mash some of the chickpeas and potato with a masher, then incorporate into the rest of the mix. Pop in the frozen spinach lumps, then whack the lid on to let everything come together.

Pump up the paratha → Once the spinach is in the pan, prepare the paratha. Heat the ghee in a medium–large frying pan, ideally large enough to fit two paratha at a time. When the ghee is foaming (working in batches as needed), snuggle in your paratha, swirling to coat in the ghee. Cook for 1–2 minutes per side, until golden brown, puffed up and further caramelised. Repeat with the remaining paratha.

If using the nigella seeds, add them to the pan once all the paratha are done and let them toast a little in the residual heat. Sprinkle them over the warm paratha, along with a scattering of salt flakes.

Back to the curry → When the spinach has fully thawed into the sauce, give the curry a little swirl to help distribute the greenery, while keeping some delineation. Season to taste with more salt flakes.

Bring it home → Divide the curry between bowls. Garnish with coriander leaves and serve with the paratha, and a small bowl of yoghurt on the side for blobbing on top.

Double duty → The best thing about today's curry for dinner? Yesterday's curry for tomorrow's lunch! The flavours will intensify, the sweet potato and chickpeas will thicken up the broth, and you could even mash the curry a little more for a different texture. Wrap any leftover paratha in foil, and store the curry in the fridge. They will happily keep for 3–4 days.

What you'll love about this tray bake, besides the 'set and forget' of it, is that you probably already have most of the ingredients in your pantry. It's a great one to whack on for visiting vegos – and you can make it vegan by crumbling planty cheese over the top instead of feta. It would also be delish as a side dish with lamb cutlets or the like. You could even nestle in some chicken marylands (leg quarters) and roast for about 40–50 minutes, until the juices run clear. Panzanella is designed to be made with yesterday's bread, so anything crusty you need to use up will work perfectly. You can also use any tins of white beans you've got handy – so butter beans, borlotti or pochas will work just fine, as will chickpeas.

This tray bake can be prepared a day ahead, sans bread, then gently reheated with the bready bits to serve.

Capsicum & Cannellini Panzanella Tray Bake

Serves → 4

Chop + stir → 15 MINUTES

Set + forget → 30 MINUTES

2 × 400 g (14 oz) tins cannellini beans, rinsed and drained
400 g (14 oz) tinned or fresh cherry tomatoes
1 small jar (about 200 g/7 oz) roasted red capsicums (peppers), cut into strips, liquor reserved
1 red onion, cut into 1 cm (½ in) wedges, keeping the base intact
6–8 garlic cloves, unpeeled, lightly bruised
1 teaspoon smoked or sweet paprika
½ heaped teaspoon salt flakes
¼ teaspoon freshly cracked black pepper
small drizzle of honey (or hot honey, page 219); optional but excellent
¼ cup (60 ml) extra virgin olive oil
200 g (7 oz) creamy feta
150 g (5½ oz) crusty bread
1⅓ cups (50 g) rocket (arugula)
¼ bunch flat-leaf parsley, finely chopped from stem to leaf

Home stretch
crusty bread
lemon wedges

Heat is on → Preheat your oven to 180°C (350°F) and line a baking tray with baking paper.

Prepare the tray → While the oven heats up, toss the cannellini beans, cherry tomatoes, capsicum, onion and garlic cloves together in a large mixing bowl. Sprinkle with the paprika, salt, pepper and honey, if using. Drizzle in half the olive oil and toss to coat. Tip the mixture onto the lined baking tray, holding space in the middle for the feta.

Pop the feta block into your mixing bowl and coat in the leftover spicy schmutz, then nestle in the centre of your baking tray, keeping the schmutzy bowl handy.

Get roasting → Slide the tray into the oven and bake for 20 minutes, until the beans start to burnish and the garlic softens.

Crunch time → Tear the bread into bits and add to the schmutzy bowl. Drizzle in the remaining olive oil, tossing about to coat with your hands. When your tray's ready to come out of the oven, grab your oven mitts, pull the tray out and tumble the bread chunks over the bake.

Pop your mitts back on, return the tray to the oven and bake for another 10 minutes.

Finish strong → When the bread is golden brown and starting to burnish at the edges, remove from the oven and stir half the rocket and all the parsley through. Break up the feta, mixing it through the bake.

Bring it home → Scatter with the remaining rocket, and sprinkle with more salt flakes and freshly cracked pepper from a height. Serve hot or warm, with crusty bread, and lemon wedges on the side to squeeze over for extra tang.

Ikra is one of Dad's favourite dip-sauce hybrids, harnessing the intensity of summer nightshades (capsicum, tomato and eggplant) as a very veggie accompaniment to whatever's on the table. The meatballs are a fun way of adding protein without schvitzing over a frying pan – or swap for jammy hard-boiled eggs to keep it vego. For shortcut ikra, stir the flesh of two roasted eggplants through a 300 g (10½ oz) jar of ajvar instead.

Capsicum & Eggplant Ikra + Ćevapi Meatballs + Pitas

Serves → 4

Chop + stir → 15 MINUTES

Set + forget → 45 MINUTES

800 g (1 lb 12 oz) cevapi sausages, or other spicy sausages
4 soft Greek-style pita pockets

Ikra

¼ cup (60 ml) neutral oil
2 medium eggplants (aubergines; about 800 g/1 lb 12 oz), halved lengthways
2 red capsicums (peppers), halved
1 red onion (1 small whole cheek reserved for the salad), roughly chopped
1 carrot, roughly chopped
4 garlic cloves, finely sliced
¼ cup (70 g) tomato paste (concentrated purée)
2 teaspoons salt flakes
2 teaspoons ground coriander
½ teaspoon sweet or hot paprika
2 teaspoons red wine vinegar
½ bunch parsley, stems roughly chopped (reserve the leaves for the salad)

Parsley salad

½ bunch parsley leaves (reserved from the ikra)
1 small red onion cheek (reserved from the ikra), finely sliced with the grain
1 teaspoon red wine vinegar
2 tablespoons olive oil

Home stretch

extra virgin olive oil

Double duty → This makes plenty of ikra, so you could siphon some off as a topping for tomorrow's toast, or to enjoy in other ways. It will keep for up to 5 days in the fridge.

Start on your ikra → Preheat your oven to 180°C (350°F) and line a large baking tray with baking paper. Drizzle half the oil over the eggplant halves and place face down on the baking tray. Add the capsicum halves, cut side down, then roast in the bottom third of the oven for about 40 minutes, or until soft.

Cevapi papi → While the nightshades are roasting, pinch and roll the cevapi mince into meatballs about the size of in-shell macadamias and place on a second lined baking tray. Whack into the oven above the veg for about 20 minutes, until browned and shrivelled.

Sweat the veg → While the oven's doing everything, get back to the ikra. Heat the remaining oil in a heavy-based frying pan. Add the onion and carrot, put the lid on, set the timer for 10 minutes and leave to sweat over medium heat, stirring occasionally. Once softened and starting to colour, stir in the garlic, tomato paste, salt, coriander and paprika. Cook for a few more minutes, or until the garlic is aromatic and the paste is cooked out. Switch off the heat.

Prep the salad → Toss the parsley and onion together in a bowl with a pinch of sugar, salt flakes and black pepper, then drizzle in the vinegar and taste. (Hold the oil for now, using it to dress the salad just before serving.)

Oven overtime → When the capsicum and eggplant are done, take them out of the oven to cool a bit. Turn the oven off, but leave the meatballs in there. Wrap the pita pockets in foil and pop them in the oven to warm while you finish the ikra.

Blitz together → When cool enough to handle, drop the capsicums (skin and all) into a food processor (or a bowl, if using a stick blender). Scoop out the flesh of the eggplant and add that too, along with the sweated onion and veg mix. Add the vinegar and parsley stems and blend to your desired degree – some texture and chunk is welcome. Taste and adjust the seasoning and acid levels to your liking.

Bring it home → Spoon the ikra onto a platter, then tumble the meatballs over. Finish with a drizzle of olive oil and a good sprinkle of salt flakes and serve straight away, with the warm pita pockets and parsley salad on the side.

Although japchae is traditionally served on special occasions in Korea as a banchan (side dish), with each constituent vegetable stir-fried individually, I was inspired to try it as a far more fuss-free tray bake by Erik Kim's sheet-pan version in the NYT. *Starting the oven cold and using it to toast the sesame seeds is a great way of utilising your time – and the oven's – or you could use pre-toasted Korean sesame seeds instead.*

This recipe is easily veganised if you swap the omelette for firm tofu, sliced into thin strips. Since we're using dangmyeon, Korean glass noodles, which are made of sweet potato starch rather than flour, it's also easy to turn gluten-free – just make sure your soy sauce is gluten free, or switch to tamari. You could also swap the soy in the sauce for 3 tablespoons soy maple glaze (page 219), if you have some handy.

You'll find the japchae pictured overleaf.

One-Tray Japchae

Serves → 4

Chop + stir → 15 MINUTES

Set + forget → 40 MINUTES

1 medium sweet potato, scrubbed
4 spring onions (scallions), roots trimmed
2 capsicums (peppers), any colour you like
200 g (7 oz) fresh shiitake mushrooms, woodier stems discarded
2 tablespoons neutral oil
1 tablespoon light soy sauce
½ teaspoon freshly ground black pepper
340 g (11¾ oz) dried sweet potato noodles (dangmyeon)
2⅔ cups (120 g) baby spinach leaves

Omelette

4 eggs
1 teaspoon light soy sauce

Cold oven start → Get the sesame seeds prepped for your sauce. Line your biggest baking tray with baking paper and scatter the sesame seeds on top. Whack into your oven, then crank the temperature up to 200°C (400°F). Set a timer for 4 minutes, and pull the sesame seeds out as soon as they are golden. Use the baking paper to funnel the seeds into a small bowl and set aside.

Omelette you finish → Return the baking paper to the baking tray. In a small bowl, whisk the eggs with the soy sauce, then pour onto the lined baking tray, tilting the tray to spread the mixture. Bake for 8–10 minutes, or until just set. Slide the omelette onto a clean cutting board and allow to cool.

Prep the veg → While the omelette is cooking, start slicing your veg. Cut the sweet potato into 3 mm × 3 cm (⅛ in × 1¼ in) batons. Chop the spring onions into 3 cm (1¼ in) lengths, finely slicing the dark green tops and reserving these for the sauce. Cut the capsicums into 1 cm × 3 cm (½ in × 1¼ in) strips, following the natural shape of the capsicum. Finely slice the shiitake, following the shape of the mushrooms. Tumble all the veg into a large mixing bowl. Add the oil, soy sauce and pepper and toss about until well coated.

Replace the (mangy but functional) baking paper in the baking tray, transfer the veg onto the lined baking tray, and roast for 20–25 minutes, or until everything's tender and slightly burnished.

Soy sesame sauce

¼ cup (40 g) sesame seeds
⅓ cup (80 ml) light soy sauce
4 garlic cloves, minced
1 tablespoon toasted sesame oil
1 tablespoon maple syrup (or 1 teaspoon brown sugar)
½ teaspoon freshly ground black pepper
1 teaspoon mirin
spring onion tops (reserved from above)

Saucy sauce → Grab that schmutzy mixing bowl and dump in all the sauce ingredients. Sprinkle in the toasted sesame seeds, reserving some to garnish, and the reserved spring onion greens. Mix well, then taste for seasoning.

Get noodling → About 10 minutes before the vegetables finish roasting, bring a large saucepan of water to the boil over high heat and cook the noodles according to the packet instructions (typically about 6–8 minutes).

Pop the baby spinach leaves in a colander and pour the noodles in, then blast the noodles and spinach with cool water while tossing about to mix and drain.

Use kitchen scissors to snip the noodles into smaller lengths, to make them easier to toss and coat, then tip the lot into your big bowl of sauce.

Bring it home → Roll the cooled omelette into a log, slice into fine ribbons, then tumble into the noodle bowl, along with the roasted veg. Toss well to combine. Taste and adjust the seasoning again – it should be sweet, salty, savoury and warmingly spiced.

Divide the japchae between bowls and serve.

Double duty → Like a noodle salad, the japchae can be served warm or cold. It's excellent for lunch-boxes and lunch à-la-desko the next day, if you can manage to save any.

One-tray japchae → pages 52–3

I like to think of capsicum and tomatoes as gateway veg: when they're in the peak of their season, their naturally high sugar content makes them very easy for our tastebuds to love at any age. More alluring still is teaming them (together or separately) with a salty cheese like feta, to play against this natural sweetness.

As a shortcut, I'm using jarred roasted capsicums in this soup, but you can roast fresh ones at home if you've the time – just halve, deseed, oil, then roast cut side down for 40 minutes at 200°C (400°F). Slip off the skins, and away you go.

Quality tinned tomatoes are worth the extra coin. Australian organic toms can stand up to the best of them, and Italian or Spanish premium tins will usually have the right sweetness and viscosity (but you can fake it with a pinch of sugar too). If your soup tastes too acidic, add ⅛ teaspoon bicarbonate of soda (baking soda) to help neutralise this.

Roasted Red Pepper Soup + Feta Cream

Serves → 4–6

Chop + stir → 10 MINUTES

Set + forget → 20 MINUTES

2 tablespoons olive oil
1 red onion, finely sliced
2–3 garlic cloves, roughly chopped
2 tablespoons tomato paste (concentrated purée)
1 teaspoon smoked sweet paprika
2 × 350–400 g (12–14 oz) jars roasted red capsicums (peppers), liquor reserved
2 tablespoons sherry vinegar
2 cups (500 ml) stock (veg/chicken)
2 × 400 g (14 oz) tins quality whole peeled tomatoes
6–8 oregano sprigs
2 bay leaves

Feta cream

100 g (3½ oz) sour cream
3 oregano sprigs, leaves picked and finely chopped
1 garlic clove, minced
½ teaspoon cracked black pepper
100 g (3½ oz) Greek feta, crumbled

Home stretch

extra virgin olive oil
oregano leaves
smoked sweet paprika
warmed flatbreads (shop-bought or MYO, page 226)

Make the base → Heat the olive oil in a large heavy-based pot over medium heat. Add the onion, listen for the sizzle, then whack a lid on and drop the heat to low. Set a timer for 6 minutes. When the onion has softened, stir in the garlic, tomato paste and paprika. Bring the heat back to medium and stir for a few minutes, until the garlic and paprika are aromatic and the rawness has been cooked out of the tomato paste. Splash in the loose liquor from the tops of the capsicum jars, along with the sherry vinegar, using a wooden spoon or spatula to deglaze the pan and lift up all the flavour from the base.

Soup it up → Pour in the stock, along with the tinned tomatoes, sloshing out the tins with a splash of water to extract every lick of flavour. Tie the oregano sprigs and bay leaves together using kitchen twine and plonk them into the pot. Dump in the roasted capsicums along with any leftover liquor in the jars. Stir well and bring everything to the boil, then simmer for 10 minutes, to let the ingredients mingle and feel like you've actually done some cooking.

Better with feta → To make the feta cream, stir together the sour cream, oregano, garlic and pepper until smooth, then fold in the feta and taste for seasoning. If it needs a lick of acid, spoon in a little of the capsicum liquor.

Blitz → Fish the bay leaf bundles out of the soup. Purée using a stick blender, or blitz in batches in a food processor. Taste and season as needed with salt, pepper, sugar and more sherry vinegar.

Bring it home → Ladle into bowls and drizzle with olive oil. Add a dollop of feta cream, some fresh oregano and a sprinkle of paprika. Serve immediately, with warmed flatbreads.

Double duty → This soup keeps well in the fridge for 3–4 days, or frozen for up to 3 months. Keep the feta cream separate and use within a few days; you'll need to make the feta cream fresh when reheating the soup from frozen.

This dish is inspired by Kylie Kwong's 'Uncle Jimmy's hokkien noodles', which helped untether me from cornflour (cornstarch) as a sauce thickener for stir-fries. For my own contribution, may I suggest overcrowding the pan with capsicum, which is ordinarily a stir-fry no-no, but works surprisingly well, as each differently coloured capsicum benefits from a different amount of heat, moisture and burnish. You'll find fresh hokkien, like the kind Uncle Jimmy has produced in Sydney for decades, in the fridge section at most major supermarkets and indie grocers, and of course South-East Asian grocers.

Poaching the chicken means you avoid the pan spitting hot oil at you, and once the chicken's coated in the glossy sweet-salty sauce, you won't notice the difference. Velveting the chicken with bicarb is the secret to that tender, bouncy, stir-fried protein, something Kylie doesn't ordinarily do with hers, but I can't resist incorporating. You could swap in 500 g (1 lb 2 oz) beef strips or prawns instead.

To turn this vego, poach some firm tofu in well-salted water instead – no need to velvet!

Traffic-Light Hokkien

Serves → 4

Chop + stir → 25 MINUTES

Set + forget → N/A

500 g (1 lb 2 oz) skinless, boneless chicken thighs, sliced against the grain into 1.5 cm (⅝ in) thick strips
¼ teaspoon bicarbonate of soda (baking soda)
500 g (1 lb 2 oz) hokkien noodles
2 tablespoons neutral oil
3 small capsicums (peppers), green, yellow and red, kept separate, sliced into strips about 5 mm (¼ in) thick, following the shape of the capsicum
1 red onion, peeled, halved and finely sliced with the grain
1½ tablespoons soft brown sugar
1 bunch Vietnamese mint (or Thai basil), leaves picked

Stir-fry sauce

⅓ cup (80 ml) soy sauce, plus extra for seasoning
2 tablespoons shaoxing rice wine or dry sherry
1 tablespoon Chinese black vinegar
1 teaspoon toasted sesame oil

Home stretch

2 good handfuls bean sprouts
Vietnamese mint (or Thai basil) leaves (reserved from above)

Double duty → This dish is surprisingly delish cold the next day! Or you could refry to activate some more caramelisation on the noods.

Touch of velvet → Toss the chicken strips with the bicarb soda and set aside to velvet for about 10 minutes, which helps make the chicken super tender and juicy.

Strips + noods → Bring a large pot of water to the boil. Plonk in the noodles and follow the cooking time suggested by the packet instructions (usually about 2 minutes). Using tongs or a pasta scoop, fish the noodles out of the water and into a large bowl. Drizzle with a tablespoon of the oil and toss to coat.

Bring the noodle water back to the boil. Carefully add your chicken strips, then drop the heat to a simmer, skimming the foam from the top. Set the timer for 3 minutes – you want the chicken to poach to just opaque, as it'll keep cooking in the wok. As soon as it's done, scoop the chicken out into your big noodle bowl.

Wok on the veg → Meanwhile, heat a large high-sided, heavy-based pan or wok over medium heat. Splash in the remaining tablespoon of oil. Add the green capsicum and crank the heat to medium–high, letting it burnish on the edges for 3–5 minutes. Toss in your yellow capsicum for another 2 minutes, then add the red capsicum for a final 3 minutes.

Add the onion, sugar and a small splash of the water from the chicken-poaching pot. Toss about for another 2 minutes, or until the onion softens.

Saucy sauce → Combine all the sauce ingredients in a bowl or jug.

Bring it home → Tumble the noodles and chicken into the pan or wok. Pour in the sauce and toss about to coat well. Scatter the bean sprouts and two-thirds of the picked herbs over and switch off the heat.

Taste for seasoning and serve, topping each bowl with the remaining picked herbs.

This is a fresh tomato sauce that's perfect for hot evenings when you need to keep stove time to a minimum but still want something substantial on the table. It's the kind of dish that always feels bougie, even if you've used vac-packed or tinned crab! I made a version with finely chopped prawn (shrimp) meat for actress Mary Coustas (who played Effie in the TV sitcom Acropolis Now*) and she absolutely loved it – when she sang its praises in full Effie voice, my '90s emigré heart was so full, I thought I could hear angels singing!*

The pangrattato and the tomato sauce can both be pre-prepped and just brought together when you're ready to boil the pasta. Make the sauce in the food processor if you can't be bothered faffing with the grater.

Fresh Tomato & Crab Angel Hair + Zingy Pangrattato

Serves → 4

Chop + stir → 10 MINUTES

Set + forget → 20 MINUTES

300 g (10½ oz) dried angel hair or curly pasta
100–150 g (3½–5½ oz) picked crab meat, drained
50 g (1¾ oz) butter
¼ bunch parsley, finely chopped

Fresh tomato sauce

3–4 garlic cloves, peeled
1.2 kg (2 lb 10 oz) ripe, aromatic tomatoes
1 teaspoon salt flakes
¼ teaspoon freshly cracked black pepper
¼ teaspoon sugar (optional)
¼ cup (60 ml) olive oil

Zingy pangrattato

2 tablespoons olive oil
1 tablespoon butter
50 g (1¾ oz) panko breadcrumbs, or 100 g (3½ oz) stale bread, crusts removed, grated
zest of 1 lemon (reserve the nude lemon for serving)
¼ bunch parsley, finely chopped

Home stretch

nude lemon (reserved from the pangrattato), cut into wedges

Sauce those tomatoes → Sit a box grater in a large mixing bowl. Using the fine side, grate the garlic into the bowl. Switch over to the coarse side, then grate half the tomatoes into the bowl, popping the tomato skins into your stock bag. Dice the remaining tomatoes and add them to the bowl. Season with the salt, pepper and sugar, if using, stirring about to dissolve. Stir in the olive oil and set aside for the flavours to develop while you get the rest of the dish together.

Get the panko in the pan-grattato → In a large deep heavy-based pan, warm the olive oil and butter over medium heat. Sprinkle in the panko crumbs, tossing regularly for about 5 minutes to toast and tan. Once the crumbs are bronzed, add the lemon zest and parsley and switch off the heat. Scoop out into a small serving dish and set aside.

Pasta time → Bring a large pot of well-salted water to the boil. Drop in the pasta and cook according to the packet instructions, less 1 minute. Drain the pasta into a colander.

Return the empty pasta pot to the stove. Pour in your tomato sauce and bring up to the boil, then switch the heat off. Tip in the cooked pasta. Add the crab meat, butter and parsley and toss about in the sauce until the pasta is evenly coated. If the sauce feels too wet, remember that the pasta will soak up the juiciness with residual heat.

Bring it home → Serve immediately, topped with the pangrattato and another glug of olive oil, with the nude lemon wedges on the side.

Cans give you a can-do attitude on a weeknight because so much of the work's been done. But instead of tinned baby corn, you can of course use fresh baby corn, frozen corn, or fresh kernels sliced off a cob – in which case, toss them in for the last 5 minutes of simmering. And in summer you can swap in fresh cherry tomatoes in place of tinned.

Tom kha goong – Thai coconut soup with prawns (shrimp) – is my favourite kind of tom kha, and I'm cheating here by using frozen prawn dumplings from the shops! You can use any kind of dumpling you'd like, shred some cooked chicken into this soup for a cheat's tom kha gai, or keep it planty using fysh sauce, vego dumplings and/or cubes of firm tofu.

Triple-Tin Tom Kha

Serves → 4

Chop + stir → 5 MINUTES

Set + forget → 15 MINUTES

2 tablespoons coconut oil
2 tablespoons red curry paste (or 4 tablespoons MYO, page 212)
10 makrut lime leaves
2 stock cubes (veg/chicken)
410 g (14½ oz) tin baby corn
400 g (14 oz) tin cherry tomatoes
400 ml (14 fl oz) tin coconut milk
¼ cup (60 ml) fish sauce
½ tablespoon brown sugar
12 frozen dumplings (prawn/veg/chicken)
200 g (7 oz) dried flat rice or vermicelli rice noodles
½ lime

Home stretch

crispy fried shallots (shop-bought or MYO, page 225)
chilli crisp oil (shop-bought or MYO, page 221); optional
Thai basil sprigs
lime cheeks

Build your base → In a large heavy-based saucepan, heat the coconut oil and curry paste, stirring about for a minute or two until fragrant.

Squish the lime leaves between your hands to unlock their aroma, then toss them into the pot. Add the stock cubes, and empty in your tins: baby corn, tomatoes, coconut milk. Pour in 1 litre (4 cups) water, season with the fish sauce and sugar, then bring the lot to the boil.

Dumpty dumplings → Dump in the frozen dumplings and let them boil away for 5–7 minutes, until they float to the top and are completely translucent.

Plump the noods → While the dumplings are bubbling about, pop the noodles in a heatproof bowl, cover with warm water and leave to rehydrate for the time allotted on the packet. Drain the noodles and distribute among your bowls.

Crown the noods → When the dumplings are done, fish them out of the broth and arrange over the noodles.

Balancing act → Taste the broth and season again. Squeeze in the lime juice, then taste and add more if needed. You're aiming for a pleasing balance of sweet, salty, sour and a touch of heat.

Bring it home → Ladle the broth into the bowls. Add some crispy fried shallots, and a drizzle of chilli crisp oil, if you're up for it. Garnish with Thai basil and serve with lime cheeks for squeezing over.

Tomatoes are stupendous for adding savouriness (aka 'umami') to dishes across the planet. The more concentrated the tomato – say, in a passata or a paste – the more concentrated the glutamates. Omurice, hailing from Japan, where 'The Fifth Taste' of umami was discovered, takes full advantage by loading up refried rice with ketchup!

This is a terrific way of using up last night's rice (everything from sushi rice to basmati will work here). And if starting from scratch with no time to cook rice, you could use a couple of pouches of cooked rice from the shops. Feel free to also toss in any chopped-up bits of leftover roast meat, or add extra frozen veg.

Tomato Omurice

Serves → 4

Chop + stir → 15 MINUTES

Set + forget → 15 MINUTES

1½ cups (300 g) raw jasmine rice, washed well (or 4 cups of leftover rice)
1 cup (140 g) frozen peas
¼ cup (60 ml) neutral oil
1⅓ cups (100 g) finely chopped wombok or white cabbage
2–3 garlic cloves, finely sliced
4 spring onions (scallions), finely sliced, whites and greens kept separate
¼ cup (60 ml) tomato ketchup
1 tablespoon worcestershire sauce
2 tablespoons light soy sauce
400 g (14 oz) ripe fleshy tomatoes (such as roma), diced
25 g (1 oz) butter

Omelettes

8 eggs
¼ cup (60 ml) milk
1 teaspoon salt flakes
1 heaped tablespoon butter

Home stretch

toasted sesame seeds or furikake
spring onion (scallion) greens (reserved from above)
tomato ketchup (optional)
spring onion & ginger chunky oil (page 222; optional)

If using raw rice → Cook the rice in your rice cooker, or following the method on page 228. Spread the cooked rice on a baking tray and leave to steam out and cool on the kitchen bench, or in the fridge to speed things up.

Peas please → Pop the peas in a heatproof mixing bowl, cover with 3 cups (750 ml) of just-boiled hot water and leave to thaw.

Fry the veg → Set a high-sided heavy-based pan or wok over medium heat. Glug in the oil and wait for it to shimmer before tumbling in the wombok, garlic, spring onion whites and most of the greens – save your best knifework for garnishing. Stir about for a couple of minutes over medium–high heat until the garlic is fragrant, and the cabbage is softened and translucent.

In goes the rice → Toss in the cooked rice and sauté over medium–high heat for 5 minutes, constantly stirring. Splodge in the ketchup, worcestershire and soy sauce and mix until everything is uniformly crimson.

Finish the rice → Drain the peas and stir them through with the diced tomatoes. Cook down for another 2 minutes, then stir the butter through. Switch off the heat, whack a lid on and leave until serving.

Omelettes to go → In a bowl, whisk together the eggs, milk and salt. Place a medium non-stick frying pan over a gentle heat. Melt 1 teaspoon of the butter in the pan, then add one-quarter of the egg mix and cook for about 3 minutes, until the top just starts to set.

While the omelette sets, scoop one-quarter of the rice mix into a small bowl (such as a cereal bowl), and flatten the rice down, to mould it. Place a serving plate firmly over the bowl, then flip them both over, so the bowl is on top. Gently remove the bowl, leaving a set mould of rice.

Gently spread the cooked omelette over the top, like a floppy hat.

Bring it home → Repeat with the remaining egg mix and rice. When all are cooked, serve sprinkled with sesame seeds and reserved spring onion greens, with the ketchup bottle and spring onion oil on the table for those who celebrate life.

There's something very cheeky-chops about this tray bake, and it's probably because of the chipolatas, which I associate with hors d'oeuvres and breakfast buffets. Ordinarily, I'm of the BBQ legend Bob Hart 'blanch and grill' school of sausages, but here the teenie sausages steam for the first 30 minutes of baking, nestled in with the tomatoes and coddled under a foil lid to create a moist environment to stop them drying out, and are then finished with a hot blast to crisp up some edges and dial up the flavour too. Look for 'gluten free' sausages at the butcher, to indicate they're not packed full of filler. Vegan sausages could be substituted too, if so inclined.

This works best with quality organic tinned cherry toms, but if fresh tomatoes are in abundance, sub in 750 g (1 lb 10 oz) whole cherry tomatoes, or quartered roma (plum) tomatoes. Add a sprinkle of sugar if your cherry toms are a little too tangy.

Tomato, Spud & Chipolata Tray Bake

Serves → 4–6

Chop + stir → 10 MINUTES

Set + forget → 45 MINUTES

- 750 g (1 lb 10 oz) kipfler (fingerling) potatoes, sliced into 1 cm (½ in) coins
- 1 rosemary sprig
- 4–5 bay leaves
- 1 red onion, cut into 8 wedges
- 2–3 garlic cloves, finely sliced
- ⅓ cup (80 ml) olive oil
- 1 teaspoon salt flakes
- ¼ teaspoon freshly cracked black pepper
- 400 g (14 oz) tin cherry tomatoes
- 500 g (1 lb 2 oz) chipolata sausages

Start your bake → Preheat your oven to 200°C (400°F). Dig out a deep baking dish that's large enough to hold the potatoes in a single layer. Pop the potatoes in, along with the rosemary, bay leaves, onion and garlic. Drizzle with 2 tablespoons of the olive oil, and sprinkle with the salt flakes and pepper. Dump the tinned tomatoes over and nestle in the chipolatas. Cover loosely with foil and bake for 30 minutes, until the spuds are fork-tender.

Time to burnish → Remove the foil from the baking dish. Crank the oven grill (broiler) up to 220°C (425°F) fan grill or 240°C (475°F) fan bake.

Drizzle the lot with the remaining 2 tablespoons of oil and whack the tray back into the oven for 15 minutes, spinning the sausages halfway through. Grill (broil) until the chipolatas are burnished and the bits underneath are starting to singe too.

Bring it home → Pull out the rosemary sprigs and bay leaves. Taste a potato, adjust the seasoning as needed and serve right away. A green leafy salad on the side wouldn't go astray.

Though I'm calling this a soup, it's somewhere between a soup and a stew, where the chunks of tomatoey bread become almost meaty – a beneficiary of the naturally occurring glutamates (umami!) in tomatoes, alongside the spongey tang of quality ciabatta.

You can find Italian polpa (finely chopped tomatoes) in the tinned tomato section at the shops, but you could also use good passata (puréed tomatoes) or two 400 g (14 oz) tins of quality crushed tomatoes. If you want a shortcut and have some PG paste (page 214) in the fridge, this would be a great addition instead of the pesto oil.

Tuscan Tomato Soup + Pesto Oil

Serves → 4

Chop + stir → 5 MINUTES

Set + forget → 30 MINUTES

¼ cup (60 ml) extra virgin olive oil
1 red onion, chopped
4 garlic cloves, peeled
800 g (1 lb 12 oz) tomato polpa
60 g (2¼ oz) parmesan wedge, with rind
1 bunch fresh basil (about 40 g/1½ oz), leaves picked, stems reserved
1 teaspoon salt flakes
¼ teaspoon freshly cracked black pepper
pinch of sugar (optional but nonna-approved)
200 g (7 oz) stale ciabatta bread

Pesto oil

¼ cup (40 g) pine nuts
1 cup (45 g) baby spinach leaves
1 bunch basil leaves (reserved from above)
1 small garlic clove, peeled
½ cup (125 ml) extra virgin olive oil

Home stretch

pretty basil leaves (reserved from above)
grated parmesan (reserved from above)

Blitz and sizzle → In a food processor, blitz the olive oil, onion and garlic to a paste. Scoop the paste into a large heavy-based pot, keeping the schmutzy processor bowl handy. Heat the pan over medium–low heat until you hear a sizzle, then whack the lid on and set the timer for 6 minutes. Stir occasionally until the mixture has softened and is starting to caramelise.

Build the soup → Stir the tomato polpa into the pot, sloshing out both tins with half a tin of water and pouring that in too. Lop the rind off the parmesan and add it to the pot, reserving the block of parmesan for grating over the soup. Add the basil stems. Season with the salt flakes, black pepper and sugar. Place the lid halfway on the pot and simmer for 20 minutes, then switch off the heat and whack the lid on to keep warm. (You can do all this the night before – or even the morning of, while you're getting breakfast going.)

Hey presto, the pesto → Heat a small pan until smoking. Switch the heat off, then throw in the pine nuts and leave to toast in the residual heat, tossing occasionally while prepping the other ingredients.

Boil a kettle of water. Pop the spinach into a colander in the sink, along with most of the basil leaves, reserving some prettier leaves for garnishing. Pour the boiling water over the leaves to speed-blanch them, then spray with cold tap water to chill them down right away and help set the vibrant green colour. Press the leaves with the back of a spoon to expel the water.

Scoop the greens into the schmutzy food processor. Add the garlic, oil and a pinch of salt, along with 3 tablespoons of the pine nuts. Blitz on high until the leaves and nuts are paste-y, the garlic assimilates and a vibrant green colour emerges. Scoop into a bowl, add the remaining pine nuts and set aside.

Back to the soup pot → After the soup has had its 20-minute simmer, tear the ciabatta into the pot and leave to simmer and soften for another 5 minutes or so, stirring regularly, until the bread breaks down and the soup has a porridge-like consistency. Remove the parmesan rind and basil stems and taste for seasoning.

Bring it home → Ladle into bowls right away. Top with a good blob of the pesto, the reserved pretty basil leaves, a crack of black pepper and some freshly grated parmesan.

This shortcut risotto will absolutely have purists shaking their fists, but I like to live dangerously. Unlike most risottos where you stir the whole time, this one gets bunged in the oven with all of its liquid, and then, right at the end, you use a whisk to release the starches and ensure a creamy finish.

Using a Microplane to grate the parmesan over the risotto will yield you the nicest cloud-like consistency, but you could also just blitz it to a crumb in the food processor before grating the veg. I'd avoid buying pre-grated parmesan, as it's kept crumby with anti-caking agent, and the aroma on a pre-grate is ... not great.

For extra flavour, sub in a litre (4 cups) of vegetable or chicken stock. And if you've got herbs growing in the garden, some parsley or chives won't go astray – even chervil would be lovely.

Grate, Bake 'n' Shake Beet Risotto

Serves → 4

Chop + stir → 10 MINUTES

Set + forget → 30 MINUTES

1 brown onion, peeled and quartered
1 beetroot (about 200 g/7 oz), top 'n' tailed, scrubbed and quartered
1 tablespoon extra virgin olive oil
2 tablespoons butter
1–2 garlic cloves, peeled and minced (crusher welcome)
1 heaped cup (250 g) raw carnaroli or arborio rice
½ cup (125 ml) white wine
2 stock cubes (veg/chicken)
2 bay leaves
¼ bunch dill, stems finely chopped, half the fronds roughly chopped (reserve the remaining fronds for garnishing)
60 g (2¼ oz) finely grated parmesan or pecorino

Home stretch

4 tablespoons mascarpone or sour cream
finely grated parmesan or pecorino
dill fronds (reserved from above)
¼ cup (35 g) slivered pistachios (optional)
extra virgin olive oil

Oven goes on → Preheat your oven to 220°C (425°F).

Grate the veg → Grate the onion and beetroot using a box grater or the coarsest setting of your food processor. Chop up any chunkier bits or stash them into your stock bag.

Start your base → Glug the olive oil and half the butter into a shallow flameproof casserole dish over medium heat. Dump in the grated veg and the garlic and stir about until you hear a sizzle. Whack the lid on and set the timer for 6 minutes, stirring halfway. Meanwhile, bring a kettle of water to the boil.

When the onion and beetroot have softened and released a sweet aroma, stir in the rice and toss vigorously for a few minutes for the rice to get toasty and turn a provocative shade of pink.

Splash in wine 'n' stock → Splash in the wine and crumble in the stock cubes. Let it all bubble for another minute, to break up the stock cubes and cook out the booziness of the wine.

Bay 'n' bake → Stir the bay leaves and dill stems through the rice, then pour in 1 litre (4 cups) of the just-boiled kettle water, which will boil and bubble again in no time. Whack the lid back on, transfer to the middle of the hot oven and set the timer for 12 minutes.

Take a whisk → Pull the pan out of the oven. Remove the bay leaves, then whisk in the remaining tablespoon of butter, along with the cheese. Continue whisking for a minute or two, whipping the lot (and risotto purists) into a frenzy. As you whip, the extra liquid in the pan will be absorbed and react with the starch in the rice and the fat in the cheese and butter, helping to encourage a silky, creamy texture.

Put the lid back on and leave for another 12 minutes to let the risotto rest and wait for the magic to happen.

Taste for seasoning, then give the mix a final stir.

Bring it home → Spoon this magenta marvel of a risotto onto plates with a lip. Top each with a spoonful of mascarpone, an extra grating of cheese, dill fronds, and some pistachios if you have them. Finish it all off with freshly ground black pepper and a drizzle of your best olive oil.

The intention of a 'minestrone' is more canonical than the ingredients – you're just looking to make a BIG, hearty serve. Typically you'd use pancetta, or some other kind of smoked meat, but here the smoky beans alleviate the need for that and keep the dish vego. I like using 'campfire' baked beans because of the lovely smoky flavour they add, but regular baked beans or other flavoured beans – even tinned cannellini beans or chickpeas – will do. The beetroot is earthy and meaty too, giving this a touch of borsch – particularly the way it dyes the pot purple! For flexitarians, parmesan rind brings the umami, while vegans will love the extra funk of nutritional yeast.

Fregola is a short Sardinian pasta. Pearl couscous, or any very small dried pasta, works here – you could even break up longer strands or crush to the size of beads. The kid-friendliest option would be alphabet pasta, so they're looking for the letters and chowing down on sweet, soft veg and pasta.

Midweek Magenta Minestra

Serves → 4 (with leftovers)

Chop + stir → 10 MINUTES

Set + forget → 45 MINUTES

1 brown onion, quartered
1 carrot, quartered
1 beetroot, peeled and quartered
1 small to medium fennel bulb, chopped into chunks (reserve the fronds for garnishing)
6 garlic cloves, peeled
¼ cup (60 ml) olive oil
2 tablespoons tomato paste (concentrated purée)
¼ cup (60 ml) worcestershire sauce
400 g (14 oz) tin polpa (finely chopped tomatoes) or passata (puréed tomatoes)
2 large waxy potatoes, scrubbed and cut into 1 cm (½ in) cubes
2 fresh bay leaves
1 hard cheese rind, or 2 tablespoons nutritional yeast
2 stock cubes (veg/chicken)
420 g (15 oz) tin smoky BBQ campfire baked beans
½ cup (50 g) fregola or pastina
1 bunch cavolo nero, leaves stripped and finely shredded

Home stretch

parmesan or other hard cheese
extra virgin olive oil
fennel fronds (reserved from above)
chopped parsley (or even better, some PG paste, page 214)
crusty bread
butter

Blitz the veg → Chuck the onion, carrot, beetroot, fennel and garlic into your food processor and blitz to a chunky paste.

Sweat the veg → In a large heavy-based pot, heat the olive oil over medium heat. Scoop the chunky veg paste into the pan and sweat with the lid on for 8 minutes, stirring occasionally. Add the tomato paste and stir about for a few minutes, until the raw astringency is cooked out and everything is glistening and richly red. Meanwhile, boil a kettle of water.

Build the soup → Deglaze the pot with the worcestershire sauce, then pour in 1.5 litres (52 fl oz) of the just-boiled kettle water. Stir in the polpa, swishing out the empty tin with another few tablespoons of water and pouring that in too. Add the potato, bay leaves and cheese rind. Crumble in the stock cubes, along with a pinch of sugar (optional but excellent).

Bring to the boil, then drop the heat to medium and keep the soup at a burble for 20–25 minutes, stirring occasionally, so any scum that floats up will get reincorporated. You'll know you're getting close when the potato cubes can be poked through with a fork.

Chunky bits → Dump in the beans, fregola and cavolo nero and simmer for another 8 minutes, or until the pasta is al dente. Taste for salt and add freshly ground black pepper as needed.

Bring it home → Ladle your magenta minestra into bowls and grate some cheese over. Finish with a generous drizzle of extra virgin olive oil, a sprinkling of fennel fronds and parsley, and another crack of pepper. Serve with fresh or toasted crusty bread and butter.

Double duty → This soup is even better the next day, when it turns into a delicious vegetable stew, which you can loosen with a splash more liquid. If you're planning on serving it the next day, add the dried pasta and fresh cavolo nero when you're bringing it back to the boil.

In the pantheon of layered bakes, moussaka is one of the cosiest. It also takes hours to make, which is less cosy for a Wednesday. So, let's take all the flavours of moussaka and make it midweeky. Spices such as nutmeg and cinnamon are a traditional inclusion – to be extra authentic, you could even sprinkle a little ground allspice into the sauce. What's inauthentic is turning the mince into meatballs, sweating the eggplant down into a rich sauce, and adding potato chippies (or crisps, depending on where you are). The crisps are a great gluten-free puffer for the meatballs, which stay super juicy and moist, and make a fab addition as a topping too. You could crush yours finer, or keep them broad like we have in the photo overleaf.

Greek oregano is the one in a bag, sold as a dried bunch – though you can sub in Mexican dried oregano. I know it looks like there are lots of ingredients here, but you'll actually notice that many are double-ups, so the recipe itself doesn't require as many things out on the bench as you think.

The Greatest (Gratest!) Moussaka Meatballs

Serves → 4–6

Chop + stir → 15 MINUTES

Set + forget → 35 MINUTES

Eggplant & tomato sauce

1 medium eggplant (aubergine), peeled and quartered
1 brown onion, halved
¼ bunch parsley, stems finely chopped (reserve the leaves for the salad)
2–3 garlic cloves, minced
2 tablespoons olive oil
1 teaspoon dried Greek oregano
¼ teaspoon ground cinnamon
2 × 400 g (14 oz) tins chopped tomatoes

Meatballs

500 g (1 lb 2 oz) minced (ground) lamb
2–3 garlic cloves, minced
1 teaspoon dried Greek oregano
½ teaspoon salt flakes
¼ teaspoon freshly cracked pepper
¼ teaspoon ground cinnamon
¼ whole nutmeg, finely grated
90 g (3¼ oz) potato crisps, crushed in the bag; save half for topping the meatballs

Feta crumble

250 g (9 oz) Greek feta, crumbled
100 g (3½ oz) hard mozzarella (the type that looks like a cute little duck)
zest of 1 lemon (reserve the lemon for the salad)

Good to grate → Start with the sauce. Using a food processor fitted with the coarse grater attachment, or a box grater, coarsely grate the eggplant and onion and place in a large shallow cast-iron casserole dish – a 28 cm (11¼ in) one is okay, 32 cm (12¾ in) is ideal. Stir in the parsley stems and ¼ cup (60 ml) water and bring to a rapid boil. Leave to bubble for about 6–8 minutes, until the liquid evaporates and the veg softens. Add the garlic and olive oil and stir about until fragrant.

Put the lid on and cook down over medium heat for 10 minutes, stirring and adding the oregano and cinnamon halfway through. Pour in the tomatoes, sloshing out each tin with a tablespoon of water, then adding that too. Stir in a teaspoon of salt flakes and a good crack of pepper, along with a small pinch of sugar, and leave to gently burble away over low heat while you prep the rest of the moussaka.

Meatball magic → While the sauce is cooking, preheat your oven to 180°C (350°F).

Combine all the meatball ingredients in a bowl, adding only half the potato crisps, and squish together thoroughly. Shape into walnut-sized balls, place on a lined baking tray and whack into the hot oven for 10 minutes to brown.

To the oven → Once the meatballs are browned, pull them out of the oven and tumble them into the eggplant and tomato sauce.

Crispy crumble → In a small bowl, toss together the feta crumble ingredients, then scatter the mixture over the meatballs. Sprinkle with the reserved potato crisps, which you can crumble or keep whole, and pop back in the oven for another 20 minutes. You want the cheese to be melted and golden, and the sauce bubbling.

EGGPLANT

Iceberg lettuce toss (maroulosalata)

100 g (3½ oz) feta, plus 1 tablespoon of the brine
1 nude lemon (reserved from the feta crumble)
1 teaspoon dried Greek oregano
½ teaspoon salt flakes
¼ teaspoon freshly cracked black pepper
½ iceberg or cos lettuce, shredded
parsley leaves (reserved from the sauce), finely chopped
¼ cup (60 ml) extra virgin olive oil

Home stretch

lemon cheeks (reserved from the salad)

Iceberg ahead → While the meatballs are baking, make up your salad. Crumble the feta into a large salad bowl and toss in the brine. Squeeze in the juice from half the lemon, then slice the remaining lemon half into cheeks for serving. Add the oregano, salt, pepper and, if you like, a pinch of sugar (I do like) and whisk together. Taste for seasoning, adding a squeeze more lemon juice and whatever else you need for balance.

Tumble in the lettuce and parsley, then taste again. Just before serving, drizzle the olive oil over and toss to coat – or serve the salad unoiled and pop the olive oil bottle on the table to let eaters dress their own like they're on a Greek island holiday.

Bring it home → Take your midweek moussaka and salad to the table and serve the reserved lemon cheeks on the side.

The greatest (gratest!) moussaka meatballs
→ pages 74–5

CRUMBLE

This is a laksa-style broth, simplified for midweek and store cupboard-friendly. Tofu puffs are perfect for sponging up flavour but they're not a non-negotiable here, as the eggplant does its share of heavy-lifting in the edible-sponge department. Malaysian-style noodle soups often use egg noodles, so hokkien noodles are a fun option here – though vermicelli rice noodles are always welcome if you've got some in the pantry. I do love the extra flavour chicken stock can bring to a speedy, yet flavour-packed, soup like this – but you can switch to veg stock if need be. For a richer broth, use coconut cream.

If you want to up the protein, add some frozen dumplings to the broth alongside (or instead of) the tofu.

Hawker-Style Red Curry Eggplant Noodle Soup

Serves → 4

Chop + stir → 20 MINUTES

Set + forget → 20 MINUTES

- 2 medium glossy eggplants (aubergines; about 600 g/1 lb 5 oz)
- ½ teaspoon salt flakes
- 100 g (3½ oz) fried tofu puffs, halved (optional)
- 1 tablespoon lime juice
- 2 tablespoons fish sauce
- neutral oil, for shallow-frying
- 450 g (1 lb) hokkien noodles

Laksa-style broth

- 2 tablespoons neutral oil
- ¼ cup (65 g) red curry paste (or ½ cup/130 g MYO, page 212), or laksa paste
- 2 cups (500 ml) chicken stock
- 800 ml (28 fl oz) coconut milk
- 1 tablespoon brown sugar (or maple syrup)

Home stretch

- 100 g (3½ oz) bean sprouts, soaked and chilled
- ¼ cup coriander (cilantro) sprigs
- 2 jammy boiled eggs (boiled for 6–7 minutes; see page 82), halved
- chilli crisp oil (shop-bought or MYO, page 221)

Eggplantsellence → Cut the eggplants into 4–5 cm (1½–2 in) chunks and place in a large mixing bowl. Sprinkle the salt over the exposed eggplant faces, rubbing it in a little, then leave the eggplant to sweat while you make the broth.

Make the broth → Heat the oil in a large saucepan over medium heat and add the curry paste. Cook, stirring, for 3–4 minutes, or until the paste is aromatic and the oil separates from the paste. Stir in the stock, coconut milk and sugar and bring to a gentle boil.

Add some puff → Add the tofu puffs to the broth now, if using. Allow the broth to simmer for 10 minutes, for the flavours to mingle.

Stir in the lime juice and fish sauce, then taste for seasoning and adjust for balance of flavour.

Marty McFry → Line a large high-sided, heavy-based frying pan with baking paper. Pour in 1 cm (½ in) of oil and heat over medium–high heat until shimmering. Grab handfuls of the eggplant, squeeze the liquid out and fry in batches for 8–10 minutes, or until golden and crisp on the outside yet soft in the middle. Remove with a slotted spoon and drain on paper towel.

Noodle about → Boil a kettle, dump the noodles into a colander in the sink and pour the just-boiled water over the top, using tongs to separate them.

Divide the noodles among serving bowls and pile the fried eggplant chunks on top.

Bring it home → Ladle the laksa broth into the bowls, dividing the tofu puffs between them. Top with the bean sprouts, coriander and jammy egg halves and serve with a dollop of chilli crisp oil.

This dish uses the silky meatiness of eggplant to offer a wonderful vego/vegan alternative to one of my favourite Cantonese dishes, duck with ginger and pineapple. The chunky veg makes for a marvellous mouthfeel, and the vibrant colours of the capsicums and purple onion against the broody burnish of the eggplant creates an impressive result that's marvellous midweek or when people are coming around. You could fry the eggplant the night before, have the sauce prepped, then bring it together for the quickest 10-minute meal. You can also add chicken to this dish, poached following the same method on page 58.

Ginger-Pineapple Eggplant

Serves → 4

Chop + stir → 30 MINUTES

Set + forget → N/A

2 glossy eggplants (aubergines; about 600 g/1 lb 5 oz), cut into 3–4 cm (1¼–1½ in) chunks
1 teaspoon salt flakes
¼ cup (30 g) cornflour (cornstarch)
¼ cup (60 ml) neutral oil
1 red onion, cut into 1.5 cm (⅝ in) chunks
1 red capsicum (pepper), cut into 1.5 cm (⅝ in) chunks
1 green capsicum (pepper), cut into 1.5 cm (⅝ in) chunks
2 cm (¾ in) thumb of ginger, peeled and finely sliced against the grain, into rounds
440 g (15½ oz) tin pineapple pieces in juice (not syrup), juice reserved

Ginger & pineapple sauce

2 cm (¾ in) thumb of ginger, peeled and minced
1–2 garlic cloves, minced
¾ cup (180 ml) pineapple juice (reserved from above)
¼ cup (60 ml) tomato ketchup
2 tablespoons light soy sauce
2 teaspoons rice wine vinegar
¼ teaspoon finely ground white pepper

Home stretch

steamed jasmine rice (page 228)
toasted sesame seeds (optional)
chilli crisp oil (shop-bought or MYO, page 221)

Nuke the eggplants → Pop the eggplant chunks into a large mixing bowl and sprinkle with the salt flakes. Transfer to a microwave-safe plate, reserving the schmutzy bowl, and microwave on high for 2–3 minutes, until softened. (Zapping the eggplant in the microwave ensures it cooks through quickly. Alternatively, salt the eggplant chunks and leave to sweat for 15 minutes, then squeeze the excess liquid out before coating – they'll just need an extra 5–10 minutes to fully cook through.)

Dump the tenderised eggplant back into the schmutzy mixing bowl, then sprinkle in the cornflour and toss about to coat.

Fry the veg → Dig out a large deep pan or wok. If using a pan, line it with baking paper, so you don't lose as much oil to the pan and the eggplant fries more efficiently. If using a wok, there's no need to line it.

Pour in 2 tablespoons of the oil and heat over medium–high heat until shimmering. Add half the coated eggplant and cook, turning occasionally, for 6–8 minutes, until crisp and browned on all sides. Scoop the eggplant from the oil to a plate lined with paper towel. Repeat with the remaining eggplant, adding more of the oil if your pan's a little parched.

Sassy sauce → Meanwhile, combine all the sauce ingredients in a jug, mixing well. Taste for seasoning, as tomato sauce can vary in sweetness, then set aside.

Flash in the pan → Once all the eggplant is done, return the pan to medium–high heat with the remaining oil. Tumble in the onion and cook for 2 minutes, then toss in all the capsicum. Set the timer for 4 minutes and toss the veg occasionally, until they relax. Add the ginger and toss about for 1 minute, or until just fragrant.

Bring it home → Add the sauce to the pan, along with the pineapple pieces and fried eggplant. Crank the heat up high and cook for 2–3 minutes, until the sauce bubbles and thickens. Remove from the heat and taste for seasoning and balance.

Divide the gingery eggplant among bowls of steamed rice and sprinkle with toasted sesame seeds, if desired. Serve with chilli crisp oil or other condiments of your choice.

Though this 'sabich' looks nothing like the 'breakfast sandwich' iterations served nowadays by street food vendors and restaurants, the original sabich was likely closer in form to what you'll see overleaf. Iraqi Jews would traditionally serve a breakfast spread for Sabich ('first light') on the Sabbath, featuring pre-prepared foods such as boiled eggs, cold fried eggplant, chopped salad, hummus, soft laffa flatbreads and amba – a spiced mango chutney popularised by Jewish merchants trading between Bombay and Baghdad, and found today in Middle Eastern and specialty delis (though the MYO mango chutney on page 216 is a very delish addish). It was an Iraqi-born Israeli, Sabich Zvi Halabi, who brought the modern iteration of sabich to the world in the 1960s, sticking the lot into a sanga that's easy to carry and even easier to love, any time of day.

If you're out of tahini, you can sub in a tablespoon of sesame oil and loosen with water as needed. If you'd prefer to mellow out the garlic flavour, try wrapping the garlic in foil and roasting it with the eggplant for 20 minutes. And if you're in a hurry, you could use shop-bought hummus – just taste and add garlic or whatever else it needs to make it yours. Or, if you've got PG paste (page 214) in the fridge already, meet me halfway by blitzing 3–4 tablespoons with the tahini and a tin of chickpeas.

Sabich Sheet-Pan Dinner

Serves → 4

Chop + stir → 10 MINUTES

Set + forget → 25 MINUTES

3 medium eggplants (aubergines; about 900 g/2 lb), cut into 2 cm (¾ in) cubes
1 × 400 g (14 oz) tin chickpeas, rinsed and drained
¼ cup (60 ml) olive oil
½ teaspoon sweet paprika
1 teaspoon salt flakes
6 eggs

Herby hummus

1 × 400 g (14 oz) tin chickpeas, rinsed and drained
4 garlic cloves, peeled
zest and juice of 1 lemon
¼ bunch coriander (cilantro), roughly chopped (reserve some leaves for garnishing)
¼ bunch parsley, roughly chopped, including stems (reserve some leaves for the salad)
3 tablespoons extra virgin olive oil
3 tablespoons tahini
1 heaped teaspoon salt flakes
1 teaspoon ground coriander
½ teaspoon ground cumin
1–2 ice cubes

Bake up → Preheat your oven to 200°C (400°F) and line a large oven tray with baking paper. In a large mixing bowl, toss together the eggplant, chickpeas, olive oil, paprika and salt flakes until coated. Spread the mixture on your lined oven tray in a single layer, reserving the schmutzy bowl, and roast for 20 minutes. Give them a quick flip and toss, then roast for another 5 minutes, until the eggplant is soft and quite burnished.

Boil up those jammy eggs → While the eggplants are roasting, gently slide the eggs into a pan of simmering water. Leave to cook for 6 minutes (or 7 minutes, if your eggs just came out of the fridge). Transfer the eggs to a sieve and run cold water over them until they stop steaming and are cool to touch. Peel, quarter and set aside for serving.

Time for a dip → To make the herby hummus, place the chickpeas in a food processor or blender with the garlic, lemon zest and juice, coriander and parsley stems. Add the remaining ingredients and blitz together for at least 5 minutes to form a fluffy hummus. Taste for seasoning and balance and set aside until ready to serve.

Salad, chop chop! → Toss the tomato, capsicum, cucumber and onion into the same big schmutzy bowl you spiced the eggplant in. Drizzle in the olive oil, add a pinch of salt and a crack of freshly ground black pepper and toss about to coat. Tumble most of the pretty parsley leaves on top, so they don't wilt under the weight of the oil, stirring them through just before serving.

EGGPLANT

Israeli salad

3 firm sweet tomatoes (such as roma), diced
1 red capsicum (pepper), diced
1 Lebanese (short) cucumber, diced
½ red onion, diced
1 tablespoon extra virgin olive oil
parsley leaves (reserved from the hummus)

Home stretch

4 soft pita mini pockets, halved (or MYO flatbreads, page 226)
coriander (cilantro) leaves (reserved from the hummus)
⅓ cup (95 g) amba (shop-bought, or MYO mango chutney, page 216)

Hot pita pockets → Wrap the pita pockets in a clean tea towel (dish towel) and zap in the microwave for 1 minute to warm through – or simply warm them in the residual heat of the oven.

Bring it home → Smear the herby hummus over a wide serving platter, then tumble the roasted eggplant mix over. Arrange the quartered eggs around the place. Scatter some coriander leaves over the top, from a height. Serve the amba and salad alongside, with the warm pitas still wrapped in the tea towel, and let diners choose their own adventure.

Double duty → This dish can be eaten cold for days. Or you can repurpose any leftover salad, flatbreads and hummus into the falafel flatbreads on page 120.

Sabich sheet-pan dinner
→ pages 82–3

If you're a fan of what a dash of wine can do for a dish, then it's time to cut out the middle man and try roasting grapes! When roasted on high, grapes are rendered surprisingly meaty, mixing with the schmaltzy skin-on chicken fat here to yield a rich garnet gravy, perfectly mopped up by spongy, crusty croutons.

If you can't find bone-in chicken thighs, chop marylands (leg quarters) into drumsticks and thighs, or get your butcher to chop them for you. For the best crispy-skinned result, let your chicken thighs dry out, skin side up, uncovered in the fridge overnight, then pull them out at least half an hour before cooking to take the fridge chill off.

Chicken, Grape & Radicchio Tray Bake

Serves → 4

Chop + stir → 15 MINUTES

Set + forget → 45 MINUTES

1 kg (2 lb 4 oz) bone-in, skin-on chicken thighs, patted dry
1 medium radicchio
¼ cup (60 ml) extra virgin olive oil
1 red onion, cut into wedges
1 whole garlic bulb, cut in half
3 thyme sprigs
400 g (14 oz) seedless red grapes, pulled off the vine
1½ teaspoons smoked sweet paprika
½ teaspoon salt flakes
½ sourdough baguette, torn into 3 cm (1¼ in) chunks

Home stretch

PG paste (page 214); optional but excellent!
radicchio leaves (reserved from above)

Oven goes on → Preheat your oven to 220°C (425°F).

Chicken comes out → While the oven is preheating, pull the chicken out of the fridge.

Prep the tray → Trim the base of the radicchio. Shred one or two of the outer leaves and set aside for serving. Slice the radicchio into eight wedges and toss into your largest mixing bowl. Pour in the olive oil, then tumble in the onion wedges, garlic bulb halves, thyme sprigs, grapes, paprika and salt, tossing about to coat.

Tip the mixture into a large deep baking dish (cast iron is great!), arranging the veg like a trivet. Sprinkle a teaspoon of salt flakes into the schmutzy bowl, then toss the chicken thighs in, swirling about to coat in the remaining oil and spices. Place the chicken thighs, skin side up, on top of the veg.

Into the oven → Roast for 40–45 minutes, until the grapes are blistered, the chicken skin is browned and the juices are running clear.

Crunchy bits → At the 30-minute mark, spread the sourdough chunks on a baking tray and bake underneath the chicken tray for 10 minutes, or until golden and crunchy.

Bring it home → Once the chicken is cooked through, pull the garlic halves and thyme sprigs out of the pan. Squeeze the garlic flesh back in, then smush it into the pan juices. Toss the crunchy sourdough croutons through the mix, encouraging it underneath the thighs to soak up the purple-tinged schmaltz.

Blob on some PG paste, if using, and snuggle the reserved shredded radicchio around the place too, for refreshingly bitter pops of purple; some more fresh salad leaves on the side never hurt. Finish with some more salt flakes and a fresh crack of pepper from a height.

One of the biggest blunders that people make when browning their shrooms in a pan is adding fat too early. All that does is seal in all the natural moisture within the spongy flesh, eventually leading to the dreaded slimy texture that mushroom-averse folk dislike. Before you add any fat, crank up the heat and BOIL the shiitake out of your mushrooms with a bit of water in the pan to help evaporate excess internal moisture, infusing them with aromatics (like the worcestershire sauce here) as they boil.

I've chosen to use a stroganoff-y combination to illustrate this method, serving the shrooms twirled through fresh fettuccine. Get creative with the condiments, and the mushroom varieties too – you could easily sub in exotics like fresh shiitake, shimeji, chestnut and the like. The world's your oyster (mushroom)!

Mushroom Stroganoff Fettuccine

Serves → 4

Chop + stir → 15 MINUTES

Set + forget → 25 MINUTES

- 500 g (1 lb 2 oz) button mushrooms (or any combo of exotics)
- 1 golden shallot (or brown onion), unpeeled
- 4 garlic cloves, unpeeled
- 2 thyme sprigs
- 2 tablespoons worcestershire sauce (or soy, for vegos)
- ½ cup (125 ml) water or stock (veg or chicken)
- 1 tablespoon brandy
- 1 tablespoon extra virgin olive oil
- 1 tablespoon butter
- 1 tablespoon tomato paste (concentrated purée)
- 1 teaspoon dijon mustard
- 200 g (7 oz) crème fraiche or sour cream
- 50 g (1¾ oz) parmesan (or other hard cheese), grated
- ¼ teaspoon sweet paprika
- 400 g (14 oz) fresh fettuccine

Home stretch

- grated parmesan
- 2 tablespoons soft herbs, such as fresh chives and/or parsley
- extra virgin olive oil

Bath time → While you get organised, soak the mushrooms, shallot, garlic cloves and thyme in your salad spinner or a bowl of cold water, to dislodge the mushroom grit and make the alliums easier to peel – 5 minutes is plenty.

Pan time → Remove the mushrooms from the water, leaving the shallot and garlic soaking. Slice the mushrooms finely, keeping the stalks intact. Toss them into a deep, wide heavy-based pan with the thyme sprigs and worcestershire sauce, and splash in the water or stock. Crank the heat up to medium–high and wait for the liquid to start boiling, then set the timer for 15 minutes.

Meanwhile, drain, peel and slice the garlic and shallot.

Once all the liquid has evaporated from the pan and the mushrooms are colouring up, stir in the brandy to deglaze the pan. Mix in the olive oil, butter, garlic and shallot. Season with a pinch of salt and fry for about 5 minutes, until everything is a glistening golden brown.

Stir in the tomato paste and mustard and fry off for 1–2 minutes.

Get creamy → Remove the pan from the heat, add the crème fraiche, parmesan, paprika and a good crack of black pepper, then stir about to incorporate. Taste for seasoning.

Pasta pot → While the mushrooms are simmering, bring a large pot of well-salted water to the boil. Once the pasta water's boiling, switch off the heat until you've stirred the crème fraiche into the sauce, then resume transmission. Bring the pot back to the boil, drop in your fettuccine and boil for 2–3 minutes, stirring to help the strands separate.

Give us a twirl → Transfer the cooked pasta straight into your mushroomy stroganoff pan. Stir about until well coated, then taste for seasoning.

Bring it home → Serve with a sprinkle more parmesan, a flourish of soft bright green herbs, a glug more olive oil and freshly cracked pepper.

Double duty → If you're a small household or planning on leftovers, keep the sauce and fettuccine separate, then combine after reheating. Toss the leftover fettuccine in oil before storing – or just cook half now, half later.

Traditionally, a chicken dish like this uses the whole bird, which is quite impractical for a whip-up Wednesday situation. Which is why creator Xiao Feng's version, using inexpensive and flavoursome chicken drumsticks, caught my eye. Because steaming is an indirect, wet heat, it keeps whatever is under-lid nice and juicy, and in this dish helps to infuse warming ginger and umami-rich shiitake flavours into the chicken.

To keep this dish vego-friendly, you could swap the drummies for a slab of silken or soft tofu, steaming it for 10–15 minutes to warm through, then slicing and drizzling on chilli or spring onion oil to serve.

The cucumber salad provides a wonderfully crunchy, cooling contrast against the delicately steamed chicken. When the weather cools, some steamed gai lan or broccolini would be perfect alongside instead.

Chicken + Shiitake Broth + Cucumber Whack Salad

Serves → 4

Chop + stir → 15 MINUTES

Set + forget → 40 MINUTES

- 100 g (3½ oz) fresh shiitake mushrooms, finely sliced
- 3–4 spring onions (scallions), whites and light greens finely sliced, dark greens kept separate
- ¼ bunch coriander (cilantro), stems roughly chopped (reserve the leaves for the salad)
- 2 cm (¾ in) thumb of ginger, peeled
- 8 chicken drumsticks (about 1.5 kg/3 lb 5 oz)

Cucumber whack salad

- 1–2 garlic cloves, peeled
- 2 cm (¾ in) thumb of ginger, peeled and finely grated
- 1 tablespoon light soy sauce
- 1 tablespoon toasted sesame oil
- 4–5 Lebanese (short) cucumbers
- spring onion (scallion) whites and light greens (reserved from above)
- coriander (cilantro) sprigs and leaves (reserved from above), roughly chopped

Home stretch

- steamed jasmine rice (page 228)
- chilli crisp oil (shop-bought or MYO, page 221)
- XO sauce or mushroom XO (store-bought or MYO, page 220)

Construction zone → Find two heatproof bowls – a shallow bowl that just fits into a bamboo steamer, and a second much smaller one that's deep enough to hold the aromatics. Pop the dark green spring onion tops, chopped coriander stems and half the ginger into the smaller bowl.

Place the larger bowl upside down on top of the small one, then flip the lot, so that the small bowl is upside down inside the bigger one. (When steaming, the water vapour will be magically sucked up into the inverted bowl, percolating into an aromatic broth.)

Drum up the drummies → Arrange the mushroom slices and chicken in the big bowl, around the smaller bowl. Cut thin rounds of the remaining ginger to place on top of each drumstick.

Place the lot in the bamboo steamer, and set it over a deep pan or wok. Pour about 2 cups (500 ml) water into the pan, under the steamer. Put the lid on, followed by a layer of foil to really keep in the steam. Bring to the boil over medium–high heat, then set the timer for 35 minutes.

Get whacking → While the chicken is steaming, make the dressing for the cucumber whack salad. Grate the garlic and ginger into a salad bowl. Add the soy sauce and a pinch of sugar, stirring to dissolve the sugar, then mix in the sesame oil. Taste for seasoning.

Place the cucumbers on a board and smack them with the flat of a knife until they burst (highly therapeutic!). Slice and dump into the bowl to soak up the dressing.

Leave the spring onion and coriander to languish on top of the salad, stirring them through just before serving.

Back to the steamer → When the timer goes off, check that the chicken is cooked – the meat should be tender and opaque, with no signs of pink at the bone.

Bring it home → Arrange the steamed rice on a large platter. Carefully tong the drummies and mushroom over the rice. Using a tea towel (dish towel) to protect your hands from the hot steam, lift the inverted bowl out of the steamer and marvel at the schmaltzy broth underneath. Taste for seasoning.

Pour the broth over the chicken and shrooms through a sieve and top with your choice of condiment. Serve with the cucumber whack salad for a full-steam dinner ahead.

Have a squiz at the image next door, and tell me what you see. Those waggly little bits of fried enoki tendrils ... they look just like ET's fingers, reaching out and glowing, right? This dish is certainly something to phone home about, all fizzy five-spice, crispy bites of exotic mushroom and tender tofu, with fresh pops of sweet veg from the capsicum, spring and salad onion. The contrast from these veggie accoutrements were my favourite part of the five-spice squid at Lau's Family Kitchen, and it didn't take long to realise that the five-spice tofu gave us the same amount of satisfaction at half the price.

If you're not a tofu household, this might just be the dish to tip you over.

Five-Spice Enoki + Tofu

Serves → 4

Chop + stir → 10 MINUTES

Set + forget → 20 MINUTES

MUSHROOM

375 g (13 oz) block organic regular (or firm) tofu
½ teaspoon salt flakes
1 red capsicum (pepper)
½ white or red onion
2–3 spring onions (scallions)
200 g (7 oz) enoki mushrooms
neutral oil, for shallow-frying (about 1½ cups/375 ml)

Five-spice salt

1 teaspoon salt flakes
1 teaspoon Chinese five-spice

Coating mix

⅓ cup (50 g) plain (all-purpose) flour
⅓ cup (40 g) cornflour (cornstarch)
1 teaspoon salt flakes

Home stretch

steamed jasmine rice (page 228)
1 lemon, cut into cheeks
mushroom XO (shop-bought or MYO, page 220); optional
chilli crisp oil (shop-bought or MYO, page 221); optional

Prep the tofu + veg → Cut the tofu into 1 cm (½ in) cubes, pop onto a plate, sprinkle with the salt flakes and place back in the fridge to dry out for 5–10 minutes while you get on with the rest of your prep. Dice the capsicum and onion, and finely slice the spring onion on the bias. Trim the very bases of the mushrooms and tear the enoki into chopstick-friendly clumps (err on the side of smaller).

Fantastic five → To make your five-spice salt, grind the salt flakes and five-spice together using a mortar and pestle and tip into a large bowl – or crush the salt flakes between your fingertips and toss through the five-spice to combine.

Fry time → Line a wide heavy-based pan with baking paper, then pour in about 5 mm (¼ in) oil and heat to 180°C (350°F) over medium heat – you don't need a thermometer, just drop in a mushroom and if it immediately starts to curl up and turn golden, you're all set.

Get your coat on → While the oil heats, combine the flours and salt flakes in a bowl, mixing with your hands to combine. Toss the tofu about in the flour coating.

Line one end of a baking tray with paper towel, and set a cooling rack over the other end. Working in batches, fry the tofu in the hot oil for 5–6 minutes, or until golden on all sides. Scoop out and drain on the paper towel side.

Toss the mushrooms through the flour mix, then fry for 2–3 minutes, until they're golden too, draining them straight onto the cooling rack.

While the tofu's still warm, toss it through the five-spice salt. Add the mushrooms and give that one more toss.

Bring it home → Just before serving, toss the capsicum, spring onion and salad onion through the ET tower. Serve over steamed jasmine rice, with the lemon cheeks and condiments of your choice.

This one began as a play on words ... in recipe form! Dauphinoise potatoes are usually sliced and baked as a creamy casserole, while d'affinois cheese is a double-cream brie-style French cheese that you buy by the gooey slice. Together, they make the best bougie baked potatoes! Once I'd stopped congratulating myself on the pun, I knew I had to deploy Stephanie Alexander's technique, which blew my mind – roasting the halved spuds on the rack, uncovered, un-oiled, unseasoned. Crunch on the outside, fluff in the heart. I prefer starting this with a cold oven; just chuck the halved spuds in as soon as you get home, crank the temp, then get on with your business until you can squish their tuchuses.

You can use PG paste (page 214) instead of garlic butter, if you've got some in the fridge – in fact, any compound butter or condiment can be squished into the fluffy spuds to melt under the cheese.

It's also a fun, playful option for a big dinner gathering, particularly if you've got people with dietaries and/or cautious eaters coming round. Give it a go – you'll never roast jackets in sweaty foil ponchos again!

Bougie Baked Potatoes + Very Fine Slaw

Serves → 4

Chop + stir → 10 MINUTES

Set + forget → 50 MINUTES

6–8 medium-sized high-starch potatoes (such as nicola or dutch cream), scrubbed
200 g (7 oz) Fromager d'Affinois cheese (or double/triple cream of your choice)

Very fine slaw

¼ white cabbage
juice of ½ lemon
½ teaspoon salt flakes
¼ teaspoon freshly cracked black pepper
2 dill sprigs, fronds picked, stems reserved

Garlic dill butter

3 garlic cloves, peeled
dill stems (reserved from the slaw)
100 g (3½ oz) good butter

Bake the spuds → Slice the potatoes in half lengthways, in whatever direction you'll get the most surface area (some are girthier than others through their middle). Pop them, cut side down, straight across a (clean) oven rack, then crank the temperature to 200°C (400°F). Set a timer for 50 minutes for medium spuds. They may need extra time if they're bigger. They're cooked when their faces are glassy and the insides feel fluffy when you give their bums a squish.

Meanwhile, pull your cheese and butter out of the fridge to take the chill off.

Toss that slaw → Slice the cabbage as finely as you can, using either a very sharp knife or a mandoline (if your mandoline doesn't have a guard, use a tea towel (dish towel) to hold the cabbage and protect your hand). Toss into a bowl, squeeze in the lemon juice and toss the salt and pepper through. Taste the slaw: some cabbage is sweet enough, others need a pinch of sugar, so you do you. Sprinkle in the dill fronds and swish about. I like to toss this slaw with my clean hands to ensure everything's mixed evenly and to massage the cabbage a little.

Butter up → For the garlic dill butter, mince the garlic and finely slice the dill stems, then fold these through the butter with a fork. If your butter is unsalted, fold in a little pinch of salt too.

Bring it home → Arrange the spuds, cut side up, on a platter or individual plates. Squish from top and bottom to expose a gash in the middle, and fill this with a good scoop of garlic butter. Top with a slice of cheese, then finish with a heaping of slaw. Merci merci, me.

This is my favourite kind of late spring, early summer picky-picky potato salad, where fork-sized bits of everything good to eat and good for you come together with a dressing that's a beneficiary of someone else's good pickling handiwork. 'Chat' potatoes, as they're known in Australia, are new-season baby potatoes that hold their shape well. Desiree would be perfect here, as would small kipflers (fingerlings), or any kind that will hold up against a gentle toss. If you can't find chats, quarter a low-starch 'boiling' potato.

Flavour-wise, there's something a little noughties fillet-o-fish going on here. If you can't find bread and butter pickles, you could instead use finely sliced dill pickles, gherkins or cornichons, or even piccalilli.

Serving the lettuce separately keeps it super crunchy against the creaminess of the other ingredients, and also invites san choy bow sandwiching behaviour, which is welcomed and encouraged.

Chat Potatoes + Green Beans + Smoked Trout + B 'n' B Pickle Dressing

Serves → 4

Chop + stir → 10 MINUTES

Set + forget → 25 MINUTES

1 kg (2 lb 4 oz) small chat (new) potatoes, halved
400 g (14 oz) green beans, topped, then torn or sliced in half
1 butter lettuce (or cos or oak leaf lettuce)
200–300 g (7–10½ oz) hot smoked trout
1 small red onion, peeled, halved and finely sliced with the grain
250 g (9 oz) baby cucumbers, sliced into coins
¼ bunch parsley, leaves finely sliced, stems finely chopped
¼ bunch dill, fronds picked (reserve some for garnishing)

Bread & butter pickle dressing

1 heaped teaspoon hot English mustard
1 cup (245 g) sour cream
½ cup (40 g) bread and butter pickles

Home stretch

dill fronds (reserved from above)

Bubbly chats → Pop the potatoes into a large pot, three-quarters filled with well-salted water. Bring to the boil, then drop to a gentle simmer and set a timer for 15 minutes.

In with the beans → Once the timer goes off, check that you can almost stick a fork through a spud, then toss in the green beans for another 3 minutes. Scoop out ½ cup (125 ml) of the water and reserve.

Drain and steam → Set a colander in the sink and drain the spuds and beans, then leave to steam-dry for 5 minutes or so while you get on with the salad.

Lettuce rejoice → Pick the butter lettuce leaves into your salad spinner or large bowl. Cover with plenty of cold water and leave to soak, draining and spinning (either in a spinner, or wrapped in a tea towel/dish towel and shaken or swung about) just before you're ready to serve.

Get dressing → Scoop the mustard into a large mixing bowl. Splash in a few tablespoons of the hot potato cooking water and stir into a paste. Stir in the sour cream and pickles and taste for seasoning.

Flake the trout → Flake the fish on top of the dressing, feeling about for bones. (These are more of a bother with river trout; if you're using ocean trout, no need to get too finicky.)

Meet and greet → Transfer the dry hot steamed potatoes and beans to the dressing and trout bowl. Then top with the onion, cucumber, parsley and dill. Leave everything layered so the spuds can warm the dressing and fish.

Just before serving, fold everything together to coat. Taste again to make sure the choir is singing in harmony.

Bring it home → Tumble the salad into a serving bowl. Top with the reserved dill fronds, a crack of pepper and some flaky salt. Serve the lettuce leaves in another bowl and allow eaters to help themselves.

If reading 'chowder' makes you want to say it in a fancy French accent – 'chowderrrrr' – then you're picking up what I'm putting down. I've cut out the need to head to a fishmonger, and lots of faffing about, by simply using smoked mussels. Their smoky flavour pairs beautifully with the creaminess of the potato-enriched soup, leading our six-year-old spawn to declare: 'I liked this even better than I expected', which I notch down to a win. Of course, you could also serve the mussels (or even smoked oysters or hot-smoked trout) on the side, and allow eaters to add as much or as little as they'd like ... a bit like 'sea-seasoning'. You could also leave it vego by stirring some dried seaweed or furikake through instead. And a bouquet 'zesti' is a bouquet garni, with lemon peel. Have I made it up? Oui. Am I sticking with it? Also oui.

Mashing potatoes are high-starch ones. You can test whether yours will pass muster by applying The Sticky Spud Test: slice a spud in half, then see if it sticks to the knife. If it slips off, save it for salads (like the one on page 96). If it sticks, it's starchy enough to break down beautifully for roasting, mashing or chowdering.

This chowder could be made a day or so in advance and reheated before adding the mussels. For a bonus taste sensation, try stirring in some PG paste (page 214) before serving.

POTATO

Smoked Mussel Chowder

Serves → 4

Chop + stir → 15 MINUTES

Set + forget → 40–45 MINUTES

1 leek, darker green tops trimmed
2 tablespoons olive oil
1 celery stalk, finely sliced
1 large-ish fennel bulb (about 400 g/14 oz), diced (reserve the fronds for garnishing)
2 medium mashing potatoes (about 450 g/1 lb), such as sebago (russet), peeled and cubed
¼ cup (60 ml) white wine
2 cups (500 ml) stock (veg/chicken)
200 ml (7 fl oz) thick (double) cream
120 g–150 g (4¼–5½ oz) smoked mussels (vac-packed ones are the juiciest!)

Bouquet zesti

2 bay leaves
4–5 thyme sprigs
peel of ½ lemon, pith removed

Home stretch

fennel fronds
extra virgin olive oil
baguette or ciabatta slices – either fresh, or grilled and rubbed with a garlic clove

Fix your leek → Split the leek down the middle, keeping it whole at the base, then wash between the papery layers under running water. Finely slice into discs against the grain.

Sauté away → Heat the olive oil in a large heavy-based flameproof casserole dish or soup pot over medium heat. Add the leek and celery. Cook with the lid on for 10 minutes, or until softened, stirring occasionally but not allowing to brown; reduce the heat if necessary. Stir in the fennel and potato and sauté over high heat for 2 minutes.

Bouquet, you stay → Make a bouquet zesti by wrapping the bay leaves around the thyme sprigs, packing the lemon peel behind, then tying the lot together with kitchen twine.

Simmertime → Add the wine to the dish and cook out the booziness for about a minute, until it stops stinging your eyes. Pour in the stock and 2 cups (500 ml) water and drop in the bouquet zesti. Increase the heat to high and bring to the boil, then reduce to a simmer. Pop the lid on ajar (so not too much liquid evaporates) and set the timer for 25 minutes.

When the timer goes off, squash the potato and fennel with a fork, and check they both squish beneath easy pressure. If they don't, cook for another 5 minutes.

Blitz → Fish out the bouquet zesti, then use a stick blender to whiz the chowder to your desired consistency (chunks are encouraged). Stir the cream through and taste for seasoning.

Bring it home → Bring the chowder back to a simmer. Drain the mussels and set aside eight whole ones. Roughly chop the remaining mussels and divide among your serving bowls, then ladle the warm soup over. Pop two whole mussels on top of each bowl. Finish with the fennel fronds, a lick of olive oil and crack of black pepper. Serve with fresh or grilled baguette or ciabatta slices.

The real hero here, beyond the carb-on-carb of pasta AND potatoes, is the walnut mince, which looks, tastes and feels decidedly meaty. *And since walnuts are the moment, their freshness is paramount. It pays to invest in the best you can find, or take the extra couple of minutes to shell your cup's worth (for this recipe, you'll need to start with about 2 cups unshelled walnuts). If buying shelled walnuts, look for the bags with the least amount of crumby bits – this'll tell you the walnuts haven't been sitting around for long.*

To make this pasta vego, pull out the anchovies, use a non-animal-rennet pecorino, and splash in some fysh sauce or soy sauce for extra funk. If you wanted to add some meat, squeeze in the filling from 250 g (9 oz) pork and fennel sausages. Instead of dried pasta, you could use 400 g (14 oz) fresh pasta; this only requires about 3 minutes of boiling time, so simmer the potatoes for 10 minutes before adding the pasta.

Potato & Cavolo Nero Orecchiette + Lemony Walnut Sauce

Serves → 4

Chop + stir → 15 MINUTES

Set + forget → 25 MINUTES

200 g (7 oz) kipfler (fingerling) potatoes, washed and sliced into 5 mm (¼ in) coins
300 g (10½ oz) dried orecchiette (or other short pasta)
1 bunch cavolo nero, leaves stripped and finely sliced

Lemony walnut sauce

1 cup (115 g) freshly shelled walnuts (2 cups unshelled)
½ teaspoon fennel seeds
2 tablespoons extra virgin olive oil
3–4 quality anchovies (optional but excellent)
1 small fennel bulb, finely diced, fronds reserved
3 garlic cloves, finely sliced
¼ teaspoon mild chilli flakes (optional but excellent)
½ cup (125 ml) white wine
100 g (3½ oz) chilled butter, diced
½ cup (50 g) finely grated pecorino
zest of 1 lemon (reserve the nude lemon for serving)
¼ whole nutmeg, grated (optional but excellent)

Home stretch

nude lemon (reserved from the sauce)
finely grated pecorino
fennel fronds (reserved from the sauce)
extra virgin olive oil

Make your sauce → Wrap the walnuts and fennel seeds into a clean tea towel (dish towel) and give them a whack with the base of your olive oil bottle to break them up into a chunky 'mince' consistency. Pour the olive oil into a large high-sided heavy-based pan and heat until shimmering. If using anchovies, stir them into the oil until dissolved.

Toss in the walnut mince, fennel seeds and diced fennel and cook over medium heat for about 15 minutes, until the walnuts start to caramelise and turn golden and the fennel softens.

Add the garlic and chilli flakes, if using, and stir about for a minute until fragrant. Crank the heat up to high, splash in the wine and wait for the waft of alcohol to stop stinging your eyes.

For the carb on carb → Meanwhile, add the potato coins to a large pot of well-salted cold water and bring to the boil. Toss in the pasta, stirring to stop the pasta sticking, then set the timer to cook according to the packet instructions. In the last minute of cooking, reserve a mugful of pasta water, add the cavolo nero, then drain through a colander.

Back to your sauce → Splash in the reserved mug of pasta water, then stir in the butter, pecorino, lemon zest and nutmeg, if using, to meld into a sauce.

Bring it home → Tip the drained pasta, potato and cavolo nero into your big pan of sauce, tossing to coat. Cut your nude zested lemon in half, squeeze the juice from one half into your sauce, then slice the other lemon half into wedges for serving. Taste for seasoning, then finish with an extra cloud of pecorino, fennel fronds, a lick of olive oil and a crack of black pepper. Serve with the lemon wedges.

Double duty → Any leftover sauce can be reheated and stirred through a fresh batch of pasta the next day. You could also cook more pasta than you'll need, quickly cool it on a tray, toss it with olive oil and turn the leftovers into a potato and pasta salad.

On those nights when I'm home alone and not in the mood to go full fanfare, something brothy, eggy and green is exactly what I crave. 'Choy' is the Chinese word for vegetable, which is why it's part of the names of many Asian greens, such as bok choy ('white vegetable') and choy sum ('vegetable heart'). These veg bring me JOY, through their sweet, gentle flavour and vibrant colour that helps to rewire the system after zappy days. If you're making this for yourself, just quarter the recipe – or make a two-person portion: one for today's you, and one for tomorrow's breakfast for future you. This'll be done and dusted within 20 minutes because there's no sweat on the alliums – you're just using shop-bought crispy shallots. Look for the crispy shallots that haven't been fried in palm oil, or make a batch of your own (page 225). While you're raiding your reserves, if you've got some spring onion oil (page 222) in the fridge, use that instead of (or as well as) the ginger and garlic; some mushroom XO (page 220) wouldn't go astray either.

Crispy Omelette + Choy-Ful Broth

Serves → 4

Chop + stir → 10 MINUTES

Set + forget → 10 MINUTES

BOK CHOY

Choy-ful broth

1 litre (4 cups) stock (veg/chicken)
2–3 bok choy, shredded against the grain, then soaked and spun dry
3 tablespoons crispy fried shallots (shop-bought or MYO, page 225)
2 cm (¾ in) thumb of ginger, peeled and finely grated
2 garlic cloves, finely grated
¼ bunch coriander (cilantro), sprigs reserved, stems roughly chopped

Crispy omelette

6 eggs
1½ teaspoons light soy sauce
1 tablespoon toasted sesame oil
¼ cup (60 ml) neutral oil

Home stretch

coriander (cilantro) sprigs (reserved from the broth)
crispy fried shallots
chilli crisp oil (shop-bought or MYO, page 221)

For the choy-ful broth → Pour the stock into a large saucepan and bring to just below the boil. Pop the shredded choy into a fine-mesh sieve, then lower the sieve into the simmering broth and leave for 2 minutes. Scoop the choy out, into your serving bowls, keeping the sieve handy.

Pop the crispy shallots, ginger, garlic and coriander stems into the simmering stock and leave to burble away gently while whipping up the omelette. Just before serving, taste for seasoning, pinch in some salt or splash in some soy and a sprinkle of ground white pepper or a crack of black pepper if need be. Switch the heat off.

For the omelette → Meanwhile, in a bowl, use a fork to whisk together the eggs, soy sauce, sesame oil and a pinch of white or black pepper. Pour the oil into a heavy-based pan or wok and heat until shimmering, then pour in the egg mixture. Let it cook undisturbed for 1–2 minutes over medium heat, then gently lift the sides and tilt the pan to let the uncooked mix flow underneath. Cook for another 1–2 minutes, until the egg is just set and the base is golden. Slide the omelette onto a chopping board and slice into four wedges, then distribute among the bowls.

Bring it home → Grab your sieve again and strain the broth into each bowl. Scatter with the coriander sprigs and more crispy shallots. Add a drizzle of chilli crisp oil, or serve it at the table along with your favourite flavour-infusing, joy-inducing condiments, so eaters can choose their own adventure.

The beauty of this recipe (pictured overleaf) is that it takes advantage of every grating side of a box grater, breaking down the ingredients to eke out maximum flavour, in minimum time, with minimum fuss and washing up. The grated broccoli becomes jammy, its natural sweetness brought up with currants and out with salty little capers and parmesan. Pangrattato literally translates to 'grated bread', which is much easier to do when the bread is stale. You're welcome to use panko breadcrumbs if you've no stale bread handy (check your freezer for parcelled breadcrumb trails from past you!).

If you're a proficient pasta cook, you should be able to whack the pasta water on to heat as you start the rest of the prep to save time, and have the whole kit and caboodle boxed off within 20 minutes; otherwise, make the sauce, then get onto the pasta, which'll mean an extra 15 minutes or so at the end.

Box Grater Brocc Pasta + Brocc Fuzz Pangrattato

Serves → 4

Chop + stir → 15 MINUTES

Set + forget → 15 MINUTES

2 small heads of broccoli
¼ cup (60 ml) extra virgin olive oil
2 shallots (any kind), or 1 brown onion, coarsely grated
2 garlic cloves, finely grated
½ bunch parsley, stems finely chopped (reserve the leaves for the pangrattato)
¼ cup (50 g) lilliput capers, drained and dried
½ cup (75 g) currants
400 g (14 oz) dried casarecce (or other short pasta)
1 cup (100 g) finely grated parmesan

Brocc fuzz pangrattato

50 g (1¾ oz) salted butter
1 tablespoon extra virgin olive oil
100 g (3½ oz) stale bread, crusts removed, coarsely grated
heaped ½ cup grated broccoli fuzz (reserved from above)
2 garlic cloves, finely grated
zest of 1 lemon (reserve the nude lemon for serving)
½ bunch parsley, leaves chopped

Home stretch

nude lemon wedges (reserved from the pangrattato)
chopped parsley
extra virgin olive oil

Time to box → Coarsely grate the broccoli 'fuzz' (the dark-green furry outer layer of the florets), leaving the tight inner florets intact. Set a heaped half-cup of the broccoli fuzz aside for the pangrattato.

Trim and peel the broccoli stalks. Coarsely grate the stems and florets.

On the boil → Bring a large pot of salted water to the boil.

Pangrattato please → Meanwhile, heat a large high-sided frying pan over medium–high heat. Add the butter and oil. When foaming, add the breadcrumbs, reserved broccoli fuzz and garlic. Cook and toss for 10 minutes, until golden. Remove from the heat. Stir in the lemon zest and parsley, then tip into a bowl and set aside.

Schvitz in the pan → Wipe out the pan and place back over medium heat. Add the olive oil, shallot, garlic and parsley stems and sauté for 5 minutes. Toss in the capers, currants and the rest of the grated broccoli florets and stems. Sauté over medium–high heat for another 5 minutes, until jammy.

Pasta pot → Meanwhile, once the water is at the boil, drop in the pasta, stir about, return the water to the boil and cook for a minute less than the packet directions suggest. Reserve a mugful of the pasta water, then drain the pasta.

Bring the gang together → Add half the reserved pasta water to the broccoli sauce and sauté for another minute over medium heat; the starchy liquid helps emulsify and season the sauce. Gradually add more pasta water if desired and simmer until it reaches your preferred texture. (I like my sauce runnier because the pasta sucks up the juices while it keeps cooking in the residual heat of the sauce – which is why we don't cook the pasta for as long as the packet tells us to.) Tumble in the drained pasta, most of the parmesan and half the pangrattato.

Bring it home → Squeeze some lemon wedges over the pasta, stir and taste for seasoning. Tumble the pasta onto a serving platter and sprinkle with the remaining pangrattato and parmesan. Add a final flourish of parsley and drizzle of olive oil and serve with any remaining lemon wedges.

This recipe is a riff on the Asian-fusion frittata I learnt to make in the kitchens of Two Good Co., a social enterprise that provides a pathway to employment and empowerment for women who've experienced true hardship. I've added one of my favourite hack sauces – KSC, a creamy kimchi and sour cream combo that's a bit of a sweet-chilli-Philly situation – along with chunks of sweet potato, which turn this into a meal for any time of day. Sustainably sourced fish goes without saying but particularly when it comes to salmon. You want your fish to come from somewhere with very cold waterways, like New Zealand for the southern hemisphere or Canada for the North. I like to use pa-kimchi (the one with spring onion/scallion) for this, but just use whatever you have – even some sweet chilli sauce would do it.

Broccolini & Salmon Frittata + Chunky Sweet Potatoes + KSC

Serves → 4–6

Chop + stir → 15 MINUTES

Set + forget → 45 MINUTES

700 g (1 lb 9 oz) small to medium sweet potatoes
1 tablespoon neutral oil

Frittata

1 tablespoon neutral oil
1 red onion, finely sliced with the grain (reserve some for garnishing)
2 garlic cloves, minced
½ long red chilli, deseeded and finely chopped
250 g (9 oz) frozen peas
1 bunch broccolini, halved lengthways, then chopped into 1 cm (½ in) lengths
9 eggs
1 tablespoon soy sauce
2 teaspoons sesame oil
180 g (6½ oz) smoked salmon/trout
2–3 spring onions (scallions), finely sliced
¼ bunch parsley, finely chopped (reserve some pretty leaves for garnishing)
1 tablespoon white sesame seeds

KSC (kimchi sour cream)

½ cup (80 g) quality kimchi
½ cup (125 g) sour cream or crème fraiche

Home stretch

red onion slices (reserved from the frittata)
parsley leaves (reserved from the frittata)

Hot potato → Chop the sweet potatoes into jaunty 2 cm (¾ in) chunks by rolling them on a cutting board and slicing on opposite angles. Toss in a large bowl with the oil, a pinch of salt flakes and a crack of black pepper.

Tumble them onto a baking tray lined with baking paper, leaving space around each, and whack into the bottom third of a cold oven. Crank the temperature up to 170°C (350°F) and roast for 45 minutes, or until soft through the middle and lightly burnished in parts.

To the frittata → While the sweet potato bakes, heat the oil in a frying pan over medium heat and cook the onion and garlic with the lid on for 8 minutes, or until softened, stirring now and then. Add the chilli and cook for a further 2 minutes, until aromatic, then set aside to cool.

Prep the green stuff → Boil a kettle of water. Pop the peas and broccolini into a colander in the sink. Pour the boiling water over, then toss about to drain well and thaw the peas.

Stir the greens through the aromatics in the pan. Line a medium deep baking dish with baking paper and scoop the greens into the dish.

Finish the frittata → Crack the eggs into a bowl, splash in the soy sauce, sesame oil and a pinch of salt and pepper, then whisk to combine. Pour into the baking dish, then flake the smoked salmon over the top. Sprinkle with the spring onion, chopped parsley and sesame seeds.

Place into the top third of the oven and bake for 25–30 minutes, or until set, turning the dish halfway through if your oven has hot spots.

Creamy kimchi → In a small bowl, combine the kimchi and sour cream, tasting for balance. Add more heat or creaminess to your liking.

Bring it home → Slice the frittata and serve warm with the roasted sweet potato chunks, garnished with the reserved onion slices and parsley leaves, with the kimchi sour cream on the side.

Double duty → This frittata and its accoutrements can also be eaten cold as an easy breakfast on the go, lunch à-la-desko, or a lunchbox legend.

I've always felt the best part of a double cheeseburger isn't the burger but the cheese! Brassicas such as broccoli, when burnished, offer plenty of chargrilled flavour in these surprisingly 'meaty' fritters. You'll be happy to know a food processor or box grater does most of the work, and happier still to see how kids love scoffing these for dinner.

Cheesy Brocc Smash Burgers + Ruby Slaw + Dilly Dipper

Serves → 4

Chop + stir → 15 MINUTES

Set + forget → 30 MINUTES

3–4 spring onions (scallions), whites roughly chopped (reserve the greens for the dilly dipper)
½ bunch parsley, roughly chopped
2–3 garlic cloves, peeled
zest of 1 lemon (reserve the nude lemon for serving)
2 tablespoons olive oil, plus extra for brushing
1 large head of broccoli (about 500 g/1 lb 2 oz); you could also use broccolini or cauliflower
2 medium zucchini (courgettes; about 400 g/14 oz)
½ cup (50 g) grated hard cheese, such as parmesan
1 cup (120 g) chickpea flour (besan)
1 teaspoon baking powder
1 teaspoon chicken-style stock powder (or 1 crumbled cube)
8 slices tasty cheese

Ruby slaw

¼ red cabbage, finely shredded
425 g (15 oz) tin baby beetroot, drained, then coarsely grated
¼ red onion or red shallot, finely sliced

Dilly dipper

3–4 spring onion (scallion) greens (reserved from above)
1–2 dill sprigs
¾ cup (185 g) sour cream

Home stretch

pretty dill fronds (reserved from above)
nude lemon (reserved from above), cut into cheeks

Squish your veg → In a food processor or blender, blitz the spring onion whites, parsley, garlic, lemon zest and olive oil to a fine paste, then transfer to a mixing bowl.

Switch to the coarse grating attachment (or a box grater) to coarsely grate the broccoli, zucchini and hard cheese. Dump the grated veg and cheese over the herby paste in the mixing bowl. Stir a teaspoon of salt flakes through, give everything a good squish, then leave for 5–10 minutes to get really juicy.

Oven goes on → While the veg mix steeps, preheat your oven to 200°C (400°F).

Fritter away → Sift the chickpea flour, baking powder and stock powder over the squishy veg. Crack in some black pepper and stir together with a spatula until well incorporated, ensuring there are no dry spots. If your batter feels a bit too loosey-goosey, mix in another tablespoon of chickpea flour.

Line a large baking tray with baking paper and brush with oil. Scoop eight ¼ cup mounds of mixture onto the tray, leaving 2 cm (¾ in) of room around each burger, to allow air to circulate for crispy edges. Flatten slightly into 'smash burger' patties.

Bake it 'til you make it → Bake the burgers for 12–15 minutes. Using a spatula and another utensil as a cantilever, gently flip the fritters, then bake for another 12–15 minutes, until golden and firm.

Cheesy finish → Switch the oven off and top each fritter with a cheese hat, leaving them in the still-warm oven to get melty.

Meanwhile, back at the ranch → Toss the ruby slaw ingredients together in a bowl, then set aside.

Do the dilly dipper → Finely slice the spring onion greens and toss in a small bowl. Reserve the prettiest fronds from the dill sprigs, then finely chop the rest. Add to the bowl with the sour cream and a pinch of salt and pepper and stir together. Taste and adjust if needed.

Bring it home → Arrange the cheesy smash burgers on a board or platter. Sprinkle salt flakes and a crack of black pepper over the top, finishing with a smattering of pretty dill fronds. Serve with the ruby slaw, dilly dipper and lemon cheeks.

Double duty → These make great burgers in a bun too! Just sandwich the warm smash burgers in the buns with the slaw and dipper inside.

Across the Caucasus and the Near East, versions of tolma or dolma (depending on the dialect) see all manner of veg and leaves stuffed with rice, aromatics, and occasionally minced (ground) meat, served with a yoghurt sauce. In the Mediterranean, they pop up as dolmades: vine leaves stuffed with rice, then boiled. The tang of the vine leaves and the creaminess of the rice and yoghurt sauce is deeply invigorating, but stuffing and rolling any kind of tolma midweek is expecting too much. Enter this one-pan wonder – somewhere between a pilaf (page 188) and a tolma, with a touch of kale chip. Instead of rainbow chard, beetroot leaves or silverbeet (Swiss chard) are welcome here, or you could even replace half the leafy greens with preserved vine leaves for more authenticity.

Cheat's Chard Tolma Bake

Serves → 4 (with leftovers)

Chop + stir → 15 MINUTES

Set + forget → 35 MINUTES

2 cups (400 g) basmati rice, washed well
1 teaspoon salt flakes
¼ cup (60 ml) olive oil
1 brown onion, sliced into half-moons against the grain
¼ bunch coriander (cilantro), stems finely chopped (reserve the leaves for garnishing)
1 bunch rainbow chard, washed
3–4 garlic cloves, peeled and crushed
1 tablespoon khmeli suneli (page 211) or mild madras curry powder
700 g (1 lb 9 oz) jar tomato passata (puréed tomatoes)

Yoghurt drizz

2 cups (520 g) natural yoghurt
¼ cup (35 g) roughly chopped dried apricots
1 garlic clove, minced

Home stretch

seeds from ½ pomegranate (optional but excellent)
coriander (cilantro) leaves (reserved from above)

Heat is on → Preheat your oven to 200°C (400°F).

For the rice → Dump the well-washed rice, salt and 3 cups (750 ml) cold water into a medium saucepan. Bring to the boil, then switch the heat off, put the lid on and leave for 10 minutes to par-cook.

For the veg → Meanwhile, heat the olive oil in a large high-sided, heavy-based pan or shallow flameproof casserole dish over medium heat. Add the onion and coriander stems and wait for the sizzle. Drop the heat to medium–low, pop a lid on and set the timer for 8 minutes.

Wash the chard well, then strip the leaves off the stems. Finely slice the stems against the grain, then chuck them in the pan with the onion, giving the lot a stir. Reset the timer for another 5 minutes, stirring occasionally. Finely slice the leaves while you wait and set them aside.

Stir in the garlic and spice mix and cook for a minute or so, until fragrant. Stir in the par-cooked rice and passata, sloshing out the dregs in the jar with about 1 cup (250 ml) water and pouring that in too. Season with a good pinch of salt flakes and a crack of black pepper. Pile in the chard leaves and press them down on top, without stirring through.

Bake that beauty → Place the pan in the oven and bake, uncovered, for 15 minutes.

Yoghurt drizz → While the pan's in the oven, stir together the yoghurt, apricots and garlic. Loosen the mix with a splash of water to a drizzle-able consistency.

Bring it home → Pull the pan out of the oven and fluff up the contents with a big spoon, stirring the slightly crispy chard on top through to distribute and absorb. Taste and season, then allow to cool for 5 minutes or so. Drizzle with the yoghurt drizz, sprinkle with pomegranate seeds, if using, and coriander leaves from a height. Serve with a big scoopy spoon at the table.

Double duty → This makes a great cold or reheated bowl lunch. Just save some drizz to rehydrate the rice the next day.

This dish (pictured overleaf) is an exercise in economising: on ingredients, time and washing up. And it's all due to fond. Otherwise known as fonds de cuisine *(loosely, the foundation of the kitchen), fond is the tasty stuff in the bottom of the pan that too often ends up down the sink. Harnessing the schmaltzy bits through sweating and deglazing can take a surprisingly spartan ingredient list and make the sum far greater than its parts.*

For whirlwind Wednesdays, chicken thighs are a great option, particularly when flattened with something heavy to help maximise the Maillard reaction. In the Georgian kitchen, this method is applied for whole spatchcocked birds in a dish called chicken tabaka, where Mum's usual weight of choice is a pizza tray topped with her granite mortar, wrapped in a reusable bag, giving her handles to lift it off when done.

Marinated feta acts as both marinade and creamy funk. Chuck in the zest and juice of a lemon and you've landed on the classic combination of a Greek horta, replacing dandelion greens with silverbeet. This is a vegetable best treated as two separate species: the stalks closer to celery, and the leaves like spinach. Don't be deterred by the amount of bulk in a bunch – once sautéed, it performs the same magic trick as any spinach, wilting down to a wonderfully savoury, brightly bitter accompaniment to the chicken.

For a vego option, sub out the chicken and feta, and use a block of haloumi instead, drying, oiling and flattening it against the pan as above to sear, then slicing and scattering over the silverbeet to serve.

Flat-Chat Chicken + Feta + Silverbeet

Serves → 4

Chop + stir → 15 MINUTES

Set + forget → 20 MINUTES

100 g (3½ oz) marinated feta in oil
1 lemon
500 g (1 lb 2 oz) boneless, skin-on chicken thighs
1 large bunch (about 700 g/1 lb 9 oz) silverbeet (Swiss chard), well rinsed
1 small brown onion, finely sliced
2 garlic cloves, finely sliced

Home stretch

extra virgin olive oil
lemon wedges

Swish the chicken → Pour ¼ cup (60 ml) of the oil from the marinated feta into a shallow dish. Grate the lemon zest into the bowl, then cut the lemon in half and squeeze in the juice, reserving the squeezed-out lemon halves. Season with salt to taste. Swish the chicken through the marinade, then leave to absorb all the flavours while you prepare the silverbeet.

Silver slivers → Strip the leaves off the silverbeet stalks, then roughly chop and reserve. Finely slice the stalks, then pop these into your salad spinner or a bowl with cold water, adding the squeezed-out lemon halves to acidulate the water; this helps to dislodge any gritty bits, infuse lemony flavour and keep the stalks extra juicy and white. Set aside.

Flat chat → Place a large heavy-based frying pan over medium heat for 2–3 minutes, or until you can hover your hand above and feel the heat radiating. Add the chicken thighs, skin side down, reserving the marinade. Flatten the thighs by placing something heavy on top – I use a fish weight that I rotate around the pan, but you could use a clean smaller frying pan with something heavy on top of it – or even go full *Backyard Blitz* using a clean brick wrapped in foil!

Cook the chicken for 6 minutes, until the skin underneath is sufficiently golden brown. Remove your weight. Flip the thighs over and fry the other side for another 4–5 minutes (no flattening needed), until the juices run clear. Transfer to a plate with a lip, cover loosely with a foil hat, and leave to rest until the silverbeet is done.

Sweaty stalks → Loosen the reserved marinade by mixing in ¼ cup (60 ml) water, then swish this into the pan, using a firm spatula to deglaze the chickeny pan juices (aka fond!). Drain the silverbeet stalks (no need to spin), then add to the pan with the sliced onion. Sauté over high heat for 4 minutes in the schmaltzy juices.

Whack the lid on, drop the heat to medium, and sweat for another 5 minutes, until the stems are soft, the onion translucent, and the liquid has evaporated. Throw the garlic in now, along with another ½ cup (125 ml) water.

Sweaty leaves → Crank the heat back up and toss in the silverbeet leaves. Put the lid back on and leave to sweat for 5 minutes.

Last blast → Using tongs, turn the leaves over and sauté uncovered for another couple of minutes, until cooked to your liking. I prefer to pull mine off while still quite bright green and toothsome, then let the residual heat soften it off. Taste for seasoning.

Slice the thighs → Pour the rested chicken juices into the pan with the silverbeet. Place the chicken on a clean cutting board and slice against the grain; for thighs, this usually means on the shortest edge.

Bring it home → Tumble the greens onto a platter or individual plates, then top with the sliced chicken. Crumble the feta over and finish with a drizzle of olive oil and an extra flourish of salt flakes and black pepper. Serve with lemon wedges for squeezing at the table.

Flat-chat chicken + feta + silverbeet
→ pages 114–15

Mkhlovani is Georgia's answer to spanakopita, where wild greens are sautéed and stuffed into a dough. But baking stuffed things midweek means too much waiting around, so I'm dividing and conquering, baking crunchy 'sails' of shop-bought puff pastry while the greens schvitz in the pan.

When you buy beetroot, remember to stash the washed leaves in the freezer for this dish. You can also use greens such as silverbeet, chard, cavolo nero or English spinach, or add another 100 g (3½ oz) of other foraged (unsprayed!) leaves – anything from warrigal greens or saltbush to nettle or dandelion greens.

Traditionally, you would use suluguni, a saltier mozzarella-style Georgian cheese, but I've made up a more globally available mix of cheeses, including cottage cheese for bonus protein.

Green Team Sailboat Mkhlovani

Serves → 4–6

Chop + stir → 15 MINUTES

Set + forget → 30 MINUTES

- 375 g (13 oz) packet all-butter puff pastry
- 2 tablespoons extra virgin olive oil
- ½ bunch spring onions (scallions; about 200 g/7 oz), finely sliced
- 1 kg (2 lb 4 oz) bunch of greens, such as silverbeet (Swiss chard), rainbow chard or beet greens
- 3–4 garlic cloves, chopped
- 1 tablespoon khmeli suneli (shop-bought or MYO, page 211); optional but excellent
- 250 g (9 oz) frozen spinach
- 200 g (7 oz) mozzarella, grated
- 200 g (7 oz) cottage cheese
- 100 g (3½ oz) feta
- ½ bunch dill (about 40 g/1½ oz), stems and fronds finely chopped
- zest of 1 lemon (reserve the nude lemon)
- 1 teaspoon salt flakes
- ¼ teaspoon freshly ground black pepper

Home stretch

- nude lemon (reserved from above), cut into cheeks

Oven goes on → Preheat your oven to 200°C (400°F) and line two baking trays with baking paper.

Sail away → Cut the frozen puff pastry into isosceles triangles; you should get at least eight 'sails'. Place on the baking trays and bake for 15 minutes, or until golden and puffed to the hilt.

Remove the pastry from the oven and rest for 15 minutes before bringing it home.

For the greens → While the pastry is puffing in the oven, heat the olive oil in a large deep heavy-based pan over medium heat. Add the spring onion and wait for the sizzle, then drop the heat to medium–low, pop a lid on, and set a timer for 5 minutes.

Meanwhile, rinse your greens well (they get especially gritty towards the root end), then strip the leaves off and finely slice against the grain. Finely slice the stems as well.

Add the greens stems to the pan, mixing well, then reset the timer for another 5 minutes, stirring occasionally. Stir in the garlic and khmeli suneli, if using, and cook for another minute.

Pile in the finely chopped leafy greens and the spinach (frozen or thawed). Put the lid on and leave to wilt for 3 minutes. Using pan-friendly tongs, move the softened leaves from the bottom of the pan to the top, then replace the lid and cook for another 3 minutes. Stir again, then cook, uncovered, for another 3–4 minutes, until the leaves are completely wilted, thawed and well mixed through.

Cheese please → In a large bowl, mix together the mozzarella, cottage cheese, feta, dill and lemon zest, using a wooden spoon to break up the feta and combine. Season with the salt flakes and black pepper.

Make the mix → Switch the heat off under the greens and stir the cheese mix through, letting the residual heat bring it all together. Check again for seasoning.

Bring it home → Poke the pastry sails over the top of the pan. Serve at the table on a trivet, with the reserved lemon cheeks in a small bowl alongside. Using a serving spoon, scoop the cheesy greens onto each plate, then top with a pastry sail or two.

Double duty → Store the pastry sails separately from the greens mix, and reheat gently for serving. You could also serve leftovers on toast and be thrilled.

While fried falafel requires dried chickpeas be soaked overnight, this one's got a can-do, midweek attitude. Usually, if you forget to soak chickpeas, it's not as simple as swapping in a tin – I once watched a whole batch's worth of falafel batter disintegrate in my frying oil because I thought I'd get clever with a can. With this recipe, there's no need to worry about them falling apart because the flatbreads form your base, and the falafel mix your 'schmear'. To get the crispiest crust that stays on the mix, rather than your pan, you'll need to use a well-seasoned heavy-based pan, or something with a non-stick (non-toxic!) coating, such as ceramic or the like. If your pan is not non-stick, you can add an extra layer of insurance by cutting a piece of baking paper to fit in the bottom of the pan, and adding to the heated pan before plopping the pitas on top.

Squashed Green Falafel Flatbreads

Makes → 8 (serves 4–6)

Chop + stir → 15 MINUTES

Set + forget → 15 MINUTES

8 small soft pita pockets
olive oil, for pan-frying

Squashed falafel mix

1 brown onion, quartered
1 tablespoon ground coriander
1 tablespoon ground cumin
1 teaspoon salt flakes
2–3 garlic cloves, peeled
1 bunch parsley (about 75 g/ 2½ oz), roughly chopped, reserving a handful of leaves for the salad
1 bunch coriander (cilantro; about 75 g/21/2 oz), roughly chopped, reserving a handful of leaves for the salad
400 g (14 oz) tin chickpeas, rinsed and drained well

Chopped salad

½ red onion, finely diced
4 firm sweet tomatoes (such as roma), roughly chopped
1 Lebanese (short) cucumber, roughly chopped
parsley leaves (reserved from the falafel mix)
coriander leaves (reserved from the falafel mix)
2 tablespoons extra virgin olive oil

Garlicky drizz

½ cup (130 g) natural yoghurt
juice of ½ lemon
1 garlic clove, minced

Blitz your mix → Pop the onion, ground spices, salt, garlic and fresh herbs – in that order – in a blender or food processor. Blitz until the onion starts to break down to a sludge, and the herb stems have yielded to the blades. Add the chickpeas and blend to the consistency of a smooth paste. Taste for seasoning and set aside in a bowl to get friendly.

Chop chop salad → In a bowl, toss together the onion, tomato and cucumber with a pinch of salt and freshly ground black pepper. Roughly tear the parsley and coriander leaves over the top and leave them be, so they don't go soggy.

Drizzle ahead → Mix the garlicky drizz ingredients together in a small jug, ready for pouring.

Squash + fry → Heat a wide frying pan over medium heat with 2 tablespoons water in the base. (Once the water evaporates, you'll know your pan is hot enough and you won't void some non-stick warranties!)

While the pan heats, divide the falafel mix into eight equal portions. Take your pita pockets and smear one side of each pita with one portion of the falafel mix.

Splash a tablespoon of olive oil into the hot pan. Working in two batches, swish the schmeared side down onto the pan and heat for 2–3 minutes, until the falafel mix is golden but still has bits of green poking through. Flip the pitas out of the pan, onto a plate, stacking them under a clean tea towel (dish towel) to stay steamy warm.

Bring it home → When ready to serve, toss the salad in the olive oil and plonk on the table with the garlicky drizz and pitas-under-towel. Instruct lucky diners to tumble some salad over the falafel mix, drizz on some drizz, fold and eat. Smashing!

Double duty → Reheat the fried flatbreads the next day to keep the party going. You can also leave some pre-made mix in the fridge the night before, ready for frying as soon as you get home.

Considering cucumbers originated in the foothills of the Himalayas around 5000 years ago, it's no surprise there's no shortage of cuke inclusions in the cuisines of India and Nepal. Here I've teamed cucumbers with chickpeas – a protein-packed legume that flips this from a side into a substantial summertime dinner.

I've used chaat masala, a spice blend that's like garam masala, with the addition of amchur (green mango) powder. You can use garam masala instead, spiking with some acid from a lime or lemon if need be. If you have date and tamarind sauce in the fridge, feel free to sub this in rather than heading out for mango chutney, though you could also double-down and MYO on page 216.

Indian-Style Cucumber & Chickpea Salad

Serves → 4

Chop + stir → 15 MINUTES

Set + forget → 10 MINUTES

3 tablespoons neutral oil
½ cup (80 g) cashews
2 sprigs curry leaves, stripped
¼ teaspoon black mustard seeds
400 g (14 oz) tin chickpeas, rinsed and drained
1½ teaspoons chaat masala
4 Lebanese (short) cucumbers, cut into chunks
4 firm sweet tomatoes (such as roma), cut into chunks
½ red onion, finely sliced

Raita drizz

½ cup (130 g) natural yoghurt
¼ bunch well-washed coriander (cilantro) stems, finely chopped, (reserve the leaves for garnishing)
handful of mint leaves, finely chopped
1 garlic clove, minced
½ teaspoon ground cumin

Home stretch

mango chutney (shop-bought or MYO, page 216)
coriander (cilantro) leaves (reserved from the drizz)
mint leaves
1 long green chilli, finely sliced (optional but excellent)

Fry your nuts + spice → Place a saucepan over low heat and pour in 2 tablespoons of the oil. When warm, toss in the cashews and toast for 5 minutes, stirring about. Sprinkle in a pinch of salt flakes and the well-dried curry leaves, stirring about until they're glistening (careful – they might spit, so pop a lid on, or throw in from a distance). Tumble in the mustard seeds and cook together for another minute, until the seeds pop like popcorn. Scoop the mixture into a small bowl.

Chaat up your chickpeas → Keeping the pan over low heat, add the remaining tablespoon of oil, followed by the chickpeas. Fry up for a few minutes, then stir in the chaat masala and cook for another minute. Turn off the heat and scoop the chickpeas into a large mixing bowl.

Tumble the cucumber, tomato and onion through the spiced chickpeas. Check for seasoning, remembering that there'll be seasoning in the raita too.

Right to the raita → Mix all the raita drizz ingredients together in a small bowl. Taste for seasoning and leave to get friendly.

Bring it home → Tip the salad onto a platter with high sides and liberally pour the raita drizz all over. Blob the mango chutney around, scatter the cashew and curry leaf mix over and finish with coriander and mint leaves, and green chilli if desired.

Double duty → This is perfect for packing for work the next day – just combine the ingredients with the dressing in the morning, then give them a good shake in your lunchbox to reincorporate before tumbling out onto whatever bowl's left in the staff kitchenette. Or, stuff the salad into a flatbread of your choice and enjoy as a wrap!

Every time I think of this dish, I remember cabaret queen Rhonda Burchmore shivering with delight at her first taste when I made it for her on my show. The cavolo nero and butter beans are the hero here, and the fish is the 'garnish', which is why there's only about 125 g (4½ oz) fish per person. The deep forest green of the cavolo nero against the creamy butter beans, combined with the zip of lemon, make this an irresistible combo that could also be enjoyed as a hearty vego side if you leave the fish in the sea.

Lemony Cavolo Nero Butter Beans + Capered Fish En Papillote

Serves → 4

Chop + stir → 15 MINUTES

Set + forget → 15 MINUTES

500 g (1 lb 2 oz) smaller fish fillets, such as flathead, mullet or whiting (roughly 4–6 fillets)
¼ cup (15 g) finely chopped dill
1½ tablespoons lilliput capers, rinsed and drained
30 g (1 oz) butter

Lemony cavolo nero butter beans

20 g (¾ oz) butter
1 tablespoon olive oil
1 brown onion, finely sliced against the grain
3 garlic cloves, finely sliced
2 × 400 g (14 oz) tins butter beans, rinsed and drained
200 ml (7 fl oz) vegetable stock (or water)
½ bunch cavolo nero or other kale (about 3 large leaves), leaves stripped and finely sliced
zest of 1 lemon (reserve the nude lemon for serving)

Home stretch

nude lemon (reserved from the beans), cut into wedges
crusty baguette
lashings of butter

Fire up → Preheat your oven to 210°C (400°F) and pull the fish out of the fridge.

Butter bean butter boom → Make a start on those lemony butter beans by melting the butter and oil together in a large heavy-based pan over medium heat. Add the onion and listen for the sizzle. Drop the heat to medium–low and whack the lid on. Set the timer for 8 minutes, stirring occasionally until translucent; a little colour here won't hurt.

Fishy parcels → Meanwhile, tear off four sheets of foil and four sheets of baking paper, each roughly 20 × 30 cm (8 × 12 in) in size. Layer the baking paper sheets over the foil ones. Pop a fish fillet in each parcel. Arrange the dill, capers and butter on top of the fish, along with a sprinkling of salt flakes and a crack of black pepper. Fold the foil up into a parcel around each fish fillet, like a Cornish pasty, and tuck the edges and crimp the foil while leaving a bit of a ceiling so the air won't escape but the fish isn't squished. It doesn't have to look pretty – it just needs to be secure. Place the fish parcels on a baking tray.

When the oven has come up to temperature, slide the tray in and bake the fish for about 8 minutes, or until the flesh just flakes apart.

Kale yeah → Once the buttery onion is sufficiently softened, add the garlic and stir about for a minute, until fragrant. Reduce the heat to low, tumble in the butter beans and stir in the stock. Bring to the boil, then add the shredded cavolo nero and stir until lovely and coated. Drop the heat to medium, whack the lid back on and set the timer for 3 minutes.

Switch off the heat and stir in the lemon zest, along with salt flakes and freshly cracked black pepper to taste.

Bring it home → Serve the beans and fish parcels at the table so eaters can help themselves – or pop a tumble of bean 'n' green onto each plate, top with the fish fillets, drizzle the sauce from the parcels over and finish with a lemon wedge or two. Crusty bread, generously buttered, will help to mop up the sauce and bring it all together.

Double duty → Leftover lemony beans and greens also make a perfect bed for poached eggs!

These pan pies are a loose play on khachapuri imeruli, a type of Georgian cheese bread that's a cousin to the iconic cheese and egg boats known as khachapuri adjaruli. Though traditionally an imeruli uses a yeasted dough to encase cheeses like suluguni, I've adapted the dough into a speedy yoghurt flatbread and the cheeses to suit a midweek cook anywhere – you could even use a mix of pizza cheese and feta. And for a speedier shortcut, you could use shop-bought pizza dough … my favourite hack is buying some straight from my local pizza place!

Spinach breaks down to almost nothing *as it cooks, so unless you have lots growing in the garden, use frozen spinach for recipes requiring a large amount. If you have time, thaw the frozen spinach overnight in the fridge on kitchen towel, to absorb the liquid around the spinach as it melts and help it to better retain its colour and texture. If you're in a hurry, run a tap over the frozen spinach clumps. Once thawed, drain and squeeze out the excess moisture before using.*

If serving in a heat-avoidant household, hold the hot honey and sprinkle the pies with salt flakes and a little drizzle of honey instead.

Spinach & Cheese Pan Pies + Hot Honey Drizzle

Makes → 4

Chop + stir → 20 MINUTES

Set + forget → 40 MINUTES

¼ cup (60 ml) olive oil
2 tablespoons butter

Yoghurt dough

2 cups (300 g) self-raising flour, plus extra for dusting
1 cup (260 g) Greek-style or natural yoghurt
1 teaspoon salt flakes

Cheese & spinach filling

500 g (1 lb 2 oz) frozen spinach, thawed
150 g (5½ oz) block of feta (creamy or crumbly, whatever you've got)
1 cup (100 g) grated cheddar
100 g (3½ oz) firm mozzarella, grated
3 spring onions (scallions), greens finely sliced (reserve the whites for the salad)
1 teaspoon freshly cracked pepper

Hot honey drizzle

¼ cup (90 g) mild-flavoured honey
1 teaspoon mild chilli flakes

Dough! → Combine the dough ingredients in a medium bowl and mix with a wooden spoon until it all forms a shaggy mess. Get your hands in there to form a ball of dough, then turn out onto a clean floured surface and knead for about 2–3 minutes. You'll want some extra flour on hand for the kneading. The dough's ready when it's smooth and springs back when you pop a fingerpad into it. Be careful not to overwork it. Place a clean tea towel (dish towel) over it while you make your filling.

Filling time → Wrap the thawed spinach in a tea towel and squeeze out as much excess moisture as you can. Tip the wrung-out spinach into a mixing bowl, add the other filling ingredients and mix to combine with your wooden spoon. Taste for seasoning.

Hot honey → Combine the hot honey drizzle ingredients in a small saucepan and place over low heat. Cook gently for a few minutes, until the honey is warmed through and runny. Switch off the heat and leave the chilli to infuse into the honey.

Ship shape → Using a board scraper or knife, divide the dough into four even pieces. Pull out a dough quarter, then cover the rest with your tea towel again.

Sprinkle flour on your rolling pin (or wine bottle!) and bench to prevent sticking. Roll out the ball of dough into a 12 cm (4½ in) round. Pop one-quarter of the filling mixture in the middle of the dough, then fold the edges over the filling so it's covered, flattening down to seal it all together. Try to avoid any holes here, otherwise the filling will escape. Tighten the edges to make a round shape. You can roll out all the pies here and keep them under a tea towel if prepping ahead, or make the rest on the fly as you're waiting for each to fry.

Continued overleaf →

→ Continued

Baby spinach salad

125 g (4½ oz) baby spinach
3 white spring onion (scallion) stems (reserved from the filling), sliced on an angle

Fry time → Heat a medium frying pan over medium–low heat. Add a drizzle of olive oil and a teaspoon of the butter and wait for it to foam and melt. Pop a pan pie into the pan and cook for 3–5 minutes on each side, with a drizzle more oil if needed; you want a deep golden colour and the edges to be creamy white (if they're still opaque, your dough hasn't fully cooked through yet).

Cook the remaining pan pies in the same way. To keep your cooked ones warm, stack them in a tea towel in a warm spot.

Toss up → Just before serving, toss the baby spinach and spring onion in a large mixing bowl with a sprinkle of salt flakes, black pepper and a drizzle of olive oil.

Bring it home → Serve the warm hand pies drizzled with the hot honey, with the salad on the side.

Double duty → Leftover pies are great for lunch the following day, either cold or reheated, and will last for up to 5 days in the fridge.

What you gain from a rolled barley risotto ('barlotto'), besides time, is a dish very reminiscent of Heston Blumenthal's snail porridge – comforting, vibrantly verdant and vibrating with vitality and nourishment.

You can turn the whole thing plant-based by subbing in vegan butter and a plant-based hard cheese. If you'd prefer, instead of the stock cubes, you can use 1 litre (4 cups) of homemade stock and supplement with 1 cup (250 ml) of extra water to make up the difference. And if you've got the time, you're welcome to make this with pearl barley for extra nutty chewiness – just increase the simmer to 35 minutes.

Spinach Barlotto

Serves → 4 (with leftovers)

Chop + stir → 10 MINUTES

Set + forget → 25 MINUTES

1 tablespoon olive oil
50 g (1¾ oz) butter
1 brown onion, finely chopped
1–2 cloves, finely chopped/minced
1½ cups (150 g) rolled barley flakes
½ cup (125 ml) dry white wine
2 stock cubes (veg/chicken)
1.25 litres (5 cups) just-boiled hot water (from a kettle)

Spinach pesto

50 g (1¾ oz) parmesan, chopped
100 g (3½ oz) freshly shelled walnuts, a handful reserved for garnishing
100 g (3½ oz) baby spinach (or frozen spinach, thawed)
100 g (3½ oz) rocket (arugula)
¼ bunch parsley, roughly chopped
4 large unsprayed nasturtium or dandelion leaves (optional but excellent)
zest of 1 lemon (reserve the nude lemon for serving)
1–2 garlic cloves, peeled
¼ cup (60 ml) extra virgin olive oil
50 g (1¾ oz) butter

Home stretch

parmesan
extra virgin olive oil
1 tablespoon mild-flavoured runny honey (or hot honey, page 219)
walnuts, roughly chopped (reserved from the pesto)
nasturtium leaves (optional)
nude lemon (reserved from the pesto), cut into cheeks

Start up the aromatics → Heat the olive oil and butter in a wide heavy-based saucepan over medium heat. Scoop in the onion, listen for the sizzle, then whack a lid on. Set the timer for 6 minutes and sweat until soft and translucent, stirring once or twice. Stir in the garlic, put the lid back on and cook for 2 minutes more.

Barley toasted → Tumble in the barley flakes and stir about for 2 minutes, until golden and lightly toasted. Pour in the wine, crumble in the stock cubes and let it all burble away and absorb into the barley flakes for another minute or so, until you've cooked out the booze and it's no longer stinging your eyes.

Simmer → Pour in the hot boiled water, stirring well. Drop the heat to low, put the lid on and leave to simmer for 15 minutes, until the barley is tender but still slightly chewy, and the liquid has mostly evaporated.

Hey pesto → While the barley cooks, get cracking on the pesto. In a food processor, blend the parmesan to a crumb, then add the remaining ingredients and whiz until you have a bright green purée.

In a swirl → Once the barley is tender and the liquid is mostly absorbed, stir the spinach pesto through. Bring it back up to a bubble, then switch the heat off. Taste and season with salt flakes and freshly ground black pepper.

Bring it home → Ladle into shallow bowls, shave some parmesan over and drizzle with olive oil and runny honey. Finish with a scattering of walnuts and nasturtium leaves, if using, and serve with the lemon cheeks.

The great thing about these fish cakes is that they're so packed with non-fishy flavours that you can use a fairly fishy fish and happily feed it to non-fish people. The crackers act like an instant crumb and binder, helping to puff these up into lovely fluffy fish cakes, juicy with zucchini, so they're more like a rissole than a Thai-style bouncer. If you're growing soft herbs in pots or in the garden, add more than just the one – the more the merrier. Bread and butter pickles are usually made with either zucchini or cucumber, and they'd both be welcome here – though if you can find a zucchini version, it's a fun way of integrating more zucchini into the recipe and adding more flavour to the tartare.

Lemony Zucchini & Tinned-Fish Cakes

Serves → 4 (makes 16)

Chop + stir → 15 MINUTES

Set + forget → 20 MINUTES

1 cup (250 ml) neutral oil

Fish cakes

150 g (5½ oz) dry crackers, such as Sao or Salada
2 medium zucchini (courgettes; about 240 g/9 oz)
2 × 125 g (4½ oz) tins pink-fleshed fish, such as smoked rainbow trout or salmon, drained
handful of soft herbs, such as dill, chives or parsley, finely chopped
zest of 1 lemon
½ cup (120 g) whole-egg mayonnaise
1 tablespoon dijon mustard
2 teaspoons worcestershire sauce
2 shakes of hot sauce
½ teaspoon salt flakes

Bread & butter tartare

½ cup (120 g) whole-egg mayonnaise
¼ cup (55 g) bread and butter pickles, roughly chopped
1 tablespoon bread and butter pickle juice
zest of 1 lemon, plus 30 ml (1 fl oz) lemon juice
1 tablespoon capers in brine, finely chopped
handful of soft herbs (dill, chives or parsley), finely chopped

Home stretch

cos or iceberg lettuce leaves
lemon cheeks
finely chopped soft herbs

Crush alert → To make the fish cakes, finely crush the crackers to a crumb, using a bag and a rolling pin or a food processor. Scatter half the biscuit crumbs over a baking tray.

Perfect match → Using a box grater, or preferably a Japanese shredder if you have one, grate the zucchini into a large mixing bowl. Toss in the remaining cracker crumbs and the rest of the fish cake ingredients. Add a good crack of black pepper and mix to combine.

Crumbs! → Using damp hands and a ¼ cup (60 ml) measure for consistency, shape the fish cake mixture into ¼ cup patties. Pop them onto the crumby baking tray to pick up the crumbs, then flip over to grab any more lone crumbs, keeping the coating fairly light.

Flash in the pan → Line a large non-stick frying pan with baking paper. Pour in the oil and heat over medium heat until shimmering. Working in batches, cook the fish cakes for about 5 minutes, until golden underneath. Using a spatula, gently turn them over and cook until golden and crispy on the other side, about 5 minutes more. Drain on a plate lined with paper towel, or on a cooling rack over a baking tray, sprinkling some salt flakes on top.

Tartare time → While the fish cakes are frying, place all the tartare ingredients in a small serving bowl and fork together. Taste for seasoning and set aside.

Bring it home → Pop the warm fish cakes onto a share plate in the middle of the table, along with the tartare, lettuce leaves and lemon cheeks. Finish with a scattering of finely chopped herbs and serve.

Double duty → These fish cakes are fab for fish sangas the next day, or you can freeze them for up to 3 months and thaw and bake as you need. Any leftover B & B tartare is great with the smoked fish potato salad on page 96.

Zucchini lends itself so well to Italian flavours, so you'll be forgiven for feeling like you've stumbled into a decidedly different book for the next few recipes. This one nods to the classic flavour combination of agrodolce ('sour–sweet'), with tangy red wine vinegar–soused red onions against juicy rehydrated currants.

By draining but not rinsing the beans, you're taking advantage of their naturally occurring aquafaba, which is like whisking an egg into your mash to enrich it. For a finer texture on the beans, use a stick blender. And if you'd prefer to keep this planty, swap the parmesan for 1 tablespoon of nutritional yeast.

This dish is delish served warm, at room temperature, or straight from the fridge. Team it with all the usual suspects, like crusty bread.

Zucchini Agrodolce + Aglio Cannellini Smash

Serves → 4

Chop + stir → 15 MINUTES

Set + forget → 25 MINUTES

4–6 medium zucchini (courgettes; about 750 g/1 lb 10 oz)
2 tablespoons olive oil

Agrodolce

2 tablespoons olive oil
3 red onions, finely sliced with the grain
4 garlic cloves, finely sliced
½ bunch flat-leaf parsley, chopped (reserve some leaves for garnishing)
3 fresh bay leaves
¾ cup (115 g) currants
1 cup (250 ml) red wine vinegar
1 tablespoon lilliput capers, rinsed and drained
1–2 tablespoons soft brown sugar

Aglio cannellini smash

2 × 400 g (14 oz) tins cannellini beans, drained but not rinsed
6 garlic cloves, sliced
1 stock cube (veg/chicken), dissolved in ½ cup (125 ml) hot just-boiled water
2 tablespoons extra virgin olive oil
100 g (3½ oz) butter
½ cup (50 g) grated parmesan
zest and juice of 1 lemon

Home stretch

pretty parsley leaves (reserved from the agrodolce)
extra virgin olive oil

Heat is on → Preheat the oven to 220°C (425°F), with an oven tray inside to heat up as well.

Roast the zooks → Slice the zucchini into quarters lengthways, so they bear a passing resemblance to Edward Scissorhands' phalanges. Pour the olive oil into a large mixing bowl, then gently toss the zucchini fingers through to coat.

Carefully pull the hot tray from the oven and line with baking paper. Arrange the zucchini fingers, cut side down, on the tray, leaving space in between for air flow. Roast for 25 minutes, or until wrinkled and roasty.

Agrodolce dreamin' → While the zucchini is roasting, glug the olive oil into a large high-sided, heavy-based pan over medium heat. Toss in the onion, garlic and a tablespoon of water, listen for the sizzle, then whack the lid on, drop the heat to medium–low and leave to sweat for about 6–8 minutes, until soft and just starting to colour. Tumble in the remaining agrodolce ingredients, along with some freshly ground black pepper. Let it all burble together, uncovered, for 15 minutes, until syrupy.

Smashin' beans → Meanwhile, dump the drained but unrinsed beans into a saucepan, along with the garlic, stock and olive oil. Stir together, then let everything get friendly over medium heat for 5 minutes. Stir the butter, parmesan and a crack of black pepper through. Stir in the lemon zest and juice and taste for seasoning.

Soak it up → When the zucchini fingers are burnished, submerge them in the agrodolce bath to coat them in the sour–sweet symphony. They can stay this way until you're ready to serve – even overnight, if making ahead.

Bring it home → Taste an agrodolce zucchini finger and adjust with extra salt, pepper, vinegar or sugar to balance the sour and sweet to your liking. Spoon the beany smash onto a platter and top with the agrodolce zucchini. Scatter some parsley over, and sprinkle with salt and pep. A final drizzle of olive oil wouldn't go astray to finish.

Double duty → This is a fab make-ahead or even bring-a-plate. Just keep all of the elements separate, and take them out of the fridge 20 minutes before serving to take the chill off.

A 'funghetto' refers to a vegetable cooked in the style of mushrooms – but the way I cook mushrooms is likely different to the original intention of a funghetto (more on my mushroom wet-fry method on page 88). Here, mushrooms are swapped for zucchini, which is first vigorously wet-fried in a little stock to infuse flavour and break down the cell structure, then pan-fried to add sweet caramel notes, before being simmered in a rich tomato sauce. Paired with a punchy polenta, this is a midweek winner worthy of regular rotation.

Zucchini Funghetto + PG Polenta

Serves → 4

Chop + stir → 15 MINUTES

Set + forget → 35 MINUTES

4 medium zucchini (courgettes; about 750 g/1 lb 10 oz), quartered lengthways, then cut into 1.5 cm (⅝ in) chunks
½ cup (125 ml) stock (veg/chicken)
⅓ cup (80 ml) olive oil
1 red onion, finely sliced
2–3 garlic cloves, finely sliced
½ cup (125 ml) white wine
400 g (14 oz) tin cherry tomatoes
2 tablespoons salted capers, rinsed and drained

PG polenta

2 cups (500 ml) milk
1 teaspoon salt flakes
1¾ cups (315 g) fine instant polenta
½ cup (50 g) grated parmesan
40 g (1½ oz) butter
¼ cup (55 g) PG paste (page 214)

Home stretch

handful of roughly torn basil, plus some pretty leaves to garnish
hot honey (page 219) or mild-flavoured honey (optional but excellent)
extra virgin olive oil
¼ cup (40 g) pine nuts, lightly toasted

Double duty → This is the kind of braise that improves overnight, so just reheat or serve cold. Scoop the polenta leftovers onto a flat tray while it's still wet and let it set overnight to fry as fingers tomorrow.

Fun with funghetto → Tumble the zucchini into a large high-sided pan, pour in the stock and turn the heat up to medium–high. Set the timer for 6 minutes, giving the mix the odd stir.

When all the liquid has evaporated and the zucchini begins to collapse, stir in 2 tablespoons of the olive oil and fry over medium heat for another 6 minutes, until caramelised. Transfer to a bowl and set aside.

Sweaty aromats → Pour the remaining oil into the pan, dump in the onion and garlic and stir, listening for the sizzle. Whack the lid on and set the timer for another 6 minutes, leaving it all to sweat and soften without colouring, stirring halfway through. Add the wine and stir to deglaze.

Simmertime, and the lovin' is easy → Plonk in the cherry tomatoes, slosh out the tin with about ½ cup (125 ml) water and pour that in too. Add a pinch of sugar. Bring to the boil, then drop back to a gentle burble, with the lid half-off, to save your cooktop from spatters. Set your timer for another 20 minutes, stirring occasionally until the tomatoes have collapsed and the sauce has thickened.

Zucchini central → Add the capers to your sauce, then gently fold in your wet-fried zucchini. Simmer uncovered over low heat for 10 minutes, stirring now and then, being careful not to break the zucchini up too much. Take the pot off the heat, popping the lid on to keep it warm.

Polenta to celebrate → While the sauce is burbling away, get the polenta party happening. Pour the milk and 3 cups (750 ml) water into a medium heavy-based saucepan. Stir in the salt flakes and bring to a simmer, then shower in the polenta and use a whisk for a few minutes to keep the mix from clumping. Then, when the polenta starts to thicken, switch to a flexible spatula or wooden spoon to scoop at the sides of the pan for another few minutes, until the polenta starts to come away from the sides. Switch off the heat and whisk in the parmesan, butter, PG paste and a good crack of black pepper.

Bring it home → Fold the torn basil through the funghetto and taste for seasoning, adding salt flakes and black pepper as needed – feel free to spike in a little extra sweetness with a drizzle of honey. Ladle over bowls of the PG polenta, drizzle with olive oil and serve sprinkled with the toasted pine nuts and some pretty basil leaves.

Few songs have immortalised dishes more decisively than Dean Martin's 'That's Amore'. Moon's hit your eye? Big pizza pie. Stars making your drool? Pasta fasule! Otherwise known as pasta e fagioli, this is a classic cucina povera dish with a pasta-and-beans base and permutations from household to household. Dean Martin's family recipe includes a quarter teaspoon of cinnamon – perhaps not so surprising when you consider his father's Abruzzo roots, where this spice is a fixture of sweets and occasionally savouries.

I love the way this soupy sauce is thickened with veg and soaked up by the pasta. I've used farfalle because the bow ties bring extra big band energy to this dish, but you could use any sort of dried pasta – short or even long – and then spiralise the zucchini into zoodles to match. I use a Japanese V-slicer (with the thicker matchsticks) for texture, but a box grater or food processor with the grating attachment works too.

If fresh sweet cherry tomatoes aren't forthcoming, use a 400 g (14 oz) tin of cherry tomatoes and sub out the polpa. The marjoram can be swapped for fresh oregano (or a pinch of dried), or fresh thyme, and while fresh basil is lovely for garnishing, it's not worth heading out to the shops for.

Italian-style chilli oil is best here, but if you don't have any, just use whatever chilli oil you'd usually plop onto your dumplings (or MYO, page 221).

Starry-Eyed Zucchini Pasta Fasule

Serves → 4

Chop + stir → 15 MINUTES

Set + forget → 10 MINUTES

- 2 tablespoons extra virgin olive oil
- 3 medium zucchini (courgettes), shredded
- 1 carrot, shredded or coarsely grated
- 4 garlic cloves, finely sliced or grated
- 210 g (7 oz) tin tomato polpa (crushed tomatoes)
- 400 g (14 oz) tin cannellini beans, rinsed and drained
- 250 g (9 oz) cherry tomatoes
- ¼ teaspoon ground cinnamon
- 2 marjoram sprigs, leaves stripped (optional but excellent)
- 250 g (9 oz) dried farfalle (or any short pasta)
- ½ cup (50 g) finely grated parmesan

Home stretch

- zest and juice of 1 lemon
- extra virgin olive oil
- 1 small bunch basil, leaves torn
- Italian chilli oil
- finely grated parmesan

Let the stars make you drool → Heat the olive oil in a wide heavy-based saucepan over medium heat. Chop in any zucchini tuchuses you couldn't quite grate, along with the carrot and garlic. Cook gently for 5 minutes, or until the garlic is fragrant and the carrot glossy.

Add the tomato polpa, rinsing and swishing in half a tin's worth of water. Stir in the cannellini beans, cherry tomatoes and a pinch of sugar. Bring to the boil and cook at a rapid boil for 5 minutes, until the cherry tomatoes begin to soften and burst.

Add the cinnamon and marjoram, plus a pinch of salt flakes and a good crack of black pepper. Simmer over medium–high heat for 5 minutes, until slightly thickened, gently squishing down any softened cherry tomatoes (deploy a splatter guard, or pop the lid on half-mast to avoid polpa polka dots). If the sauce starts to dry out, stir in a splash of water.

Pasta pot → While the sauce is simmering, bring a large pot of salted water to the boil. Add the pasta and cook according to the packet instructions until al dente.

Nuke the zook → Pop a colander in the sink with the shredded zucchini in the bottom. Reserve 1½ cups (375 ml) of the pasta water, then drain the cooked pasta over the zucchini so it softens with the hot water.

Melt 'n' mix → Gently tip the cooked pasta and shredded zucchini into your pan of simmering sauce. Add the parmesan, gently tossing to coat. Loosen with half the reserved pasta water to make a slightly creamy sauce and toss again. Check the sauce consistency: if it needs more liquid, splash in some more pasta water and mix about.

Bring it home → Add the lemon zest, lemon juice and a glug of olive oil. Toss in about half the basil and taste for seasoning. Divide between bowls, drizzle with chilli oil and crack on some black pepper. Scatter with more parmesan and garnish with the remaining basil for a flashy finish.

This shila plavi is a Third Culture take on Georgia's soupy rice that's perfect for midweek. The advantage of making a dish like this on the other side of the world is that I get to borrow from the wisdom of all the cuisines I've come to know and love. Like upping the veg as you might find in a risotto primavera, and using broken rice (typically used in Thai, Filipino and Vietnamese dishes such as cơm tấm) to speed up the cooking. You can buy broken rice, but I've also included instructions for making your own. Soaking the rice while you build up the flavours in the pan is another trick I picked up from congee-making, and the resulting shila plavi is extra fluffy and creamy.

Blitzing the veg to a mirepoix 'paste' helps build flavour and a lovely sunny colour. Coriander roots help create a grounding, earthy base – just wash them judiciously, as they can be notoriously gritty. Asparagus and broad beans are beautiful together, but you can use any greens in your fridge or freezer. Blanch or boil your veg just until they change colour; they'll continue cooking once stirred through the hot rice.

Shila Plavi + Adjika Paste

Serves → 4 (with leftovers)

Chop + stir → 5 MINUTES

Set + forget → 40 MINUTES

1 cup (200 g) raw jasmine rice
1 small brown onion, chopped
3 garlic cloves, peeled
2 carrots, roughly chopped
1 celery stalk, roughly chopped
4 coriander (cilantro) stems (with roots, if possible), chopped
4 holy basil (or Thai basil) stems (leaves reserved for garnishing)
2 tablespoons olive oil
1 tablespoon khmeli suneli (shop-bought or MYO, page 211)
2 cups (500 ml) vegetable stock
500 g (1 lb 2 oz) broad beans (fresh or frozen), podded
2 bunches asparagus, trimmed and cut into 2 cm (¾ in) batons

Home stretch

¼ cup (55 g) adjika paste (shop-bought or MYO, page 215)
coriander (cilantro) stems and leaves
holy basil (or Thai basil) leaves (reserved from above)

Double duty → This'll make a great lunch tomorrow too. Just zap in the microwave, stirring a few times, as the middle will be lava and the outside may appear cold – or reheat in a small saucepan, splashing in some water to loosen off the mix.

Rice breaker → Add the rice to a food processor and blitz until 'broken' – which will take 1–2 minutes. Transfer to a bowl, then slosh a little water around the processor bowl and pour this over the rice, keeping the processor handy. Add enough cold water to cover the rice, then leave to soak for 15 minutes while you forge ahead.

Blitz paste → In your sloshed-out food processor, make a speedy mirepoix by blitzing the onion, garlic, carrot, celery, herb stems and roots to a fine paste.

10-minute mirepoix → Heat a wide, high-sided pan over medium–high heat. Add the olive oil, khmeli suneli and the veg paste and sweat for 8–10 minutes uncovered, stirring now and then, until the onion aroma has cooked out and the veg has started to change from orange to sunny yellow.

Rice + toasty → Strain the rice, then stir it through the veg for a few minutes, toasting the rice and letting the veg start to caramelise.

Rice + tender → Stir in the stock and 1 litre (4 cups) water. Bring to the boil, then drop the heat to a simmer for 15–18 minutes, until the mixture is loosely porridge-y and the rice is tender, stirring occasionally to stop it catching. Taste for seasoning.

Blanch d'veg → In a medium pot of well-salted boiling water, boil the broad beans for 4 minutes, then scoop into a colander in the sink and blast with cold tap water to cool. Squeeze the pods from the edge that hasn't burst to double-pod them into a bowl – the bright green flesh will pop right out.

Bring the water back to the boil. Blanch the asparagus for 2 minutes, then scoop into the colander and blast with cold water to cool.

Bring it home → To serve, stir some of the broad beans and asparagus through the rice, then garnish with the remaining broad beans and asparagus. Blob on some adjika paste and finish with a scattering of herbs from a height.

The creaminess of the avo pesto against the crunch of the tamari-toasted seeds and slurp of soba noodles makes this dish a smashing springtime dinner. You could add some asparagus if you have some handy, or chuck in some strips of crispy cucumber too. If you'd like to bulk this out with more protein, some smoked tofu or smoked fish would be perfect. You'll find podded edamame beans – known as 'mukimame' – in the freezer section of the supermarket and Asian grocers.

Stone-Cold Soba Noodles + Avocado & Miso Pesto + Tamari-Toasted Seeds

Serves → 4

Chop + stir → 20 MINUTES

Set + forget → 15 MINUTES

200 g (7 oz) frozen mukimame (podded edamame)
270 g (9½ oz) soba noodles
1 tablespoon sesame oil

Tamari-toasted seeds

½ cup (75 g) pepitas (pumpkin seeds)
¼ cup (40 g) sunflower seeds
¼ cup (40 g) sesame seeds
1 tablespoon tamari or soy sauce (or soy maple glaze, page 219)

Avocado & miso pesto

1 avocado
4 ice cubes
1 bunch basil leaves (freeze the stems for your next napoli sauce)
½ bunch coriander (cilantro), washed well
2 garlic cloves, peeled
2 tablespoons lemon juice
1 tablespoon shiro miso (white miso paste)
1 tablespoon nutritional yeast
½ cup (125 ml) neutral oil

Home stretch

1 ripe avocado, sliced
coriander (cilantro) leaves
lemon cheeks

Full steam ahead → In a large pan with a steaming basket on top, bring 2 litres (8 cups) water to the boil. Add the mukimame to the steaming basket and steam for 5 minutes.

Once the water is at the boil, put the soba noodles and a good pinch of salt in the boiling water below, replacing the steaming basket and lid on top and cook for 3–4 minutes, depends on the girth of your noodle (check the packet instructions).

The big chill → Drain and rinse the noodles and mukimame under cold water, then drain well again. Toss them on a baking tray with the sesame oil, then cover and set aside in the fridge to chill together while you prepare the rest of the recipe. You could even leave the noodly mukimame chilling overnight to be halfway to tomorrow's dinner.

Tamari-toasted seeds → Tip all the seeds into a frying pan and toss about over medium heat for 5 minutes, or until they start to smell toasty. Pour in the tamari and toss about until the tamari has evaporated. Scoop the seeds out onto a small sheet of baking paper and set aside to cool.

Pesto inferno → Scoop all the flesh from the avocado into a food processor. Add ¼ cup (40 g) of your tamari-toasted seeds. Add all the remaining pesto ingredients and blitz until super smooth. Taste for seasoning. (The pesto can also be made the day before, and forked around to reinvigorate before serving.)

Bring it home → Toss half the pesto through the cold noodles, along with half the remaining toasted seeds. Divide among bowls, top with the avocado slices and coriander leaves, sprinkle with the remaining toasted seeds and serve with lemon cheeks.

Double duty → You've probably clocked that this is a great make-ahead option. Just keep the elements separate and combine when serving. You'll only need half the pesto for this recipe – keep the rest in a clean jar in the fridge, topped up with extra lemon juice, to use the next day as a dip, or as a delicious rye or sourdough toast topper with sliced tomatoes, basil and/or coriander leaves, making sure to top them both with more tamari-toasted seeds.

You'll notice that all of my avocado recipes are salads, because I don't believe avocado should be heated. This is about as close to heating as it'll get, where the avocado cubes sit against warm veg and quinoa, attaining a gentle level of ambient warmth. Quinoa is always better with a soak for digestion, preferably overnight, but any amount of soaking is better than none if you're in a hurry. Tri-colour quinoa would be fun for the look, but use any you can get your hands on. And if you have it, you could use a teaspoon of Tex-Mex spice mix (page 211) in the salad instead of the paprika and cumin.

Brocc Avo Quinoa + Zippy Green Dressing

Serves → 4

Chop + stir → 10 MINUTES

Set + forget → 35 MINUTES

1 cup (170 g) quinoa, soaked
2 bunches broccolini
2–3 curly kale stems
3–4 radishes (watermelon radish encouraged)
¼ bunch coriander (cilantro), leaves picked (reserve the stems for the dressing)
2 tablespoons olive oil
400 g (14 oz) tin black beans, rinsed and drained
400 g (14 oz) tin corn (or frozen corn, thawed)
1–2 garlic cloves, minced
½ teaspoon ground coriander
½ teaspoon ground cumin
¼ teaspoon smoked sweet paprika

Zippy green dressing

½ cup (130 g) natural yoghurt
coriander (cilantro) stems (reserved from above), very finely chopped
juice of ½ lime
¼ cup (60 ml) extra virgin olive oil

Home stretch

2 ripe avocados
juice of ½ lime
extra virgin olive oil

Quick on the quinoa → Drain the quinoa and give it a good rinse. Tip into a medium saucepan with 1½ cups (375 ml) water, bring to the boil, then cover and simmer for about 15 minutes, until all the little tails protrude. Turn off the heat and leave to steam for 10 minutes with the lid on. Uncover, fork to fluffiness and allow to steam out.

Hot water veg prep → Meanwhile, boil a kettle of water. Trim the ends off the broccolini, then slice into 3 cm (1¼ in) fork-friendly bits. Strip the kale leaves off their stems and roll tightly, then chiffonade into fine ribbons. Pop the broccolini and kale into a heatproof colander in the sink and pour the boiling water over the top, then allow the veg to steam dry.

Cold water veg prep → Using a mandoline or a sharp knife, slice the radishes into thin coins – if using larger watermelon radishes, cut the coins into quarters. Submerge the slices in a little bowl of iced water (to bump up the crunch). Toss in the coriander leaves and set aside for now.

Zippity doo dah → In a small blender or food processor, blitz all the dressing ingredients until smooth. Leave in the fridge to infuse.

Salad days → Pour the olive oil into a large heavy-based frying pan over medium heat. When shimmering, add the fluffed-up quinoa and leave it to become a bit crunchy and golden. Add the kettle-blanched veg and toss about for a minute or two with the heat cranked up high. Dump in the drained black beans, corn and garlic and mix together. Drop the heat, season with the spices and a pinch of salt flakes, then toss about to coat the lot until fragrant. Taste for seasoning and balance.

Avo good one → Just before serving, dice the avocadoes, place in a small bowl and sprinkle with the lime juice.

Bring it home → Spread the zippy green dressing over a large platter. Pile the quinoa salad on top. Drain and dry the radish slices and coriander leaves and arrange on top with the dressed avocado. Finish with a good drizzle of extra virgin olive oil and another crack of pepper for good measure.

Double duty → This is a perfect bowl lunch – just leave the coriander leaves off the leftovers and garnish with fresh ones. Wrap any extra coriander you've picked in a paper towel and pop in an airtight container, and it'll be good as new tomorrow.

Poke is the kind of dish that's more about arranging than cooking, where the 'slicing' (which is what the 'poh-keh' actually refers to) can be done with tools like mandolines and peelers, and/or outsourced to your friendly fishmonger. You can use any kind of sustainably sourced sashimi-grade fish they have, or switch to smoked tofu or marinated tempeh for a planty version. The brown rice brings an unbeatable nuttiness and heft to the dish, but you could use any steamed rice – even a couple of pre-cooked rice pouches to save time. The toasted sesame dressing is to die for; just watch the sesame seeds to make sure they don't burn.

Brown Rice Poke Bowl + Avocado

Serves → 4

Chop + stir → 10 MINUTES

Set + forget → 50 MINUTES

2 cups (440 g) raw medium-grain brown rice

Daikon & carrot pickle

1 carrot, peeled into ribbons
1 small daikon, peeled into ribbons
1 banana shallot, finely sliced into rounds
⅓ cup (80 ml) rice wine vinegar
2 tablespoons caster (superfine) sugar
1 teaspoon salt flakes

Toasted sesame dressing

½ cup (75 g) white sesame seeds
1 garlic clove, peeled
⅓ cup (80 ml) mirin
½ cup (125 ml) neutral oil
2 tablespoons light soy sauce

Home stretch

400 g (14 oz) firm-fleshed sashimi-grade fish, such as salmon, kingfish or tuna, diced or finely sliced
1½ cups (250 g) mukimame (podded edamame)
1½ cups (150 g) finely shredded red cabbage
1 Lebanese (short) cucumber, deseeded and sliced on the bias
2 radishes, finely sliced and soaked in iced water (optional)
1 avocado, halved and sliced
2 tablespoons pickled Japanese ginger
1 tablespoon furikake
1 lemon, quartered

Rice is right → Place the rice and 1 litre (4 cups) cold water in a medium saucepan. Bring to the boil, pop a lid on and turn the heat down to low. Simmer away for 40 minutes, until all the water is absorbed. Turn off the heat, leave the lid on and let the rice steam for another 10 minutes. (You can cook the rice the day before and be halfway to tonight's dinner.)

In a pickle → While the rice is simmering, place the carrot, daikon and shallot in a non-reactive bowl. Place the rest of the pickle ingredients and ⅓ cup (80 ml) water in a small stainless-steel pot. Stir over high heat to dissolve the sugar, then gently boil for 5 minutes. Pour the hot liquid over the veg mix and let sit until needed. (These pickles can also be made up to a week in advance and kept in a clean jar or container in the fridge.)

Open sesame → To make the dressing, place a frying pan over medium–low heat. Once the pan is really hot, scatter in the sesame seeds – they should start toasting straight up. Keeping a constant eye on them, toss them about until they're really golden brown, with some being close to burnt. You want this colour for the depth of flavour.

Set aside 1 tablespoon of the seeds, then tip the rest into a food processor, add the remaining dressing ingredients and blend together for about 2 minutes. You want the sesame seeds to break up, to help thicken the dressing. Pour into a serving jug, then stir through the reserved sesame seeds. Check for seasoning.

Bring it home → Pile the steamed rice into bowls and top with the fish. Arrange the daikon and carrot pickle on top, along with the mukimame, sliced vegetables, avocado and pickled ginger. Drizzle with the sesame dressing and some of the leftover pickling liquid, sprinkle with furikake and serve with lemon wedges.

The key to a really great stir-fry is in the name; it's moving things about at a vigorous pace, over a searing heat, giving the ingredients as much pan contact as possible, cooking them in batches to prevent overcrowding. Prep your ingredients while you heat the pan until it's smoking, setting them up in separate bowls as your 'mise en place' so it's easy to quickly sear them one after the other.

'Mangetout', the French name for snow peas, literally means 'eat all' – so eat allll the beans and peas, using whatever combination you have on hand! And with marinated tempeh adding marvellously umami-rich moments to this sublime spring–summer stir-fry, you won't miss the meat. Mind you, if you wanted to add chicken or beef strips, you could use the velveting then poaching technique on page 58.

Beans & Peas + Marinated Tempeh 'Mince'

Serves → 4

Chop + stir → 20 MINUTES

Set + forget → 10 MINUTES

¼ cup (60 ml) peanut oil or rice bran oil
800 g (1 lb 12 oz) mix of green beans, snow peas (mangetout) and sugar snap peas
200 g (7 oz) marinated tempeh
4 spring onions (scallions), cut into 3 cm (1¼ in) lengths

Stir-fry sauce

1 cm (½ in) knob of ginger, peeled and grated
1–2 garlic cloves, peeled and grated
1 cup (250 ml) vegetable stock
1 tablespoon light soy sauce
1 tablespoon toasted sesame oil
1 teaspoon caster (superfine) sugar
1 tablespoon cornflour (cornstarch)

Home stretch

½ cup (70 g) roasted peanuts, chopped
steamed jasmine rice (page 228)
chilli crisp oil (shop-bought or MYO, page 221)

Wok on → Heat a large wok or high-sided pan for 4–5 minutes over medium heat until smoking.

Bean scene → While the wok heats up, boil a kettle's worth of water. Top the beans, snow peas and sugar snaps, and snap the green beans in half. Pop them all into a colander in the sink and pour the just-boiled water over the top, then set aside to steam-dry.

On the sauce → In a small bowl or jug, whisk together the sauce ingredients until combined.

Mind your tempeh → Mash the tempeh in its packaging until it resembles a mince.

Wok station → Add half the oil to the smoking hot wok and squeeze in the tempeh mash, using a wooden spoon to smush it into a mince-y consistency. Stir about for 4 minutes over high heat, until nicely browned, then transfer to a bowl.

Add the spring onion to the still-hot wok with the rest of the oil and stir-fry for a minute, then remove. Stir-fry the blanched beans and snow peas (in batches if needed) for a couple of minutes. Give the sauce another whisk and add to the wok, along with the tempeh and spring onion. Bring up to the boil and cook for a minute, until the sauce is glossy.

Bring it home → Toss in half the roasted peanuts and taste for seasoning. Serve on steamed rice, topped with the remaining peanuts, with chilli crisp oil on the side.

Double duty → This stir-fry keeps really well for a couple of days. Just zap to reheat – or even stir the rice through the mix and stir-fry again into a super veggie fried rice.

If you like licking the middles out of cream-filled biscuits, or touch the sides well before you reach for the main, this one's for you! Colcannon is like a croquette who forgot her coat, but the best bit – the filling – is right there, in all her velvety, buttery glory. Traditionally, cabbage is folded through mashed potato for this dish, but you can really use any kind of brassica, from cavolo nero to broccoli – perfect for a veg-box surprise.

If you've no cream, use the same amount of milk, and add extra butter if you'd prefer a little more richness. Instead of bacon, you could slip in pancetta or smoked fish, or even bacalao, or leave the bacon out entirely to keep it vego. Turn this recipe fully plant-based by using olive oil instead of butter, and loosening the mix with some of the water you boiled the potatoes in, or folding through your vegan cream of choice.

Starchy potatoes are the sticky ones; try The Sticky Spud Test on page 98. The main thing flavour-wise is to go nuts on the nutmeg: rasp to your heart's content to access its uniquely alluring aroma.

Sprouty Colcannon Casserole + Crispy Potato Skins

Serves → 4–6

Chop + stir → 20 MINUTES

Set + forget → 40 MINUTES

- 1.5 kg (3 lb 5 oz) starchy potatoes (those good for mashing and roasting)
- ⅓ cup (80 ml) olive oil
- 100 g (3½ oz) butter
- 200 g (7 oz) smoked streaky bacon, finely chopped
- 500 g (1 lb 2 oz) brussels sprouts, very finely shredded against the grain
- 1 teaspoon salt flakes
- 1 bunch spring onions (scallions), finely sliced, greens and all (reserve some greens for garnishing)
- 300 ml (10½ fl oz) single (pure) cream
- ¼ whole nutmeg
- 100 g (3½ oz) cheddar, shredded

Home stretch

- spring onion greens (reserved from above)
- ½ bunch chives, finely chopped (optional but excellent)

Heat is on → Preheat your oven to 180°C (350°F) and line a baking tray with baking paper.

Skinny dip → Wash and scrub the potatoes. Pop a colander in your sink, then peel the spuds under gently running water, saving the skins. Place the peels in your salad spinner (or a large mixing bowl) and pour over just enough fresh water to cover. Drain, then spin well (or squish out over the sink) to dry. Dump them onto a tea towel (dish towel), wrap them up and pat them really dry (the drier the better so the oil sticks).

Skinny crisps → Tip the dried potato skins onto the lined baking tray. Drizzle with ¼ cup (60 ml) of the olive oil, add a good pinch of salt flakes, then mix together with your hands to coat. Whack into the oven and set the timer for 20 minutes. Toss about with tongs, then bake for another 10 minutes, or until browned and crispy. Set aside until ready to serve.

Boil the spuds → As soon as the potato skins go in the oven, cut the spuds into 3 cm (1¼ in) chunks, place in a pot and cover with plenty of cold water. Add a good pinch of salt and bring to the boil, then simmer for 20–25 minutes, until super fork-tender.

Time to sweat → While the potato cooks, heat the remaining tablespoon of olive oil and half the butter in a large shallow, heavy-based flameproof casserole dish over medium heat. When the butter is foaming, add the bacon, brussels sprouts, salt flakes and a pinch of ground white pepper. Toss about for a minute until everything is well coated and you can hear a sizzle, then place the lid on and sweat for 5 minutes, stirring occasionally. Add the spring onion and sweat for another minute or so.

Continued overleaf →

Double duty → If you've any left over, make the mash into fritters and coat in panko breadcrumbs, then shallow-fry for a delicious breakfast, served with avocado and a fried egg.

Mash time → Once cooked, drain the potatoes well and pop them back into the saucepan to steam-dry for a minute or two. Mash them in the pan, then place back over a gentle heat and pour in the cream and rasp in the nutmeg using a Microplane. When warmed enough to start bubbling, switch the heat off again and use a flexible spatula to whip the remaining butter into the mash.

Use the same spatula to transfer the mash to the casserole dish with the sprouty bacon mix, and to fold in half the cheese. Taste for seasoning. Once everything is friendly, scatter the remaining cheese on top and crack over some black pepper.

You're on a casserole → Leaving the lid off, place the pan in the hot oven for 10 minutes to gratinate the cheese into a bubbly melty magma.

Bring it home → When ready to roll, top with the crispy potato skin chips and sprinkle with the reserved spring onion greens from a height, along with the chives if using.

Smoked tofu has a bacony flavour, making it a fab dance partner for sweet, tender brussels sprouts that burnish up swiftly in the oven. When sprouts aren't in season, you could glaze blanched green beans, or even use fresh cucumber (no need to bake – just stir the glaze through!). The peanut glaze is addictive, so make a double batch to keep in the fridge for smushing over noodles for a quick dinner. In the glaze, instead of the soy sauce and maple syrup, you could use ¼ cup (60 ml) of the soy maple glaze on page 219, if you have some handy. If you don't have chow mein noodles, you could use two-minute noodles without the flavour sachets – just avoid those containing palm oil. You want about 100 g (3½ oz) noodles per person.

Tray-Baked Glazed Brussels Sprouts + Smoked Tofu + Saucy Noods

Serves → 4

Chop + stir → 15 MINUTES

Set + forget → 25 MINUTES

250 g (9 oz) smoked firm tofu (or regular firm tofu), cut into 1.5 cm (⅝ in) cubes
600 g (1 lb 5 oz) brussels sprouts, trimmed, halved if small, or quartered if larger
6 spring onions (scallions), whites cut into 2 cm (¾ in) lengths, greens finely sliced
2 tablespoons neutral oil
350–375 g (12–13 oz) packet fresh chow mein noodles

Peanut glaze

2 cm (¾ in) thumb of ginger, peeled and grated
3 garlic cloves, grated
½ cup (140 g) peanut butter
¼ cup (60 ml) maple syrup
2 tablespoons light soy sauce
2 tablespoons toasted sesame oil
1 tablespoon rice wine vinegar
2 teaspoons sriracha sauce (or less if you'd prefer it milder)

Home stretch

¼ cup (40 g) toasted sesame seeds
sliced spring onion (scallion) greens (reserved from above)
chilli crisp oil (shop-bought or MYO, page 221)

Heat is on → Preheat your oven to 220°C (425°F) and whack a baking tray inside to preheat too.

Toss up → In a large mixing bowl, toss the tofu, brussels sprouts and spring onion whites with a pinch of salt flakes and oil to coat. Carefully pull the hot tray out of the oven and line with baking paper. Spread the mixture on top, giving the tofu and veg as much space as possible to encourage crispy bits. Reserve the schmutzy bowl.

Roast and toast → Bake for 15–20 minutes, or until the sprouts are dark golden and crispy on the outside and tender in the middle.

Nutty notions → Combine all the peanut glaze ingredients in a small saucepan. Place over medium heat and bring to the boil, then switch off the heat and whisk together to emulsify.

Get noodling → Cook the noodles according to the packet instructions. Reserve 1½ cups (375 ml) of the noodle cooking water, then drain the noodles through a colander and tip them into your schmutzy mixing bowl.

Glaze away → Pour half the peanut glaze over the noodles, and chuck in most of the spring onion greens and ½ cup (125 ml) of the noodle water. Toss to coat, then pile the noodles on your serving platter in a triumphant heap.

Pour another ¼ cup (60 ml) of the noodle water into the remaining glaze in the saucepan, and whisk again to emulsify.

Bring it home → Once the sprouts, spring onions and tofu are golden brown, tumble them over the noodles and drizzle with the remaining glaze. Finish with a sprinkling of sesame seeds and spring onion greens and serve with chilli crisp oil on the side.

Double duty → This makes a fab lunch, reheated or served cold as more of a salad. Loosen the glaze with a little just-boiled water if it's become too stiff.

Tray-baked glazed brussels sprouts + smoked tofu + saucy noods

→ page 153

Here we're sear 'n' steaming brussels sprouts like gyoza, then combining with the kinds of flavours you'd expect to find at a Hofbräuhaus (indeed, I distinctly remember eating brassica and bratwurst on an enormous plate in Munich, where they've been pairing beer and sausages by royal decree since the 16th century), served with an indecent blot of hot mustard and soothing sour cream. To make this vego, pull out the meat and add a tin of rinsed lentils, some fennel seeds and smoked sweet paprika to taste.

You can use a mandoline to finely slice the fennel and onion, using a guard to avoid nipping fingertips. If you're in a hurry, you can sear the sprouts in a separate pan. To save time on the sausage de-robing, slice the snags through the skins lengthways. I prefer squeezing out the mix, but I'm a sicko.

Buttery Brussels Sprouts + Pork & Fennel Sausages + Apple

Serves → 4–6

Chop + stir → 15 MINUTES

Set + forget → 30 MINUTES

⅓ cup (80 ml) olive oil
600 g (1 lb 5 oz) brussels sprouts, trimmed and quartered (or halved if smaller), outer leaves reserved
50 g (1¾ oz) butter
1 brown onion, finely sliced with the grain
1 small fennel bulb, trimmed and finely sliced with the grain
1 tangy apple, peeled and grated
1–2 garlic cloves, finely diced
500 g (1 lb 2 oz) pork and fennel sausages

Home stretch

⅓ cup (85 g) sour cream
hot English mustard
fennel fronds (reserved from above)

Sprout for my love → Pour 3 tablespoons of the olive oil into a high-sided pan. Arrange the brussels sprouts, cut side down, in the pan. Turn the heat to medium–high, put the lid on and set the timer for 5 minutes, leaving them to sit until they are quite well coloured; if quartered, flip them to the other side halfway through.

Flip the sprouts onto their tuchuses. Add the butter and ¼ cup (60 ml) water and stir about until the butter melts. Place a lid on to capture the steam and shake about for 1 minute. Scoop those verdant, glossy, buttery, toasty sprouts into a bowl and set aside.

Sweat sesh → Add the remaining 2 tablespoons olive oil to the schmutzy pan. Tumble in the onion and fennel slices and put the lid on. Sweat over medium heat for 8 minutes, or until translucent and slightly golden on the edges, stirring occasionally.

When the timer goes off, toss in the grated apple and garlic and stir about for another 2 minutes, until fragrant and softened.

Sausage sizzle → Pop the sausage meat out of the casings, straight into the pan. Crank the heat up high to help render out the fat, breaking the meat up to a ballsy or bolognese-y consistency with a wooden spoon and encouraging some deeply browned and flavoursome bits below. Sizzling is good! Fry for 8–10 minutes, stirring occasionally and giving the pan the odd shake until the meat cooks through – from pink to opaque.

All together now → Return the sprouts to the pan, along with any of the buttery juices in the bowl and the outer leaves of the brussels sprouts, and toss to introduce the ingredients to each other. Keep the pan sizzling for the sprouts to absorb the flavours, then switch off and taste for seasoning, adding salt flakes and freshly cracked black pepper as needed.

Bring it home → Serve with dollops of sour cream and dabs of hot English mustard, finished with fennel fronds, salt flakes and a final crack of black pepper.

Double duty → Leftovers keep very well – just leave off the mustard and sour cream, so you can reheat in a pan or zap in the microwave. This is also the kind of thing I would LOVE to whack a poached egg on, for a bit of a Bavarian breakfast hash.

Shchi (pronounced 'she') is essentially a cabbage soup, whose etymology stems from the old Slavic 'siitii', the plural form of satiety or satisfaction. When I was growing up, a big pot of this, or borsch, was Mum's standing Sunday simmer – it was cost and time effective, and a guarantee we'd be nourished and the crisper cleared. Think of it as white borsch, where the beetroot has been subbed out for earthy sweet veg like turnip or swede, and the acid amped up with apple cider vinegar. If you have some dill pickle brine handy, or kraut that's belched up a brew, feel free to use that instead of the vinegar. Kimchi brine would also be welcome.

I've kept this recipe fully plant-based, but if you'd prefer more richness, foam in a knub of butter with the oil when sweating the veg, and use chicken stock in place of veg. If you're using a commercial stock, taste the soup before adding any extra seasoning, as some stocks can be quite salty. And don't forget to collect all the vegetable trimmings and peels (except from the cabbage and turnip) and pop into a bag in the freezer, ready to make more stock for your next shchi.

Crisper Clear-Out Shchi (Slawbag Soup)

Serves → 4 (with leftovers)

Chop + stir → 10 MINUTES

Set + forget → 50 MINUTES

- ¼ cup (60 ml) olive oil
- 1 brown onion, finely sliced
- 1 small fennel bulb, cut in half, then finely sliced against the grain all the way up to the stalks (reserve the fronds for garnishing)
- 3–4 garlic cloves, finely sliced
- ½ bunch dill, stems and fronds chopped (reserve the finer fronds for garnishing)
- ¼ cup (60 ml) apple cider vinegar
- 1 large turnip or swede, peeled, halved and cut into 2 cm (¾ in) chunks
- 2 waxy (low-starch) potatoes, peeled and cut into 2 cm (¾ in) chunks
- 2 bay leaves
- 2 cups (500 ml) vegetable stock
- 300 g (10½ oz) bag of white cabbage and carrot slaw (or ¼ small cabbage and 1 carrot, shredded)

Home stretch

- sour cream
- dill and fennel fronds (reserved from above)
- extra virgin olive oil

Double duty → This soup gets even better overnight as the flavours get friendly, and will happily last in the fridge for 5–7 days ... when you're just about ready for your next crisper clear-out.

Pot luck → Heat the olive oil in a heavy-based flameproof casserole dish or large pot over medium heat. Chuck in the onion and fennel. Wait for it to sizzle, then drop the heat to medium–low. Put the lid on and cook for 10 minutes, stirring occasionally. Once the vegetables have softened and the onion is translucent, pop in the garlic and dill stems, and stir for about 2 minutes, until fragrant.

Splash in the pan → Deglaze the pan with the vinegar, then add the turnip, potatoes and bay leaves. Pour in the stock and 1.5 litres (6 cups) water (preferably filtered). Bring to the boil, then drop back to a simmer and cook for 25–30 minutes, until the potatoes are fork-tender.

Empty the baggie → Now add the slaw bag contents (or your shredded cabbage and carrot), along with the chopped dill. Stir to combine, then switch off the heat and put the lid back on. Let the cabbage and carrot cook in the residual heat for 10–15 minutes. Season with salt flakes and black pepper to taste.

Bring it home → Ladle into soup bowls, top with a generous dollop of sour cream and garnish with the reserved dill and fennel fronds. Finish with a drizzle of olive oil and a final sprinkle of salt and pepper.

The king of cabbage dishes from my neck of the woods is 'golubtsi': sweet, tender cabbage, coddling a parcel of rice and meat, braised in a rich tomato sauce. But ain't nobody got time for rolling, folding or braising when it comes to midweek meals. So, try this short-cut version: an unrolled cabbage roll!

Cooking the meat as one big burger patty keeps it juicier, and means you can sear away, stir-free, while you get onto the whizzed-up mirepoix paste. Turn these rolls meat-free with a plant-based mince, marinated tempeh or some blitzed-up mushrooms. This is the perfect place to use up your leftover cooked rice – even brown rice works well here – or those pre-cooked rice pouches.

Deconstructed Cabbage Rolls

Serves → 4–6

Chop + stir → 10 MINUTES

Set + forget → 20 MINUTES

¼ cup (60 ml) olive oil
500 g (1 lb 2 oz) minced (ground) beef
1 brown onion
1 carrot
1 celery stalk (reserve any celery heart leaves for garnishing)
4 garlic cloves
½ bunch dill (reserve the fronts for garnishing)
½ bunch parsley (reserve the leaves for garnishing)
¼ cup (60 g) tomato paste (concentrated purée)
2 teaspoons sweet paprika (or whatever type you've got)
400 g (14 oz) tin whole peeled or cherry tomatoes
½ teaspoon sugar
2 cups (500 ml) stock (veg/chicken/beef)
¼ white cabbage (about 350 g/12 oz), core and outer leaves removed
2 cups (370 g) cooked rice

Home stretch

dill fronds (reserved from above)
parsley leaves (reserved from above)
sour cream
extra virgin olive oil

Patty pan → Grab a large shallow flameproof casserole dish or heavy-based pan that's at least 28 cm (11¼ in) wide, ideally 32 cm (12¾ in). Pour in 2 tablespoons of the olive oil and place over medium heat, then crank the temperature up to medium–high and squish the minced beef over the bottom of the pan, into a patty. Cook over high heat for about 8 minutes, until the meat starts to brown and caramelise underneath and schvitz (sweat!) on top. Flip it over and break it up with a wooden spoon, stirring for about another 4 minutes, until uniformly brown.

Blitz your base → While the meat is browning, peel and roughly chop the onion and carrot, and roughly chop the celery. Add to a food processor, along with the garlic. Roughly chop the dill and parsley stems and add those too. Pulse to a chunky paste – not soupy, still with a bit of texture.

Add another tablespoon of oil and the veg mixture to the browned meat and sauté for 5 minutes, still on high heat, stirring occasionally.

Red zone → Stir in the tomato paste and paprika until everything is a uniform shade of burnt umber. Tip in the tomatoes, then rinse out the tin with a slosh of water, adding the tommy wash to the pot, along with the sugar for sweetness. Pour in the stock and bring to a roaring boil. Taste for seasoning and add salt flakes and black pepper accordingly.

A cabbage for you → Chop the cabbage into 3 cm (1¼ in) wedges, then cut into 2.5 cm (1 in) fork-friendly flaps, following its natural curve. (Enjoy the heart of the core as a chef snack, or palm off to little hands for a first taste of cabbage's sweet, juicy potential.)

Bubble away → Stir the cabbage flaps through the bubbling brew and bring to the boil again. Cook at a rapid boil for 5 minutes, then stir in the rice, drop to a simmer and cook for another 10 minutes. (The cabbage will keep cooking in the residual heat once the pan's off, so don't be deterred if it still has a little bite.)

Bring it home → Roughly chop the dill fronds and parsley leaves and stir most of it through the mix. Blob dollops of sour cream on top, or let eaters help themselves at the table. Garnish with the remaining dill and parsley, plus any bonus celery heart leaves. Drizzle with extra virgin olive oil, and finish with a flourish of pepper, salt and paprika.

Double duty → This is definitely the kind of dish that keeps on giving – you could live on the leftovers for days. Just leave off the sour cream until you're serving.

One of my favourite ways of using up leftover slaw mix is to fry it up into an okonomiyaki – essentially a Japanese rosti. The batter is really 'as you please' – which is what its name translates to as well. It can be cooked as one big pancake, or as smaller latkes/fritters. You can add more protein to the batter, in the form of chopped-up firm tofu, last night's roast, or quick-cook seafood like prawns (shrimp), squid or firm-fleshed fish; just reduce the amount of cabbage by the same weight. To keep it fully planty, swap the oyster sauce in the okonomi sauce for mushroom sauce, and use a miso soup sans bonito flakes. Speaking of, sprinkling this pancake with bonito flakes as a dancing garnish does take it to the next level texturally.

Japanese Vegetable Pancake (Okonomiyaki)

Serves → 4–6

Chop + stir → 20 MINUTES

Set + forget → 35 MINUTES

¼ cup (40 g) sesame seeds
⅓ cup (80 ml) neutral oil, for shallow frying

Batter

450 g (1 lb) coleslaw mix (or grate 2 carrots + ¼ small cabbage)
4 spring onions (scallions), finely sliced, including the green tops
1 cup (150 g) self-raising flour
50 g (1¾ oz) rice flour
2 eggs
1 cup (250 ml) instant miso soup
½ teaspoon salt flakes

MYO okonomi sauce

¼ cup (60 ml) tomato ketchup
2 tablespoons worcestershire sauce
1½ tablespoons light soy sauce
1 tablespoon oyster sauce
1 tablespoon brown sugar
½ tablespoon toasted sesame oil

Home stretch

Japanese mayonnaise
spring onion greens (reserved from the batter)
bonito flakes (optional)
pickled ginger (optional)
furikake and/or toasted seaweed snack sheets, cut into strips (optional but excellent)

Batter believe it → Dump the slaw into a large bowl. Add most of the spring onion, reserving some green tops for garnishing. Toss well with your hands to distribute the mix. Sprinkle in the flours and toss about again, making sure all the veg is coated.

In a smallish bowl, whisk together the eggs, miso soup and salt flakes until combined. Pour it over the slaw mix and fold with a flexible spatula until there are no clumps of dry flour left.

Let the batter rest in the fridge for 15 minutes (set a timer).

Saucy wonder → While the batter is chilling, combine the okonomi sauce ingredients in a small saucepan over low heat, stirring regularly until the sugar dissolves. Taste and season to your liking, then set aside.

Seedy interlude → With 10 minutes left on the batter timer, scatter the sesame seeds in a cold 26–28 cm (10½–11¼ in) heavy-based frying pan. Place over medium–high heat and set the timer for 8 minutes, tossing the seeds occasionally until most are golden. Tip into a bowl.

Fry time → Place the pan back over medium heat and pour in enough oil to generously cover the base. Bring the oil to a shimmer. Give one last fold to the slaw batter, then pour it into the hot oil, spreading it out to the edges in a thickish round disc. Leave for 15 minutes, until golden underneath and mostly cooked through.

Drain the excess oil from the edge of the pan into a bowl (you'll use it again soon). Slip a plate on top of the pancake and carefully flip it onto the plate. Pour the excess oil back into the pan, then slip the pancake into the pan and cook for another 5 minutes to finish it off.

Bring it home → Slip the pancake onto a serving platter and give it a good crack of black pepper. Spread the okonomi sauce all over the top. Drizzle a thin but generous zig-zag pattern of mayo over the sauce, running a skewer or the tines of a fork through to make a feather pattern. Sprinkle with the toasted sesame seeds, reserved spring onion greens and your chosen garnishes. Serve immediately, cut into wedges.

Double duty → The pancake can be eaten cold the next day, and it makes a great lunchbox treat too.

Once I stopped rolling cabbage rolls and tolma, I asked myself: what else could I leave undone? Dumplings, of course. All the comforting flavours of dim sum – even the slippery pastry – yet none of the wrapping? Sign me up! Rather than a mix of pork and chicken, you can go fully chicken, or use prawn (shrimp) meat, or even pulsed firm tofu – the world's your oyster sauce. Remember to enlist any little hands in helping to separate the wrappers before you drop them into the bubbling water, for the silkiest, finest texture – but even with a few clumpy bits, it's still good: you dim sum, you lose sum.

Pork & Cabbage Dimmies Undone

Serves → 4

Chop + stir → 10 MINUTES

Set + forget → 15 MINUTES

2 tablespoons neutral oil
250 g (9 oz) minced (ground) pork (at least 20% fat)
250 g (9 oz) minced (ground) chicken
4 spring onions (scallions), greens and whites roughly chopped (reserve some greens for garnishing)
1 cm (½ in) knob of ginger, peeled
2 garlic cloves, peeled
100 g (3½ oz) fresh shiitake mushrooms – or 30 g (1 oz) dried shiitake, soaked for 20 minutes in hot water
1 tablespoon Maggi seasoning
1 tablespoon oyster sauce
¼ teaspoon ground white pepper
1 tablespoon Chinese black vinegar
¼ small white cabbage, core removed
200–250 g (7–9 oz) packet of wonton or gyoza wrappers
1 cup (250 ml) chicken stock, or 1 stock cube (veg/chicken) dissolved in 1 cup (250 ml) water
1 tablespoon toasted sesame oil

Home stretch

sliced spring onion greens (reserved from above)
chilli crisp oil (shop-bought or MYO, page 221)

Get bubbling → Half-fill a pasta pot with well-salted water and place over high heat.

Wok on → Heat a splash of water in a large high-sided, heavy-based pan or wok over medium heat. Once the water has evaporated entirely, pour in 1 tablespoon of the oil.

Pop the pork and chicken in, crank the heat up to high and set a timer for 8 minutes. Use a wooden spoon to mash the meat until broken up and starting to schvitz (sweat!), then keep frying until the liquid evaporates and the meat starts to brown, stirring occasionally.

Flavour blitz → Meanwhile, pop the chopped spring onion into a food processor, saving some greens for garnishing. Add the ginger, garlic, mushrooms, Maggi seasoning, oyster sauce and white pepper. Pulse until it all comes together into a chunky mix.

Wok of life → Once the meat is browned, deglaze the pan with the vinegar, then add the blitzed mushroom mix, splashing a few tablespoons of water into the processor bowl to help slosh out every last bit. Pour the remaining tablespoon of oil into the pan and stir about to incorporate. Cook, stirring, for another 5 minutes, to encourage more colour and bring out the aroma.

Wonton cabbage → Once the pasta pot water is at the boil, blanch the flappy cabbage leaves for 2 minutes, then drain and scoop into the wok, stirring about to incorporate into the dimmie mix.

Slice the wonton wrappers in half diagonally, bending them in their stack to make them easier to separate. Once the water is back up to the boil, drop in the separated wrappers, stirring about to keep them from sticking. Boil for 2 minutes, until they rise to the surface, then scoop them out, straight on top of the dimmie mix.

Taking stock → Pour the stock into the wok, splash in the sesame oil and crank the heat until the liquid's bubbling. Switch off the heat and gently fold the wrappers through to incorporate and coat in the juices.

Bring it home → Divide among bowls, sprinkle with the reserved spring onion greens and serve immediately, with chilli crisp oil.

This is your year-round mega veg MVP, a great way to take full advantage of abundant aromats like celery, which helps to build body texturally – a bit like a mince. Essentially, it's like an all-veg bolognese – so chances are, if your kids like spag bog, they'll like this. And you'll like that it's got eight different veg squeezed in too – over a kilo's worth! I've teamed it with a super quick polenta, the kind you can make last-minute and feel like you've slaved over. My kind of fast food!

MVP (Mega Veg Passata) + VCP (Very Cheesy Polenta)

Serves → 4–6 (with leftovers)

Chop + stir → 15 MINUTES

Set + forget → 45 MINUTES

Mega veg passata

1 brown onion
4–5 garlic cloves
1 carrot
2 celery stalks, leaves reserved
1 capsicum (pepper)
1 zucchini (courgette)
1 sweet potato
¼ cup (60 ml) olive oil
50 g (1¾ oz) butter
1 tablespoon mild-flavoured honey
¼ teaspoon ground cinnamon
140 g (5 oz) tomato paste (concentrated purée)
400 g (14 oz) tin chopped tomatoes
2 stock cubes (veg/chicken)

Very cheesy polenta

2 cups (500 ml) milk
1 teaspoon salt flakes
1½ cups (270 g) instant polenta
100 g (3½ oz) butter
1½ cups (150 g) grated parmesan

Home stretch

parmesan (reserved from the VCP)
celery heart leaves (reserved from the MVP)
extra virgin olive oil

Blitz the mega veg → Peel and roughly chop the onion, garlic and carrot. Roughly chop the celery, capsicum, zucchini and sweet potato. Tumble the veg into your food processor and pulse together, scraping the sides down a few times to get all the chunks well and truly pulverised.

Schvitz the mega veg → Add the olive oil and butter to a heavy-based pan with a lid. When the butter starts foaming, tip in all the mega veg. Stir in the honey and cinnamon and sauté until all the vegetables have a slippery coating of oil and butter. Whack the lid on and set the timer for 10 minutes in the steam room, stirring occasionally, until the vegetable mince is very soft but not browned.

Burble time → Boil 2 cups (500 ml) water in a kettle. Add the tomato paste to the veg and cook for a further 2 minutes, stirring. Pour in the tomatoes, sloshing out the tin with another ¼ cup (60 ml) water to collect the dregs and pouring that in too. Crumble in the stock cubes, add the hot boiled kettle water and bring back up to the boil.

Drop the heat to an assertive burble, half-cover with the lid and simmer for 30 minutes, stirring now and then, until all the veg is super soft, and the sauce has reduced by a third.

Polenta to love → When the sauce is nearly ready, pour the milk and 1 litre (4 cups) water into a medium–large heavy-based saucepan. Add the salt flakes and bring to a simmer. Shower in the polenta and whisk about to stop the mix clumping. When the mix is too thick to whisk, switch to a flexible spatula, stirring about for 4–5 minutes, until the polenta starts to come away from the sides. Switch off the heat and whisk in the butter and most of the parmesan – it'll look clumpy momentarily but will come back together creamy and delish. Whack a lid on and keep warm. The polenta will start to firm up as it cools, but you can loosen it off with a splash of hot water and a diligent whisk.

Bring it home → Ladle the creamy polenta into flat bowls, spoon the MVP over the top or alongside, and finish with the remaining parmesan, reserved celery heart leaves and a drizzle of olive oil.

Double duty → The MVP makes quite a bit of sauce but can happily sit in your fridge all week for reheating or repurposing into a creamy soup. Or portion it up and freeze for when you need a quick sauce for pasta, or for any braise, soup or stew that requires deeply satisfying savoury flavours.

While shawarma, or 'shaurma' as it is known in Georgia, ordinarily refers to the 'turning' of meat on a vertical spit (from the Turkish 'çevirme'). I hope you'll indulge this plant-powered version, where the only turning you'll be doing is with a spatula in the pan. Blitzing the flavour base saves time chopping, and it cooks faster too. You could also use a box grater or finely chop everything instead. The rest of this cook is really quite set and forget, so build the base, whack it on, and go on living your life for a little while.

Baharat is a traditional Middle Eastern seven-spice mix, which you can pick up from your local specialty grocer or larger supermarkets. At a pinch, you could use garam masala and ½ teaspoon sweet paprika, 1 tablespoon of the Tex-Mex spice mix or a tablespoon of khmeli suneli (both on page 211) if you've got it.

Freshen this up with a chopped veg salad, like the one with the falafel flatbreads on page 120.

Beany Shawarma + Garlicky Drizz

Serves → 4–6

Chop + stir → 15 MINUTES

Set + forget → 45 MINUTES

3 garlic cloves, peeled
¼ bunch parsley, stems roughly chopped (reserve the leaves for garnishing)
¼ bunch coriander (cilantro), stems roughly chopped (reserve the leaves for garnishing)
1 red onion, quartered
1 carrot, roughly chopped
2 celery stalks, roughly chopped
¼ cup (60 ml) extra virgin olive oil
1 tablespoon baharat spice mix
2 tablespoons tomato paste (concentrated purée)
¼ cup (60 ml) red wine vinegar
400 g (14 oz) tin brown lentils, rinsed and drained
400 g (14 oz) tin red kidney beans, rinsed and drained
1 cup (250 ml) vegetable or chicken-style stock
400 g (14 oz) tin diced tomatoes

Garlicky drizz

½ cup (130 g) natural yoghurt
1 tablespoon lemon juice
1 garlic clove, minced

Home stretch

parsley and coriander leaves (reserved from above)
4–6 large pita breads
chopped veg salad (page 120)

Blitz your base → Pop the garlic, parsley and coriander stems in a food processor and blitz for 10 seconds. Add the onion, carrot and celery and whiz until the vegetables are finely chopped, with no chunky bits lurking.

Sweat the veg → Heat the olive oil in a large heavy-based pot over medium heat. Scoop in the veg paste and stir. Whack the lid on and set the timer for 10 minutes, stirring occasionally, until softened and jammy. A little colour is welcome, but you can also drop the heat and add a dash of water to cool things down if it's all catching and browning too fast.

Spice it up → Add the baharat and tomato paste, stirring for a few minutes. Splash in the vinegar and stir to deglaze, then cook for 2 minutes to let the vinegar infuse more juicy jamminess and tang into the mix.

Get beany → Stir in the lentils and beans and sauté for a few minutes. Pour in the stock and tomatoes, sloshing out the tin with a splash of water and pouring that in too. Season with a pinch of salt and a good crack of black pepper. Bring to a gentle boil, then drop the heat, put the lid half on and gently simmer for 35 minutes, stirring occasionally. Remove the lid and cook for another 10 minutes or so, to evaporate any pooling liquid. You want this mix to be thick and spreadable but not dry. Also, pop the pita breads on top of the lid to warm through.

Chop chop → When the beany mix is nearly done, stir the garlicky drizz ingredients together in a jug, ready for pouring.

Bring it home → Toss the reserved parsley and coriander leaves through the chopped salad. Smear the beany mixture onto the warmed pita breads, add some chopped salad, then pour over the garlicky drizzle. Fold together and enjoy immediately.

Double duty → The beany mix keeps in the fridge for up to a week. Serve over rice, as a pasta sauce, baked beans, or even in a cheesy jaffle!

The bones of this recipe are a gift from nonagenerian Chinese–Australian cookery teacher Elizabeth Chong. Her mother, Jenny Lee, would often make this soup for her children in 1930s Melbourne, using the outer leaves of lettuce she'd find at the Queen Victoria Market, and the only 'noodles' she could get her hands on at the time: macaroni. Between this and her dad's gift of the dim sim (as we know it here), I think we can safely say her family has helped revolutionise Australia's relationship with Chinese cuisine. You can adapt this soup in so many ways, adding extra steamed veg or bonus flavourings. I've swapped Elizabeth's pork mince for chicken, and you could swap it back, or use grated firm tofu instead. Use the best-quality chicken stock, or make your own when you have the time and freeze in 1 litre (4 cup) portions. If you can't find fresh shiitake, rehydrate 50 g (1¾ oz) dried shiitake in 2 cups (500 ml) of just-boiled water for 20 minutes, then use the shiitake liquor as your 2 cups (500 ml) water in the broth.

Use the outer leaves of your iceberg for this, and save the tender middles for raw salads such as the maroulosalata on page 75. You could use any dried short pasta, or 400 g (14 oz) fresh pasta.

Jenny Lee's Macaroni Soup

Serves → 4

Chop + stir → 10 MINUTES

Set + forget → 15 MINUTES

200 g (7 oz) dried macaroni
1 tablespoon toasted sesame oil
1 tablespoon neutral oil
400 g (14 oz) minced (ground) chicken
3–4 spring onions (scallions), whites finely sliced (reserve the greens for garnishing)
1 cm (½ in) knob of ginger, peeled and roughly chopped
100 g (3½ oz) fresh shiitake mushrooms, finely sliced with the shape
1 litre (4 cups) quality chicken stock
1 heaped teaspoon salt flakes
¼ teaspoon ground white pepper
1 iceberg lettuce, outer leaves and larger leaves torn (reserve the heart for a salad!)

Home stretch

sliced spring onion greens (reserved from above)
chilli crisp oil (shop-bought or MYO, page 221)
XO sauce or mushroom XO (page 220); optional but excellent

Pasta, pronto → Fill your largest pot with well-salted water and bring to the boil. Drop in the pasta and cook according to the packet instructions until al dente. Drain the pasta, then toss the sesame oil through to coat and flavour the pasta and stop it sticking.

Kick off → Meanwhile, splash the neutral oil into your second biggest pot over medium–high heat. Add the chicken and flatten it into a large patty, then fry for about 5 minutes, until it releases moisture but hasn't coloured. Add the spring onion whites, ginger and mushrooms and stir about to break up the chicken; if it clumps into little balls, that's okay too!

Splash out → Pour in the stock and 2 cups (500 ml) water. Add the salt and white pepper and bring to the boil. Drop back to a simmer and tumble in the lettuce leaves, then switch off the heat. Taste and add extra seasoning if needed.

Bring it home → Pile the pasta into soup bowls, then ladle the hot soup over. Garnish with the spring onion greens and serve with chilli crisp oil, and XO sauce if using.

There is something so beachside about this sarnie, which is perfect for those teas-on-knees nights. 'Katsu' is anything crumbed in Japanese, but also means 'winning', and you'll feel like a winner when you smush in mash-up mushy peas, a classic British dish to accompany fish and chips, with a Japanese wasabi twist – PLUS roasted seaweed snacks (from the snack aisle) for bonus crunch. You can crumb and fry your own smaller fish (like flathead fillets) to cut into 'fingers', or head to the freezer aisle for a shortcut. When buying fish fingers for these, aim for the thickest-looking ones, with the usual eye on sustainability ticks and certifications. You also want a 'door-stopper' thickness on the bread – a very English term describing bread that's been sliced real thick, thanks! If you can't find shokupan (a Japanese milk bread), ask for 'toast cut' high-tin, or use brioche or milk buns if you want something a little more spesh than white bread.

Katsu-Inspired Crumbed Fish Sarnies

Serves → 4

Chop + stir → 10 MINUTES

Set + forget → 20 MINUTES

16 fish fingers (or 8 homemade crumbed fish fillets)
4 larger-sized iceberg lettuce leaves
1 loaf of shokupan milk bread (or soft white bakery bread), cut into 8 slices about 1.5–2 cm (⅝–¾ in) thick
quality butter, for spreading

Mushy pea mayo

1 cup (140 g) frozen peas
¼ cup (75 g) Japanese mayonnaise
1 tablespoon pickled ginger liquor
¼ teaspoon wasabi paste (optional but excellent)

Home stretch

2 tablespoons pickled ginger slices
lemon juice
10 g (¼ oz) toasted seaweed snacks

Flippin' fish → Cook the fish fingers according to the packet instructions – I like to pan-fry them in half butter and half oil for extra crunch, which usually only takes 8 minutes, flipping halfway through. If baking, it may take around 15 minutes once your oven is hot. (If using fish fillets, dust them with flour, dip them in beaten egg, coat them in panko crumbs, then pan-fry for about 4 minutes on each side.)

Mushy mushy → While your catch is cooking, put the peas in a small heatproof bowl and pour boiling water over them. Leave to thaw for 5 minutes, then drain and add to a small blender. Add the remaining mayo ingredients and pulse to a chunky consistency; I still like to see a few peas. Taste for seasoning, adding salt and freshly cracked pepper to your liking, remembering that the fish fingies will be salted too.

Lettuce shred → Slice the lettuce into fine chiffonade ribbons, or tear into small flaps if that's more your speed, then pop them into a salad spinner with cold water to get super crisp.

Slather up → Lay out your eight bread slices and generously butter each slice, right to the edges. Slather the mushy pea mayo onto four of the buttered bread slices.

Bring it home → Drain and spin-dry the shredded lettuce and place over the other four bread slices for your sarnie base. Top each with four fish fingers (or two crumbed fillets), the pickled ginger slices, a squeeze of lemon juice and a sprinkle of salt flakes. Place the bread lids on and press your sarnie together until you hear that satisfying crunch. Slice in half and serve with toasted seaweed snacks on the side.

Think of these creamy peas as a dal – made using frozen peas for a super easy dinner in the time it takes to fix the carb-on-carb base. When it comes to carbs like potatoes or rice, I have a hard and fast rule: always cook double for a 20-minute headstart on tomorrow's tea. You can use tinned baby potatoes and cooked packet rice here as a shortcut, but using up leftovers will always make you feel more smug.

Also known as Indian five-spice, panch phoron is a whole-seed spice mix that's delicious for adding extra crunch and spice to simple dishes like roast spuds. If you don't have it, swap in 2 tablespoons of whatever whole seeds you do have – fennel, nigella, coriander, mustard and/or cumin seeds would all be perfect.

Masala Mushy Peas + Golden Basmati + Potato Fry-Up

Serves → 4 (with leftovers)

Chop + stir → 10 MINUTES

Set + forget → 25 MINUTES

Masala mushy peas

1 brown onion, quartered
4–5 garlic cloves, peeled
2 cm (¾ in) thumb of ginger, peeled and roughly chopped
6 coriander (cilantro) roots, stems and leaves, washed
2 tablespoons neutral oil
1 tablespoon mild madras curry powder
½ teaspoon garam masala
270 g (9½ oz) tin coconut cream
1 cup (250 ml) vegetable or chicken-style stock
500 g (1 lb 2 oz) frozen baby peas
50 g (1¾ oz) baby spinach leaves

Golden basmati

60 g (2¼ oz) butter
1 tablespoon neutral oil
1 red onion, finely sliced into rings
2 tablespoons panch phoron
1 teaspoon mild madras curry powder
3 garlic cloves, minced
2 cm (¾ in) thumb of ginger, peeled and minced
1 teaspoon salt flakes
400 g (14 oz) cooked (or tinned) baby waxy potatoes
3 cups (550 g) leftover cooked basmati rice (page 227)

Home stretch

natural yoghurt
coriander leaves (reserved from above)

Masala magic → In a food processor, blitz the onion, garlic, ginger, coriander roots, stems and most of the leaves into a paste. Heat the oil in a heavy-based saucepan over medium–high heat, stir in the paste and spices, then whack a lid on for 6 minutes, stirring occasionally, until heavily fragrant.

Go for gold → Meanwhile, in a high-sided, heavy-based pan with a lid, foam a tablespoon of the butter in the oil, then add the onion slices, panch phoron and curry powder and listen for the sizzle. Whack a lid on, set the timer for 10 minutes and sweat over medium–low heat, stirring occasionally. Stir in the garlic, ginger and salt, stick the lid back on and cook for another 5–7 minutes, until the onion is super soft and glossy.

Time for peas → Stir the coconut cream into the masala base, let it come to the boil, then pour in the stock and simmer for 5 minutes. Tumble in the drained frozen peas, bring back to the boil and cook for 4 minutes. Add the spinach and wilt for a further minute.

Rice in spice → While the green pot's simmering, get back to the gold. Add the potatoes to the other pan and coat well in the spices. Stir the rice through and taste for seasoning. Warm through over medium heat, tossing now and then, until the potatoes and rice start getting crispy on the edges, being careful not to burn the onion (though a bit of caramelisation is heaven). Add the remaining butter and let it foam up before stirring through.

Pulse the peas → Once the masala peas have cooked, remove the pan from the heat and use a stick blender to carefully whiz the mixture to a chunky texture, somewhere between a dal and a soup. Season to taste, adding a pinch of sugar if it could use a little more sweetness.

Bring it home → Tumble the rice onto a serving platter, pour the mushy peas over, drizzle with yoghurt and top with the remaining coriander leaves.

Look, I know someone out there will look at this and say IS THIS COLOUR AI!? No! It's BI ... carb! Alkalising the water with a tiny amount of bicarb soda helps to lock in the greenness of the peas and spinach, so it's much easier being green. That's why I quietly call this one Kermit the Soup. Hold off on the crème fraiche and lemon wedges until you're at the table, because it's the acid in ingredients like these that gives green things a Valencia filter. For a peppery grown-up soup, take it up a notch with 'rocket' fuel instead of spinach.

Tinned potatoes are a nifty way of saving yourself 20 minutes, but you could also use about 400 g (14 oz) leftover boiled or mashed spuds instead. Feel free to add leek if you need to use it up or you're down an onion; a stick of celery wouldn't go astray either. And if you've got mint in the garden, toss in a few leaves at the end with the parsley.

Bright Green Pea Soup + Crusty Baguette

Serves → 4 (with leftovers)

Chop + stir → 10 MINUTES

Set + forget → 10 MINUTES

- 1 brown onion, roughly chopped
- 2 garlic cloves, peeled
- 2 tablespoons olive oil
- 1 tablespoon butter
- 2 stock cubes (veg/chicken)
- ¼ teaspoon bicarbonate of soda (baking soda)
- 4 cups (560 g) frozen peas
- 400 g (14 oz) tin baby potatoes or butter beans, rinsed and drained
- 100 g (3½ oz) baby spinach leaves
- ¼ bunch parsley, leaves picked, stems finely sliced

Home stretch

- ¼ cup (65 g) crème fraiche (or sour cream or yoghurt)
- extra virgin olive oil
- crusty baguette
- butter
- lemon wedges (optional but excellent)

Whiz the alliums → Blitz the onion and garlic in a food processor to a rough paste. Rinse out the processor bowl and set aside.

Sweat the alliums → In a large heavy-based pot, heat the olive oil and butter over medium heat. Pop in the onion paste, listen for the sizzle, then turn down the heat. Whack the lid on and set the timer for 4 minutes, stirring occasionally, until soft but not coloured.

In goes the veg → Add 1 litre (4 cups) boiling water and crumble in the stock cubes and bicarb. Bring back to the boil. Add the peas and potatoes and wait for the pot to come back to the boil. Set the timer for 3 minutes for frozen baby peas, and 4 minutes for regular peas – just long enough to cook the peas through but keep them brilliantly bright green.

Switch off the heat. Stir in the spinach and parsley, dunking in and about to get wilty and cool down enough to blitz.

Smooth operator → Ladle the soup into your food processor (or use a stick blender) and blend until silky smooth. If using a jug blender, blitz in batches so as not to overfill and risk a scene from *The Exorcist* on your ceiling. Taste and season with salt flakes and freshly ground black pepper.

Bring it home → Ladle into deep bowls and stir in a swirl of crème fraiche, a drizzle of your best olive oil, a crack of freshly ground black pepper and some salt flakes. Serve piping hot with baguette, simply torn and slathered with lashings of butter at the table. Don't forget some lemon wedges for squeezing in at the last moment.

Double duty → This soup will happily sit in the fridge for a couple of days, or can be portioned and frozen for up to 3 months, closing the frozen pea soup loop.

Sing it with me: When you stir creamy sauce with some tuna, of course, that's a mornay! If you grew up in Australia, you'll probably be surprised to learn that tuna mornay is actually pretty exotic for anyone who didn't, and one advantage of coming to it later in life is playing fast and loose with this canonical classic of Cucina Australiana. I've taken the best bits of a mornay (creamy, comforting, casserole), eliminated the margin for gluggy error by replacing the bechamel with a crème fraiche-based green sauce that's full of zip and zest – though you're welcome to use half a cup of PG paste (page 214) as a shortcut instead. If using tuna in spring water, drain and add ⅓ cup (80 ml) olive oil to the green sauce instead. And it's all topped off with a Friday Night fish 'n' chips vibe from the salt and vinegar crisps – bonus points if they're crinkle-cut!

Tuna Mornay + Salt & Vinegar Chippie Scales

Serves → 4–6

Chop + stir → 15 MINUTES

Set + forget → 25 MINUTES

425 g (15 oz) tin tuna in olive oil, drained (reserving the oil)
2 tablespoons brined capers, drained
250 g (9 oz) dried pasta shells
1 cup (140 g) frozen peas
1 bunch broccolini, cut into 1 cm (½ in) pieces
150 g (5½ oz) shredded cheddar
165 g (5¾ oz) packet of crinkly salt and vinegar crisps
olive oil

Green sauce

1 bunch parsley
3–4 garlic cloves, peeled
zest and juice of 1 lemon
⅓ cup (80 ml) tuna oil (reserved from above)
¼ teaspoon freshly ground black pepper
200 ml (7 fl oz) crème fraiche

Heat is on → Preheat your oven to 170°C (350°F) and bring a large pot of well-salted water to the boil.

Green with envy → To make the green sauce, roughly chop the parsley (to make it easier to blitz), then toss it in your food processor or blender. Add the garlic, lemon zest and juice, tuna oil and black pepper, then blitz together for a couple of minutes, into a green paste. Scoop in the crème fraiche and blitz again to incorporate. Transfer to your largest mixing bowl and dump the drained tuna and capers in too.

Shell be right → Once the pasta water is at the boil, rain in the pasta, stirring about for the first minute or so to stop it clumping. Cook for 1 minute less than suggested on the packet.

Before draining the pasta, pop your peas and broccolini in a colander in the sink. Drain the pasta over your greens to give them a swift blanch and take the frosty edges off the peas.

All together now → Toss the pasta, broccolini and peas into the mixing bowl. Tumble in half the cheddar and stir to thoroughly coat everything with the green sauce. Check for seasoning.

Bake it 'til you make it → Transfer to a ceramic baking dish or pie dish. Top with the crisps, standing them to jaunty attention (or crunch them over if you're in a hurry). Sprinkle with the remaining cheddar. Drizzle over a lick of olive oil and bake for 10 minutes, until the cheese is golden and the sauce is bubbly.

Wearing oven mitts, remove your catch from the oven and leave to stand for 5 minutes or so before serving at the table.

Double duty → You could enjoy this cold as a pasta salad the next day. The chippies will go a little soggy, so this is your permission slip to eat all the chips first!

This pasta salad follows the Ina Garten school of less-pasta-to-veg ratio, making every bite more interesting. For a speed-boat version, toss a drained tin of baby potatoes and a cup of frozen corn into the pasta pot for the last minute of cooking – a big time saver! And rather than making the dressing from scratch, you could loosen some PG paste (page 214) with olive oil, stir through some finely chopped anchovy and use that instead. To veer lower carb or vego, swap the spuds or tuna for a tin of butter beans or five-bean mix.

Tuna Niçoise Pasta Salad

Serves → 4

Chop + stir → 10 MINUTES

Set + forget → 30 MINUTES

400 g (14 oz) small baby potatoes
200 g (7 oz) jar tuna fillets in olive oil
2–3 corn cobs (about 600 g/1 lb 5 oz), husks removed, sliced in half
300 g (10½ oz) green beans, topped and snapped in half
200 g (7 oz) dried penne (or other short pasta)

Very nice dressing

⅓ cup (80 ml) tuna oil, from the jar above (or olive oil for vego)
1 lemon
1 tablespoon red wine vinegar
5 garlic cloves, peeled
4 quality anchovies
½ teaspoon salt flakes
½ bunch parsley (about 50 g/1¾ oz)
200 g (7 oz) sugar plum or cherry tomatoes, halved
⅓ cup (50 g) anchovy-stuffed olives (or olives of your choosing)

Home stretch

1 lemon, cut into wedges

Hot spuds! → Pop the potatoes into a large saucepan of well-salted water and quickly bring to the boil. Turn the heat down and simmer for 15 minutes.

Nice dressing! → Drain the olive oil from your tuna jar straight into your food processor or blender. Use a speed peeler to peel the yellow zest off the lemon, applying less pressure than if you were peeling a carrot, to avoid the bitter white pith. Toss the zest into the food processor, squeeze in the juice from half the lemon and splash in the red wine vinegar. Tumble in the garlic cloves, anchovies and salt flakes.

Lop the leaves off the parsley and toss them into your largest mixing bowl. Drop the headless parsley stems into the processor and blitz until smooth. Taste for seasoning, then pour the dressing over the parsley leaves, along with the halved tomatoes and the anchovy-stuffed olives (it'll look like a lot of dressing, but just you wait!).

Back to the veg → When the timer on the spuds goes off, add the corn cobs and beans to the pot and simmer for 4 minutes. Scoop out the lot, leaving the water boiling in the pan, and topping it up above halfway with water. Plonk the beans and spuds into the dressing bowl without stirring. When the corn is cool enough to handle, slice the kernels off and toss them into the bowl. Cut any larger spuds in half with a paring knife in the bowl.

Pass the pasta → Once the water comes back up to the boil, throw in the pasta and cook for a minute less than suggested on the pasta packet. Drain, then add to the mixing bowl with the rest of the party, along with the tuna, and toss everything about until verdantly speckled.

Bring it home → Tumble the salad into a serving bowl or on a platter and serve straight away, with the lemon wedges and a good sprinkling of freshly cracked pepper over the top.

Double duty → You can happily eat the leftovers the next day, or toss them with a cheat's bechamel from the tuna mornay on page 178, top with shredded cheese and chippies and bake until golden.

If you're a long-time listener/cooker of mine, you're probably wondering, 'how's she going to get herself out of a bechamel this time?'*, and the answer is: JAPANESE CURRY CUBES! These wonders already have flour and butter in them, so there's no need to cook out a roux – it's pre-rouxed. You'll find these curry cubes at the shops with differing degrees of spiciness, so choose a heat level to suit your household. You could use a Japanese curry powder (or even the curry-powder tin at the back of the cupboard) instead, but you'll have to make a basic roux from butter and flour to help thicken up the sauce.*

Frozen veg bags are a nifty way of adding colour to a bake or casserole, and they're very interchangeable; you could just use corn, or peas, or any combo you like.

Serve with a side of Very fine slaw (page 95) or Miso sesame slaw (page 30).

Japanese Mac & Cheese

Serves → 4

Chop + stir → 20 MINUTES

Set + forget → 30 MINUTES

- 3 cups (750 ml) milk (or plant-based milk if preferred)
- 5 Japanese curry cubes, roughly chopped
- 250 g (9 oz) shredded cheddar
- 200 g (7 oz) dried elbow macaroni
- 500 g (1 lb 2 oz) frozen veg of your choice
- 4 spring onions (scallions), sliced diagonally, reserving ¼ cup of the greens for topping
- ¾ cup (45 g) panko breadcrumbs
- ⅓ cup (50 g) sesame seeds
- 50 g (1¾ oz) butter, grated

Roux the day → In a medium saucepan, bring the milk to just before the boil, then stir in the chopped curry cubes until they dissolve. Give it a quick whisk if it's lumpy. Set a timer for 15 minutes and leave to thicken over a gentle heat, stirring so it doesn't stick to the bottom of the pan. Remove the pan from the heat and add half the cheddar, stirring about until the cheese is fully melted and the sauce is smooth. Taste for seasoning, adding salt flakes and black pepper to taste.

Mac attack → Cook the macaroni according to the packet instructions, less 1 minute. Drain and set aside, reserving the pasta pot.

Grill up → Preheat your oven grill (broiler) to 220°C (425°F) or 'high' – whatever your grill needs to hear from you to know it's going to do some work.

Melt 'n' mix → In the schmutzy pasta pot, combine the cooked macaroni, frozen veg and spring onion. Pour your cheesy curry sauce over the pasta, tossing to ensure the pasta is evenly coated. Using a flexible spatula, transfer every last skerrick of the mac and cheese mix into a medium baking dish. Toss the breadcrumbs with the sesame seeds, butter, reserved spring onion greens and remaining cheddar, then scatter the lot over the mac and cheese.

Grill for 5–10 minutes, until the top is golden brown and the cheese sauce is bubbly.

Bring it home → Once the mac and cheese is deliciously cooked, allow to cool for a few minutes, then serve with something leafy.

Double duty → This dish is a leftover legend, where the flavours only get better the next day – just reheat as you need, or eat cold from a container at your desk ... it's that good!

The beauty of a fried rice is that it's an anything-goes situation – an easy midweek winner. You can swap the Spam for thick-cut leg ham, or cubed leftover roast, or even marinated tempeh or mushroom 'meat' (I like Fable). It's also a good way of using up a big tin of sweetcorn, or whatever frozen veg is already in your freezer, like baby peas. When you're using shelf-stable or long-life products – whether that's canned meat or tinned beans or even frozen veg – the key is to keep tasting while you're cooking, and to balance out the seasoning to ensure everything is reinvigorated with flavour. Caramelising the Spam brings out the sweetness and makes it taste less like a salty clump, so do give it time in the pan.

Shaoxing rice wine is a useful and inexpensive Chinese condiment for infusing savouriness and tang. If you're shaoxing-less, you can also use dry sherry if you've got it (à la Kylie Kwong).

Green Eggs & Spam Fried Rice

Serves → 4–6

Chop + stir → 10 MINUTES

Set + forget → 20 MINUTES

¼ cup (60 ml) neutral oil
170 g (½ tin) Spam, finely diced
3 cups (555 g) cooked and chilled jasmine rice (page 228)
2 cups (300 g) frozen corn (no need to thaw)
2 tablespoons shaoxing rice wine (optional but excellent)

Green eggs (omelette)

4 eggs
3 spring onions (scallions), finely sliced
1 tablespoon finely chopped coriander (cilantro) stems
1 tablespoon light soy sauce

Fried rice sauce

1–2 garlic cloves, minced
1 cm (½ in) knob of ginger, peeled and finely grated
1 tablespoon light soy sauce
1 tablespoon oyster sauce
1 tablespoon kecap manis
1 tablespoon sesame oil
25 g (1 oz) butter, diced

Home stretch

coriander (cilantro) leaves
sliced spring onion greens
light soy sauce
spring onion & ginger chunky oil (page 222)

Take a whisk → Get cracking on the omelette. In a bowl, whisk together the eggs, spring onion, coriander and soy sauce.

Eggstra extra → Heat a large high-sided, heavy-based pan or wok over medium heat. Add half the oil and, when shimmering, pour in the omelette mix and swirl it around – the eggs should puff up right away. When golden underneath but still not quite cooked on top, tuck the omelette into a roll, starting from one side, then remove from the pan. (The residual heat will finish cooking the egg; so will the pan when the egg is added back in!)

Wok on → Crank the heat under the pan to medium–high. Swirl in the remaining oil, then tumble in the cubes of Spam (or ham ... or mushrooms!), leaving them to settle and caramelise for 5 minutes or so. Toss about to do the other side, then, when mostly all golden, toss in the cooked rice, mixing really well to break up any clumps, making sure everything is well coated in the oil. Stir-fry for about 5 minutes, then toss in the frozen corn and rice wine and stir-fry for another 5 minutes, or until the corn is cooked (vibrant and juicy).

Get saucy → In a small bowl, mix together all the ingredients for your fried rice sauce. The butter will be blobby, and that's okay!

Toss caution to the wind → Drizzle the fried rice sauce all over the rice. Add the omelette back in, breaking it up into bits. Toss around until the egg is heated through and the butter has melted. Taste for seasoning, remembering that Spam (if that's what you're using!) is very salty.

Bring it home → Pile the fried rice onto a serving plate and garnish with coriander leaves and spring onion greens. Serve with soy sauce and spring onion oil on the side.

Double duty → Fried rice makes a great cold lunch or reheated dinner – just keep the fresh coriander off and add it after reheating.

Somewhere between nachos, chilli-non-carne and tortilla soup, this soupy, stewy, one-tray four-tin concoction with a crisp, cheesy totopo topping and cooling, creamy whipped guac ticks all the boxes. It's also very versatile. If using fresh corn, shuck the kernels off the cob by placing the corn flat on a chopping board and slicing through with a sharp knife. For frozen corn, just run it under the tap to take the chill off before tossing it in the mix. If you don't have any black beans or lentils, kidney beans or even chickpeas will fit here. You can use plain corn chips or tortilla chips if you can't find totopos, and half 'n' half shredded cheddar and manchego instead of Mexican cheese mix.

Use your deepest roasting pan to catch all the deliciously soupy sauce.

Four-Tin Tex-Mex Totopo Tray Bake

Serves → 4

Chop + stir → 10 MINUTES

Set + forget → 25 MINUTES

420 g (15 oz) tin corn kernels, drained
400 g (14 oz) tin black beans, rinsed and drained
400 g (14 oz) tin brown lentils, rinsed and drained
400 g (14 oz) tin cherry tomatoes
1 red onion, finely sliced with the grain
1 tablespoon Tex-Mex spice mix (or 2 tablespoons MYO, page 211)
300–400 g (10½–14 oz) jar roasted red capsicum (pepper) strips, liquor reserved
2 tablespoons olive oil
200 g (7 oz) packet totopos
200 g (7 oz) Mexican cheese mix

Whipped guac

2 ripe avocados
1 garlic clove, peeled
100 g (3½ oz) natural yoghurt
1 teaspoon Tex-Mex spice mix (or 2 teaspoons MYO, page 211)
juice of ½ lime
¼ bunch coriander (cilantro), sprigs reserved for garnishing

Home stretch

coriander (cilantro) sprigs (reserved from the guac)
Tex-Mex spice mix or paprika
½ lime, cut into wedges

Roast the lot → Preheat your oven to 220°C (425°F). In a large deep roasting pan, combine the corn kernels, beans and lentils. Add the cherry tomatoes, sloshing out the tin with a splash of water to get all the juice. Toss in the onion, Tex-Mex spice mix, the capsicum strips and liquor, along with the olive oil, then toss with a large spoon or your hands to introduce the ingredients properly.

Whack the pan into your hot oven and roast for 20 minutes for all the ingredients to get really friendly and saucy, and to bronze some bits on the veg.

Whip it good → While the veg finishes baking, whip up your guac by blitzing all the ingredients together until super smooth – using a blender, food processor, molcajete (the traditional way!), or a fork and bowl, if you're so inclined. Taste for seasoning.

Top those totopos → While the totopos are still sealed in the packet, take out any of the day's aggression by giving the pack a few decisive bangs to crush up the chips to fork-sized bits – or keep them whole if you'd prefer more of a nacho vibe. Slip on some oven mitts and pull the pan out of the oven (remember it's HOT!). Scatter half the restructured totopos over the veg and do a gentle fold-through, then sprinkle with the remaining totopos and all the cheese.

Pop the pan back into the oven for another 5 minutes to bubble the cheese and bronze the odd totopo tip.

Bring it home → Once the tray's out of the oven, blob the whipped guac about. Finish with a scattering of coriander leaves and sprinkle more Tex-Mex spice mix over the top. Scoop tableside into flat bowls and serve with comforting soup spoons, with lime wedges on the side.

Double duty → These get a little soggy in the fridge, but that shouldn't stop you packing them into your lunchbox for the next day. Keep the guac separate, and fork before serving to reinvigorate the colour and whipped texture.

Pilaf, pulao, plov, paella ... if it's a loaded one-pan rice dish, chances are 'tis but a rose by any other name. For every iteration, there are infinite ifs and maybes: 'If you don't have this, try that' or, 'maybe a handful here'.

Banana shallots (the long thin ones) work best, but golden shallots will do. Soaking them helps the skins slip off, and also stops them burning, instead bronzing their faces, adding savouriness. The cauli becomes sweet and tender and soaks up the flavours of the stock and the richness of the ghee. You can bend the veg with the seasons too – pumpkin (squash) or sweet potato can replace the carrot, and beans, broccoli or brussels sprouts can go in instead of (or as well as!) the cauli. You might even slip in some bits of leftover roast veg (or meat) and, for a more authentically Uzbek version, sprinkle in a handful of chopped dried apricots.

One-Pan Golden Cauli Pilaf

Serves → 4

Chop + stir → 15 MINUTES

Set + forget → 35 MINUTES

6 banana shallots or golden shallots, soaked in cold water for 10 minutes
¼ small cauliflower (about 300 g/ 10½ oz)
4 Dutch carrots, or small-ish carrots
4 tablespoons ghee (or 2 tablespoons olive oil + 2 tablespoons butter)
1 cup (200 g) raw basmati or long-grain rice, rinsed and drained
1 tablespoon salt flakes (or ½ teaspoon fine salt)
1 tablespoon mild madras curry powder (or khmeli suneli, page 211)
¼ teaspoon brown sugar
2 cups (500 ml) vegetable stock
1 cup (150 g) frozen corn
1 cup (140 g) frozen peas

Home stretch

soft herbs, such as coriander (cilantro) or parsley
lemon cheeks

Prep the veg → Drain the shallots, lop off the tops and bottoms, then cut them into quarters lengthways (or halves if you have smaller ones).

Cup the cauliflower curds in your palm and pull the florets off towards you, so they snap off the stalk at their natural point. Halve any florets that are bigger than a golf ball.

Peel the carrots, saving their skins for stock, then use the same peeler to strip long ribbons off the carrots, popping them into a bowl of cold water. Any bits that are too hard to peel can be munched on as 'chef snacks', handed to any tiny fists in your vicinity or stashed in your stock bag.

Hot stuff → Place a large shallow flameproof casserole dish, or high-sided heavy-based frying pan with a lid, over medium heat. Leave to heat up for 2–3 minutes, until your hovering palm feels the warmth.

Spoon in half the ghee. Add the shallots and cauliflower florets, letting as much of the veg access the pan's surface as possible. Set a timer for 10 minutes and whack the lid on, then turn the veg after 5 minutes. Once the shallots are coloured and the cauliflower is burnished, pull the cauliflower and shallots out and reserve.

Spice the rice → Tip the drained rice into the pan, scoop in the rest of the ghee, and stir in the salt, curry powder, sugar and a good crack of black pepper. Swish the contents around to get friendly over medium heat, the rice going glossy.

Put a lid on it → Pour the stock into the pan, along with enough water to ensure that the rice is all covered, add the cauliflower, shallots and carrot strips and bring to the boil. Once boiling, drop the heat to very low.

If your pan looks anything like mine (heavy, lidded, little chance of steam escaping), pop the lid on, set the timer for 15 minutes and walk away. Spin some salad leaves, stir some other pots – just generally live your life. If your pan has a dodgy lid, pop a layer of foil over the top of the pan, then squash the lid down. (This is also a neat trick if you're ever cooking rice in a dodgy pot using the absorption method.)

After 15 minutes, scatter the corn and peas over the rice. Put the lid back on, set the timer for another 5 minutes and then walk away again.

Bring it home → When the timer goes off, return to the pan, gently fluff, taste for seasoning, adding an extra pinch or two of salt as needed. Garnish with herbs and serve with lemon cheeks.

Double duty → This reheats really well, and leftovers will keep a few days. You could speed things up by stirring leftover cooked rice through the cooked cauli along with the frozen veg, and popping a lid on with ¼ cup (60 ml) water to reheat.

This one's somewhere between a green curry and a noodle salad, perfect for those shoulder seasons when you want something both comforting and fresh. Roasted cauli is tender and sweet, while tofu and coconut milk provide planty protein boosts. Boiling the tofu is a bit like poaching chicken, helping to infuse flavour while keeping it tender. If you want to keep it vego, use a vego green curry paste and swap the fish sauce for fysh sauce.

Green Curry Cauliflower Rice Noodle Salad

Serves → 4

Chop + stir → 10 MINUTES

Set + forget → 40 MINUTES

1 cauliflower (about 1 kg/2 lb 4 oz)
2 tablespoons green curry paste (or 4 tablespoons MYO, page 212)
2 tablespoons neutral oil
2 tablespoons coconut cream or coconut milk
2 red capsicums (peppers), sliced into rings
1 red onion, sliced with the grain into 1 cm (½ in) wedges
300 g (10½ oz) sugar snap peas or snow peas (mangetout), topped and halved on the bias
375 g (13 oz) block firm tofu, cut into 2 cm (¾ in) cubes
200 g (7 oz) dried vermicelli rice noodles

Coconut curry dressing

1 tablespoon neutral oil
⅓ cup (100 g) green curry paste (make it 2 heaped tablespoons shop-bought or MYO, page 212)
300 ml (10½ fl oz) coconut cream
2 teaspoons brown sugar
2 tablespoons fish sauce
juice of 1 large lime

Home stretch

3 Thai basil sprigs, leaves picked (optional)
3 coriander (cilantro) stems, picked into sprigs
⅓ cup (60 g) unsalted roasted peanuts, roughly chopped
1 green chilli, finely sliced (optional)
1 lime, cut into wedges

Fire up → Preheat your oven to 180°C (350°F), with a deep oven tray inside.

Cauli-up → Bang the cauliflower stem side down on the bench, to help loosen the florets. In a heatproof colander in the sink, tear the florets into fork-sized chunks. Tear any smaller leaves in too. Pour a kettle of boiling water over the cauli and let it steam out in the sink for 2–3 minutes.

Curry up → Transfer the cauli to a big mixing bowl. Blob the curry paste, oil and coconut cream over the cauli and toss about to coat, then taste for heat and seasoning. Tumble in the capsicum and onion and toss well to combine. Transfer to your preheated oven tray, keeping your big mixing bowl handy (no need to rinse the goodness out). Roast for 35–40 minutes, or until the veg is tender and burnished on the edges. Remove from the oven and allow to cool slightly.

Poach away → While the veg roasts, in a medium saucepan, bring plenty of well-salted water to the boil. Pop the peas into a sieve and into the hot water for 1 minute; pull them out and drain, then tip the peas into your big mixing bowl.

Return the sieve to the pot, add your tofu (to make it easier to hoik out of the water), bring back to the boil and simmer for 5 minutes.

Drain the tofu through the sieve, reserving the pot. Shake off the moisture, drain well on a clean tea towel (dish towel), then tip into the bowl with the peas.

Dress up → Grab your medium saucepan again for the dressing. Add the oil and bring to a shimmer over medium heat. Add the curry paste and cook, stirring, for 2–3 minutes, until fragrant. Stir in the coconut cream, sugar and fish sauce and bring to the boil. Drop the heat to a simmer and bubble away for 3–4 minutes until lightly thickened.

Switch off the heat, squeeze in the lime juice and taste for balance. Pour the dressing over the peas and tofu and toss about to coat. Give the saucepan a quick rinse; a slick of oil in the pan is fine.

Noodle time → Boil another kettle's worth of water. Drop your noodles into your rinsed pot and cover with plenty of boiling water. Leave for about 3 minutes, or until softened and opaque.

Bring it home → Drain the noodles and dump them into your bowl of dressing, along with the tofu, peas and tray of cooled roasted veg. Add half the picked herbs and toss gently to coat. Divide between bowls and top with the remaining herbs, peanuts and chilli, if using. Serve with lime wedges.

The way these flavours and textures meld together – creamy, fragrant rice, caramelly cauli and toothsome tangy tomatoes – I guarantee you'll be licking your plate! If you've got soy-maple glaze (page 219) in your fridge but no kecap manis, it's a very dignified substitution. I've left the sambal intentionally chunky and mild – more like a salad with a hint of heat – though this heat can also be left out to keep it fam-friendly.

The sunshine rice is inspired by nasi tumpeng, a celebratory Indonesian dish of rice tinted yellow by being simmered with turmeric and aromats, and usually served in a cone shape to signify abundance and gratitude.

Speaking of, since you're only using the 'steak-y' bits in this recipe (pictured overleaf), you'll be grateful to have an abundance of roasted cauliflower florets as a halfway to another midweek dinner! If you'd prefer not to steak your cauli, this glaze works just as well as a coating on a cauliflower's worth of florets – just roast the florets for 20 minutes sans glaze, then toss about in the glaze and give them an extra 5 minutes to get friendly.

Glazed Cauliflower Steaks + Cherry Tomato Sambal + Sunshine Rice

Serves → 4

Chop + stir → 20 MINUTES

Set + forget → 35 MINUTES

2 medium cauliflowers (about 1.6 kg/3 lb 8 oz)
2 tablespoons neutral oil

Sunshine rice

3 cups (750 ml) cold water
200 ml (7 fl oz) coconut milk
1 heaped teaspoon salt flakes
2 teaspoons ground turmeric
6 makrut lime leaves
3 cups (600 g) raw jasmine rice, washed until the water runs clear

Kecap manis glaze

1 tablespoon neutral oil
⅓ cup (80 ml) kecap manis
1 teaspoon rice wine vinegar
2 garlic cloves, minced

Rice and shine! → Pour the water and coconut milk into a medium saucepan with a lid. Whisk in the salt and turmeric and bring to the boil over medium–high heat. Scrunch the lime leaves in your hands to bruise them, then add to the pan with the washed rice. Stir to combine, cover with the lid and reduce the heat to low. Set a timer for 12 minutes, leaving the rice alone, then remove from the heat, keeping the lid on. Reset the timer for 15 minutes to let the residual steam finish cooking the rice. Once the timer goes off, use a fork to fluff up the rice grains, then cover again to keep warm.

For the cauli steaks + spares → While your rice is steaming, preheat your oven to 200°C (400°F), with an oven tray inside.

Boil a kettle of water. Using a large sharp knife, carefully cut the cauliflowers straight down the middle into steaks about 1 cm (½ in) thick; you should get six in total, along with spare cauli bits on each side, which you can tear into fork-friendly florets.

Place the cauli florets in a large mixing bowl in the sink, and the cauli steaks on top. Pour the just-boiled water over them, then carefully pour the water out of the bowl, leaving the cauli to steam out until the oven is ready.

When the oven's preheated, pour the 2 tablespoons neutral oil over the cauli and rub it over the steaks in the mixing bowl. Pull the tray out with your oven mitts and leave these on the handles to remind you that it's HOT. Arrange the oiled cauli steaks on that tray and place towards the top third of the oven. Toss the cauli florets around in any oil remaining in the mixing bowl, spread them on a second baking tray, then place towards the bottom of the oven. Roast for 20 minutes, until the cauli steaks are softened through the middle and starting to colour. Pull the florets out too and stash them in a container in the fridge for tomorrow's dinner.

Dabu dabu–style tomato sambal salad

1 teaspoon rice wine vinegar
juice of ½ lime (wedge the other lime half for serving)
500 g (1 lb 2 oz) cherry tomatoes, halved
1 cup (140 g) unsalted roasted peanuts
1 banana shallot, finely sliced
1 long red chilli, finely sliced (optional but excellent)
kecap manis, to taste

Here for the glaze → While the cauli is roasting, grab your large mixing bowl again, slosh in all the glaze ingredients and stir together.

All together now → Once roasted, dip the cauli steaks into the glaze, coating both sides, then place them back onto the baking tray and back into the oven for 8–10 minutes, or until burnished.

Rock the sambal → Use the dregs of the glaze in your large mixing bowl as the base of your sambal dressing, splashing in the rice wine vinegar to loosen, along with the lime juice and a pinch of sugar to sweeten if need be. Toss in the cherry tomatoes, peanuts, shallot and chilli, if using, tumbling them into a salad. Taste and add some kecap manis and a little more lime juice to your liking.

Bring it home → Divide the sunshine rice between bowls, top with the glazed cauli steaks and serve the tomato sambal spooned around the cauli.

Double duty → Those leftover roasted cauliflower florets are brilliant in the green cauli curry on page 191, or the quattro formaggi tray bake on page 197.

Glazed cauliflower steaks + cherry tomato sambal + sunshine rice
→ pages 192–3

When people say a recipe 'came to them', they're usually referring to some kind of human-to-human exchange, from a friend or family member. In this case, this dish literally *came to me, in the night, and I woke up* having *to make it. Think of it like a four-cheese pizza, with the gnocchi acting like little bites of pizza dough, lightened up by the roasted cauli, priming you for another bite, and the cottage cheese packing in extra protein (while quietly adding a bonus cheese). The cauli's caramelised juiciness is gorgeous against the cheese's salty funk – especially the tang of blue cheese. Gorgonzola would be ace here, but a milder blue, like Blue Castello, would be very welcome too. If yours is not a blue cheese–loving household, you could consider swapping in goat's cheese. Or, you could leave the blue off the bake itself, and serve it on the side for crumbling on later. 'Pizza cheese' is sold as a package deal of mozzarella, parmesan and cheddar, but you can make your own mix by combining equal parts shredded mozza, parm and ched.*

A rocket (arugula) salad wouldn't go astray here – and if you're feeding a crowd, this cheesy bake makes a wonderful hearty side to serve with other dishes.

Quattro Formaggi Gnocchi Cauli Tray Bake

Serves → 4

Chop + stir → 10 MINUTES

Set + forget → 30 MINUTES

1 whole cauliflower (about 1 kg/ 2 lb 4 oz)
500 g (1 lb 2 oz) gnocchi
2 tablespoons olive oil
150 g (5½ oz) pizza cheese
100 g (3½ oz) blue cheese (as sharp or mild as you like)
200 g (7 oz) high-protein cottage cheese
200 g (7 oz) crème fraiche or sour cream (or even just regular cream)
1–2 garlic cloves, minced

Heat is on → Preheat your oven to 180°C (350°F) and boil a kettle of water.

Cauli-power → In the meantime, bang the cauliflower stem side down on the bench, to help loosen the florets. In a heatproof colander in the sink, tear the florets up, so they're slightly larger than the gnocchi (on the smaller-side of fork-sized). Tear any leaves in too.

Pour the just-boiled kettle of water over the cauli and let it steam out in the sink for 2–3 minutes.

Into the tray → Dump the gnocchi into a wide shallow casserole dish or oven tray, along with the steamed-out cauli bits. Drizzle with the olive oil, add a pinch of salt flakes and toss about with your hands to ensure everything is well coated.

Transfer to the oven and roast for 25 minutes, until the cauli is starting to brown at the edges.

Cheese time → While the cauli and gnocchi do their thing, toss the cheeses into a mixing bowl. Add the crème fraiche, along with the garlic, a good crack of pepper and another pinch of salt flakes. Stir about.

After 25 minutes, pull the cauli and gnocchi out of the oven, leaving the oven mitts around the tray, and either crank the oven up to 240°C (475°F), or as hot as you'd take it for pizza – or switch the oven to the fan grill (broil) setting.

Using a big spoon, top the cauli and gnocchi with your cheesy sauce mix. Depending on the constellation in your tray, you might need some extra cheese for topping.

Pop the lot back in the oven or under the grill (broiler) for another 5 minutes to get some serious goo and colour.

Bring it home → Serve the tray at the table with your big spoon for scooping all the gooey goodness out, finishing with a crack of black pepper if you're that way inclined.

Kotletki, or cutlets, are the former Soviet Union's answer to burger patties. I've combined my favourite bits of Mum's light, veg-loaded kotletki with a little Japanese hambagu magic. Japanese 'burgers' use panko breadcrumbs, which, being flatter and wider than regular breadcrumbs, crisp up to a glassy texture that is unbeatable. You could also MYO crumb by blitzing any stale bread that's hanging about. The advantage of popping veg into the mix is threefold – you're eating more veg, you're buying less meat, AND you'll end up with a juicier result. I'm using cauliflower here because of its mild flavour and pale colour. Your kids won't know that these are one-quarter cauli – it is, after all, the 'chicken of the soil'.

Chicken & Cauli Kotletki + Garlicky Green Beans & Cherry Toms

Makes → 18

Serves → 4 (with leftovers)

Chop + stir → 20 MINUTES

Set + forget → 25 MINUTES

Kotletki

¼ cauliflower (about 250 g/9 oz), broken into florets, including the core
1 onion, peeled and quartered
¾ cup (45 g) panko breadcrumbs
500 g (1 lb 2 oz) minced (ground) chicken
¼ cup (60 g) Japanese mayonnaise
2 eggs
2 teaspoons salt flakes
¼ teaspoon ground white pepper
8 good rasps of nutmeg (about ¼ teaspoon grated nutmeg)

Green beans & cherry toms

400 g (14 oz) green beans
500 g (1 lb 2 oz) cherry tomatoes
½ lemon
2–3 garlic cloves, peeled
1 tablespoon olive oil

Home stretch

panko breadcrumbs, for crumbing
neutral oil, for frying
40 g (1½ oz) butter

Rollin' rissoles → To prepare the kotletki, place the cauliflower and onion in a food processor and pulse until you have a rice-like texture. Tip the mixture into a large bowl, then add the remaining kotletki ingredients. Give the mix a good knead for a couple of minutes, until well combined. You'll wonder if your mix is too wet; the breadcrumbs just haven't had a chance to puff up and do their magic yet!

With wet hands, shape the patties into similar-sized oblongs of about ¼ cup (60 g), the size of an apricot. Squish down to about 1 cm (½ in) thick, place on a tray and chill in the fridge until ready to cook. (You could make and/or shape the mix up to a day in advance and store covered in the fridge.)

Veg out → Bring a medium pot of well-salted water to the boil. Top the green beans and snap them in half (I like to get junior burger hands onto this task). Pop them into the boiling water for 3 minutes.

Meanwhile, chop the cherry tomatoes in half and slip them into a heatproof bowl. Finely grate the lemon zest and garlic over the tomatoes, adding a pinch of salt flakes and a crack of pepper.

When the green beans are done, drain well, then dunk straight into the tomato bowl. Drizzle with olive oil and toss about to combine. The residual heat from the beans will intensify the flavours and give you a gloriously zippy side. (You can make this up to a day ahead as well; just take it out of the fridge when you fry the patties, to take the fridge chill off.)

Born to fry → When ready to cook the patties, prepare a plate or tray with panko breadcrumbs (less is more – you can always add more).

Place a large heavy-based frying pan over medium heat and line with baking paper, then splash in some frying oil to cover the bottom. Foam the butter in too.

In batches, arrange some patties in the pan and cook slowly for about 5 minutes on each side, until golden and thoroughly cooked through (opaque but still juicy). Place on a cooling rack over a baking tray and repeat until all the patties are done, finishing with a sprinkle of salt flakes.

If you're cooking these in batches to serve right away, you can keep them warm in a low oven while finishing the rest.

Bring it home → Enjoy warm, with your garlicky beans and tomatoes.

Double duty → Freeze leftover kotletki on a tray, or refrigerate for up to 3–4 days and reheat in a pan as needed. Serve in a broth with peas and a blob of chilli crisp oil, or in a bun with lettuce as 'chicky' burgers.

This luxurious one-pan panacea simmers with sunny Grecian flavours. Fennel is best looked at as three separate veg: fronds are herbage best kept for garnishing, stalks are best treated like celery in a mirepoix, and the bulb is the juicy, sweet heart, which can be sliced finely for salads or cut into chunky wedges for frying and braising.

Hold off adding any extra salt until just before serving, as the preserved lemon in the double lemon drizz is very salty. (Remember to scrape off the preserved lemon pith and flesh, as these can be bitter – the peel's your prize!) Once the drizz is stirred through at the end, taste again, and then finish off your seasoning.

To make this braise gluten-free, leave the orzo out and add an extra tin of beans for extra planty protein.

Simmery Fennel, Cannellini & Orzo Braise + Honey & Double Lemon Drizz

Serves → 4 (with leftovers)

Chop + stir → 20 MINUTES

Set + forget → 20–25 MINUTES

3–4 medium fennel bulbs with fronds (about 1.2 kg/2 lb 10 oz)
¼ cup (60 ml) olive oil
100 g (3½ oz) salted butter
1 brown onion, finely sliced with the grain
2–3 garlic cloves, finely sliced
1 stock cube (veg/chicken), or 1 teaspoon powder
½ bunch parsley, stems finely chopped (reserve the leaves for the drizz)
1 cup (190 g) orzo (aka risoni)
400 g (14 oz) tin cannellini beans, rinsed and drained

Honey & double lemon drizz

zest and juice of 1 lemon
1 tablespoon finely chopped preserved lemon peel
½ bunch parsley leaves (reserved from above), roughly chopped
1 tablespoon mild-flavoured honey

Home stretch

⅔ cup (100 g) marinated feta
feathery fennel fronds (reserved from above)
extra virgin olive oil

Double duty → This reheats a treat – just save some drizz for loosening off with olive oil and drizzling over the next day.

Wedge the fennel → Cut the stalks off the fennel, reserving any fronds, then finely slice the stalks and set aside. Carefully trim the root end of each fennel bulb, keeping all the layers intact at the base. Cut each bulb vertically into wedges, keeping each wedge attached at the base if possible. You want the wedges to be about 1.5 cm (⅝ in) at their widest, so you might end up with six to eight wedges from small–medium bulbs, or even 10 wedges from big mamas.

Get sizzling → Place a wide, high-sided, heavy-based frying pan with a lid (or a shallow flameproof casserole dish) over medium heat. Pour in a good glug of the olive oil to cover the bottom. Add half the butter and wait for the frothy sizzle. Working in batches, arrange the fennel wedges in the pan, cut side down, and cook for 3–4 minutes on each side, until lightly golden. Transfer to a bowl and repeat with the remaining wedges, adding more oil and the remaining butter as needed.

Once all the fennel wedges are golden and out of the pan, toss in the finely sliced fennel stalks and onion. Put the lid on and leave to sweat for 5 minutes, stirring occasionally, until the onion turns translucent and the fennel stems soften. During the last couple of minutes, add the garlic, stock cube and parsley stems and toss around a bit.

Braise the lot → Stir in 3 cups (750 ml) of just-boiled water. Taste for seasoning and sprinkle in some salt and pepper if needed, then bring back to the boil. Tumble in the orzo, cannellini beans and your golden fennel wedges. Stir about to ensure everything is evenly distributed, then turn down the heat to a simmer and put the lid on. Set the timer for 10 minutes and stir occasionally, until the orzo is cooked. The braise will thicken up and become lovely and glossy, and the fennel will be fork-tender and sweet.

Make your drizz → While the braise is bubbling away, prepare all the ingredients for your honey lemon drizz and mix together in a small bowl.

Bring it home → Blob the drizz over your brill braise, then stir through at the table to allow the flavours to get friendly before serving. Spoon on blobs of marinated feta, then sprinkle with feathery fennel fronds and a glug of olive oil to finish this one right off.

This is a traditional Sicilian dish from the city of Palermo – a place that sits at the crossroads of Mediterranean, Middle Eastern and even Norman (French) civilisations. You'll note those influences here: wine and butter from the French, currants and fennel seeds from the Silk Road (even a pinch of saffron wouldn't go astray), and, of course, the irresistible combo of lemon, fennel and garlic from the island of Sicily itself.

When it comes to sardines, as with anchovies, it does pay to spend a little more, especially when these small fish provide all the flavour and protein in this punchy fennel-infused pasta dish.

Bucatini is a fun pasta shape for the way it sucks up sauces and bounces about on the fork, but you're welcome to use any long pasta, fresh or dried.

Fennel & Fish-Tin Bucatini

Serves → 4

Chop + stir → 10 MINUTES

Set + forget → 20 MINUTES

¾ cup (115 g) currants
½ cup (125 ml) dry white wine
100–140 g (3½–5 oz) tin quality sardines in olive oil
¼ cup (60 ml) olive oil
1 small fennel bulb, very finely sliced against the grain, including the stalks (reserve the fronds for garnishing)
2 red shallots, finely sliced against the grain
3–4 garlic cloves, finely sliced
2–3 quality anchovies
400 g (14 oz) dried bucatini
1 lemon

Caper pangrattato

25 g (1 oz) butter
100 g (3½ oz) sourdough bread, torn or diced into small pieces
½ teaspoon fennel seeds, crushed
2 tablespoons salted lilliput or tiny capers

Home stretch

fennel fronds (reserved from above)

Currant mood → Pop the currants into a small bowl, pour the wine over them and leave to soak while you get cooking.

Pasta pot → Bring a large pot of well-salted water to the boil.

Can pangrattato → Meanwhile, drain the oil from the sardine tin into a large high-sided pan and place over medium heat. Add the butter. When the butter foams, toss in the bread bits, fennel seeds and capers and fry for about 7–10 minutes, tossing now and then, until the bread is coloured and crunchy and the fennel seeds aromatic. Scoop the mixture onto a small plate.

Sweat the veg → In the same schmutzy pan, heat 2 tablespoons of the olive oil. Toss in the fennel, shallot, garlic and anchovies and put the lid on. Set the timer for 10 minutes and leave to sweat over medium heat, stirring and checking occasionally. Once the fennel has softened, tip in the wine-soaked currants, along with the wine. Crank the heat up and give a good stir to deglaze the pan and cook out the booziness.

Pasta please → While your fennel is schvitzing (sweating), add the bucatini to your pan of boiling salted water and cook until al dente, following the timing on the packet as a guide.

Sardine squish → Keeping the drained sardines in the tin, fork in the zest of the lemon. Cut the lemon in half and squeeze in the juice from one half. Slice the other lemon half into jaunty bits for serving. Finely chop the reserved fennel fronds and squish them through the sardines, keeping the prettiest fronds aside for the final flourish.

Bring it home → When the bucatini is cooked and the fennel and onion are soft and sweet, drag the bucatini into the pan, along with some of the dripping pasta water, and gently stir about to heat through. Fold the contents of the sardine-y lemony fennel tin through, along with the remaining tablespoon of olive oil (plus a splash more, if you like). The sardines will all but disappear through the pasta, leaving a gentle flavour. Taste for seasoning, adding salt flakes and loads of freshly ground black pepper as desired.

Serve at the table, sprinkled with the crumb caper and your prettiest fennel fronds, with the jaunty lemon bits alongside.

Chickpeas are a fantastically versatile ingredient that have been delivering plant-based, protein-packed nutrient density since B-C-E. This dish takes full advantage of their transmutable texture and transformative powers, from their crunch when roasted, to their creaminess when puréed – with their aquafaba ('bean water') standing in as vegan egg whites to help fluff the chickpea purée in full flight. In that way, fennel and chickpeas are a perfect pairing, since both are so versatile and adaptable – here the fennel is roasted so that it burnishes and releases its full sweetness, while its fronds are kept fresh to let the anise notes shine.

You can make this salad up to a day ahead; just keep the roasted ingredients separate from the chickpea purée and herby toss until you're about to serve. It makes a substantial side for grilled chops or fish, and also travels well for a bring-a-plate.

Warm Fennel & Spiced Chickpea Salad + French Herby Toss

Serves → 4

Chop + stir → 10 MINUTES

Set + forget → 40 MINUTES

- 2 fennel bulbs, with fronds (reserve the leaves for garnishing)
- 1 brown onion, peeled and cut into thin-ish wedges
- 400 g (14 oz) tin chickpeas (reserve half, and the aquafaba, for the purée)
- ¼ cup (60 ml) olive oil
- 1 tablespoon fennel seeds, crushed
- ½ teaspoon salt flakes
- ¼ teaspoon freshly ground black pepper

Chickpea & almond purée

- chickpeas and aquafaba (reserved from above)
- ½ cup (125 ml) extra virgin olive oil
- ½ cup (80 g) blanched almonds
- 2 garlic cloves, peeled
- zest and juice of 1 lemon
- ½ teaspoon salt flakes
- ¼ teaspoon freshly ground black pepper

French herby toss

- ½ cup (65 g) finely chopped dried apricots
- 2 tablespoons chardonnay vinegar
- ¼ bunch parsley
- ¼ bunch chives
- ¼ cup fennel fronds
- 2 tablespoons extra virgin olive oil

Home stretch

- fennel fronds (reserved from above)

Prep the veg → Top and tail the fennel, reserving the stalks for your stock bag. Pull off and reserve the fennel fronds. Slice the bulbs in half lengthways, then into quarters, or even into sixths if the bulbs are large.

Toss the fennel and onion wedges in a large mixing bowl. Drain the tin of chickpeas, reserving the liquid (aquafaba), then rinse the chickpeas and add half of them to the bowl. Add the olive oil, crushed fennel seeds, salt and pepper and toss together.

Line a baking tray with baking paper. Tip the mixture onto the tray, then whack into a cold oven and crank the heat to 180°C (350°F). Bake for 35–40 minutes, until the fennel wedges start to soften and scorch, the onion wedges have collapsed and the chickpeas are beautifully golden.

Purée away → To make the chickpea and almond purée, tumble the remaining chickpeas into a blender or food processor, along with ½ cup (125 ml) of the aquafaba (the liquid you reserved from the chickpea tin). Add the remaining ingredients and blitz to a fine, fluffy consistency. Taste for seasoning, and splash in a tablespoon or so of water if the mix needs a little loosening.

So fines! → Make the herby toss by soaking the chopped apricots in the vinegar for at least 10 minutes while you chop the herbs finely. Just before you're ready to serve, toss all the herby fuzz together with the vinegary apricots and olive oil.

Bring it home → Spread the almond and chickpea purée across a shallow platter. Layer the roasted fennel, onion wedges and chickpeas over the top, dressing with the herby toss. Garnish with the reserved fennel fronds and finish with a sprinkling of salt flakes and freshly cracked pepper. Serve warm, or at room temperature.

Sweet, creamy, rich and sumptuous, parsnip and pear is a soup combo that's ripe for a retro revival. However, the faff with fibrous root vegetables such as parsnips is the time it takes for them to relax in the pan, which would ordinarily preclude them from midweek meal territory. But, if you can break down the fibres before *you cook them – say, by grating the veg – then you've gained yourself 20 minutes back to the future, Marty McFly.*

If you're in a hurry, keep the bread as crostini, top with the mustardy cheese mix and bake separately, so you don't have to wait for the soup to finish burbling.

A simple leafy salad would round this out for dinner.

Grate Parsnip & Pear Soup + Cheesy Mustardy Toasts

Serves → 4 (with some for the freezer)

Chop + stir → 10 MINUTES

Set + forget → 45 MINUTES

2 leeks
20 g (¾ oz) butter
2 tablespoons olive oil
4 garlic cloves, roughly chopped
1½ cups (375 ml) dry cider
½ tablespoon honey
6 small to medium parsnips (about 650 g/1 lb 7 oz)
2 firm pears (about 450 g/1 lb), cored
2 bay leaves
1 star anise
2 cups (500 ml) chicken or vegetable stock
4 good rasps of nutmeg (about ⅛ teaspoon grated nutmeg), plus extra to serve

Cheesy mustardy toasts

2 tablespoons olive oil
1 tablespoon wholegrain mustard
½ sourdough baguette, roughly torn into pieces
1 cup (100 g) coarsely grated cheddar

Wiki leeks → Cut the leeks lengthways down the middle, then give them a good rinse under running water, rubbing between the layers. Lop the dark green tops off and whack them into your stock bag. Finely slice the pale green and white bits and pop into a salad spinner to soak, or into a bowl with plenty of water for a wash and rinse, being careful to agitate the grit out. Spin out to dry or drain well when ready to cook.

Sweaty betty → Place a large heavy-based saucepan or cast-iron pot over medium heat. Toss in the butter and olive oil. Once the butter's foamy, add the leek, garlic and a splash of water and listen for the sizzle. Drop the heat to medium–low and whack the lid on. Set a timer for 10 minutes, checking and stirring halfway to keep the bottom from catching.

Cider splash → Once the leek is softened and the garlic aromatic, splash in the cider and stir to deglaze. Cook off over medium–high heat for about 5 minutes, then stir the honey through.

Grate work → Using a food processor or a box grater, coarsely grate the parsnips and pears (no need to peel). Add to the pot with the bay leaves, star anise, stock and 2 cups (500 ml) water. Cover and cook for 20–25 minutes, until the parsnip can be squashed between your fingers.

A toast to you → When your soup is nearly done, start on the toasts. Mix the olive oil and mustard in a bowl, toss in the bread and half the cheddar and mix to coat. Preheat the grill (broil) function on your oven, or crank your oven up to 220°C (425°F).

Soup yourself → Switch the heat off under your soup pot. Pull out the bay leaves and star anise, sprinkle in the nutmeg and stir about. Use a stick blender to whiz the lot to a creamy consistency in the pot – or, blitz in a food processor, in batches if need be, then return to the pot. Taste for seasoning, remembering you can always add more later.

Bring it home → Ladle your warm soup into heatproof serving bowls, scatter the mustardy bread mix on top, then sprinkle the rest of the cheddar over the bread. Cook under your hot oven grill for about 5 minutes, until the bread is golden and the cheese melted. Serve with another rasp of nutmeg and a sprinkle of salt flakes.

Double duty → You can make the soup the day before, along with the rubbed bread, then heat and gratinate for serving. You could also freeze the soup in portions, ready to be reheated and gratinated.

Tex-Mex spice mix

Khmeli suneli spice mix

Tex-Mex Spice Mix

Makes → ½ CUP (70 G)

Takes → 5 MINUTES

1 tablespoon (14 g) salt flakes, lightly crushed
1 tablespoon (10 g) ground cumin
2 teaspoons (8 g) mild chilli powder (or ½ teaspoon of a hotter chilli powder)
2 teaspoons (7 g) ground paprika (hot/smoky/sweet – whatever you've got!)
2 teaspoons (8 g) garlic powder
2 teaspoons (6 g) onion powder
2 teaspoons (4 g) ground coriander
2 teaspoons (1.5 g) dried oregano (ideally Mexican or Greek)
2 teaspoons (6 g) cornflour (cornstarch)
1 teaspoon (5 g) caster (superfine) sugar

Tex-Mex is a fusion of the chilli-pepper kick of Mexican cuisine with the sweet–savoury notes of Texan barbecue. Use this spice mix in any Mexican or Southwestern American dishes that need a savoury kick, toss through roast potatoes or sweet potatoes, use for your nachos or the totopos tray bake on page 187, and stir through taco rice, or quinoa or grainy salads like the brocc avo on page 145.

Measure all your spices into a clean jar with a tight-fitting lid. (I like to use digital scales when measuring spices for mixing, which is why I've included all the gram weights here.)

Firmly close the lid and shake the spices about until evenly mixed.

Storage + shelf life → Use right away, or store in a cool, dark nook of the pantry, where your spice mix will keep for up to 6 months. Give the jar a good shake before using.

Khmeli Suneli Spice Mix

Makes → ¾ CUP (70 G)

Takes → 5 MINUTES

2 tablespoons (10 g) ground coriander
2 tablespoons (5 g) dried basil
2 tablespoons (5 g) dried oregano
2 teaspoons (5 g) ground fennel seeds
2 tablespoons (20 g) ground fenugreek (halve if grinding the seeds yourself)
2 tablespoons (20 g) ground turmeric
½ teaspoon (2 g) cayenne pepper

Khmeli suneli is Georgia's version of curry powder or garam masala – which means every household has its own twist. You've probably got everything besides the ground fenugreek in your pantry already. If you can only find whole fenugreek seeds, halve the quantity, as freshly ground is more intensely bitter. Blue fenugreek is ideal if you can find it, as this is what we'd use in Georgia. Any time you want to bring some Georgian spice to your life, grab this out of the pantry and give it a shake over steamed greens or the shila plavi on page 140, on proteins as a rub or finishing spice, through creamy dressings and omelettes, and in your mkhlovani on page 118.

Measure all your spices into a clean jar with a tight-fitting lid. (I like to use digital scales when measuring spices, which is why I've included all the gram weights here.)

Firmly close the lid and shake the spices about until evenly mixed.

Storage + shelf life → Use right away, or store in a cool, dark nook of the pantry, where your spice mix will keep for up to 6 months. Give the jar a good shake before using.

Red Curry Paste

Makes → 1 HEAPED CUP (ABOUT 250 G)

Takes → 30 MINUTES

20 dried long red chillies
1 tablespoon shrimp paste (belacan)
4 red shallots or banana shallots, peeled
4 garlic cloves, peeled
3 cm (1¼ in) knob of ginger (peeled if super woody)
1 lemongrass stem (trim the base and use the thickest part up to the halfway mark)
1 teaspoon ground cumin
1 teaspoon ground coriander
1 teaspoon salt
1 tablespoon neutral oil

This paste has a lovely rounded heat from the dried chillies and ground spices. It's got a kick, but less so than most shop-bought curry pastes. Fry it off as a base for curries, or loosen with neutral oil as a marinade. To make it plant-based, swap the shrimp paste for 2 tablespoons fysh sauce. Use this paste in your tom kha (page 63) and hawker-style eggplant laksa (page 78).

Soak the dried chillies in boiling water for 20–30 minutes – if you'd prefer less heat, use kitchen scissors to snip the chillies and shake out any seeds before soaking. Reserve ¼ cup (60 ml) of the chilli soaking water, then drain the chillies.

While the chillies are soaking, preheat your oven to 180°C (350°F) fan-forced. Wrap the shrimp paste in foil and bake for 5–10 minutes.

Combine the chillies, chilli soaking water and toasted shrimp paste in a blender. Add the remaining ingredients and blitz to a smooth paste.

Storage + shelf life → Use right away, or freeze the curry paste in ice cube trays and it'll last for 3–6 months.

Riffs → For a Malaysian spin, add an extra lemongrass stem, six makrut lime leaves and a 2 cm (¾ in) thumb of fresh turmeric (or a teaspoon of ground turmeric).

Green Curry Paste

Makes → 2 CUPS (ABOUT 600 G)

Takes → 15–20 MINUTES

½ tablespoon shrimp paste (belacan)
10 long green chillies, split and deseeded, then quartered
4–6 makrut lime leaves, destemmed
4 red shallots, peeled
4 garlic cloves, peeled
zest and juice of 1 large lime
3 cm (1¼ in) thumb of ginger, peeled and roughly chopped
1 lemongrass stem, trimmed and roughly chopped
¼ cup coriander (cilantro) stems and roots (see recipe intro)
1 tablespoon neutral oil
1 tablespoon fish sauce
1 teaspoon ground coriander
1 teaspoon ground cumin
1 teaspoon sugar (brown or white)

Get ready for a zippy, bright curry paste with a kick, but less front-palate heat and a fresher aroma than most shop-bought pastes. If your coriander doesn't have roots, add the stems and an extra ½ teaspoon ground coriander. To make it planty, swap the shrimp paste and fish sauce for 3 tablespoons fysh sauce. Use this paste in the sunrise mussels on page 44 and the green curry cauli noodle salad on page 191, fry off as a base for all of your curries, or loosen with neutral oil as a marinade.

Preheat your oven to 180°C (350°F). Wrap the shrimp paste in foil and bake for 5–10 minutes.

Once the shrimp paste has cooked and is cool enough to handle, combine all the ingredients in a blender or food processor and blitz to a smooth paste. Taste and adjust for seasoning.

Storage + shelf life → Use right away, or freeze the curry paste in ice cube trays and it'll last for 3–6 months.

ed curry paste

Green curry paste

G paste → page 214

Adjika → page 215

PG Paste

Makes → 2 CUPS (400 G)

Takes → 10 MINUTES

1 bunch parsley (about 100 g/ 3½ oz), leaves and stems roughly chopped
40 g (1½ oz) garlic (about 10 garlic cloves), peeled
zest and juice of 1 lemon
1 cup (250 ml) olive oil
1 teaspoon salt flakes

Consider this (pictured on page 213) your base paste for any manner of dishes – swishing through pasta, whipping up a salad dressing, or simply serving atop fish or roasted veg. I like to think of garlic as the white t-shirt of aromatics because it goes with everything; parsley is a bit like the trusty silk scarf for extra colour and pop – and the lemon offers zip, while helping bring the pH of the paste down, extending its shelf life. Toss this paste through a tuna pasta salad (page 180) or a tuna mornay (page 178), or stir into the green PG polenta on page 136 for a zesty kick.

Using a food processor or blender, blitz all the ingredients together until a fine paste forms, scraping down the sides as needed. Taste and adjust for seasoning.

Storage + shelf life → Use right away, or store in an airtight container in the fridge for up to a week, or pop into ice cube trays and freeze to use over 3–6 months.

Riffs → For extra oomph, add three anchovies or a handful of grated parmesan. If you're not a big garlic fan, use half a bulb, then taste and add more if needed.

You can use either flat-leaf or curly parsley for this recipe, but with its drier, more fibrous texture, curly parsley works best. (For once, something curly parsley can be better at than continental, beyond dressing up a butcher's display!) Parsley stems can be quite wet and watery, so if you're harvesting your own, prioritise the leaves over the stems.

If you'd prefer a rougher texture, more like a chimichurri, finely chop the parsley and garlic on a board, zest and juice the lemon, and loosen with olive oil.

Adjika

Makes → 1 CUP (300 G)

Takes → 10 MINUTES

4 garlic cloves, peeled
¼ cup (40 g) sun-dried tomatoes, drained
1 cup (250 g) drained piquillo peppers
¼ teaspoon mild chilli flakes
¼ bunch (15 g/½ oz) coriander (cilantro) stems, leaves reserved
¼ bunch (15 g/½ oz) parsley stems and leaves
½ bunch (15 g/½ oz) holy basil, Thai basil or young regular basil leaves
30 ml (1 fl oz) neutral oil
1 teaspoon ground fenugreek (halve if grinding the seeds yourself)
1 teaspoon ground coriander
1 teaspoon salt flakes
½ teaspoon sugar
¼ teaspoon pepper

Adjika (pictured on page 213) is Georgia's answer to a fiery harissa or spiced chutney, which I've made milder and more fam-friendly, though you could add more heat with extra chilli flakes if so desired. Some adjika recipes use fresh chilli peppers and leave the mix overnight to ferment a little, while others char the peppers first, but I like to introduce funk and smoke by using jarred peppers and sun-dried tomatoes. Use this adjika any time you'd use a tomato chutney or sauce – especially for barbecues. It's also great on dishes like the shila plavi on page 140, and the cauliflower pilaf on page 188.

If you can't find holy basil, Thai basil still gives you the menthol-like notes that are a feature of a paste like adjika. If you can't find either, Italian basil can serve as an alternative – but try to find a bunch with softer leaves and a milder aroma, as this herb can sometimes be overpowering and will take the flavour in a totally different direction.

Place all the ingredients into a small blender and whiz until smooth. Taste and season to your liking.

Storage + shelf life → Your adjika will last for up to a week in the fridge in an airtight container.

Mango Chutney

Makes → 2 CUPS (500 G)

Takes → 70 MINUTES

2 tablespoons neutral oil
1 brown onion, finely sliced
½ teaspoon mustard seeds (brown, black or yellow welcome)
2 cm (¾ in) thumb of ginger, peeled and roughly chopped
2–3 garlic cloves, roughly chopped
1 tablespoon mild madras curry powder
¼ teaspoon ground fenugreek (optional but excellent)
500 g (1 lb 2 oz) mangoes (underripe or frozen are fine), peeled and roughly chopped
½ cup (125 ml) apple cider vinegar
¾ cup (165 g) sugar (any type)
¼ teaspoon fine salt

Welcome to sunshine in a jar – the kind that warms you from the inside out, with the heady spices of the subcontinent and tangy sweetness of mango. Fenugreek isn't always included in a mango chutney, but I love how this spice offers a herbaceous groundedness to the mix. Dog-ear this page for when mangoes are going cheap at the shops, and thank me later. This chutney is wonderful in the Indian-style chickpea salad on page 123, the sabich tray bake on page 82, and any time you need a savoury-sweet condiment, or want to add colour and interest to your cheeseboards, sandwiches, burgers and the like.

Heat the oil in a large saucepan over medium–high heat. Add the onion and mustard seeds, listen for the sizzle, then drop the heat to medium and whack a lid on. Cook, stirring occasionally, for 8 minutes, or until softened but not coloured.

Dump in the ginger, garlic, curry powder and fenugreek, if using. Cook, stirring, for a further 1–2 minutes, or until just fragrant.

Tumble in the mango flesh and stir to coat with the spices. Stir in the vinegar, sugar and salt. Bring to the boil, stirring to dissolve the sugar, then drop the heat to low. Cook with the lid slightly ajar, stirring occasionally to stop the mixture catching, for 45–60 minutes, or until the chutney is thickened and reduced to your liking.

Remove from the heat and transfer into very clean, airtight, heatproof containers. This chutney can be served right away but is best once chilled, as it'll continue to thicken and set.

Storage + shelf life → The chutney will keep for up to 1–2 months in the fridge – using a clean spoon every time you dig some out will help extend its shelf life. (And yes, you WILL want to eat this off a spoon!)

Riffs → For a chunkier South Indian spin, use green mango and jaggery (palm sugar).

Go all in on amba, the Iraqi–Jewish version that travelled to Baghdad via trade with Bombay, by adding into your spice mix a teaspoon each of ground cumin and sumac, along with a good pinch of cayenne pepper.

Or, add a Thai twist by swapping out the spices in the recipe above for 3 tablespoons of green or red curry paste (see page 212).

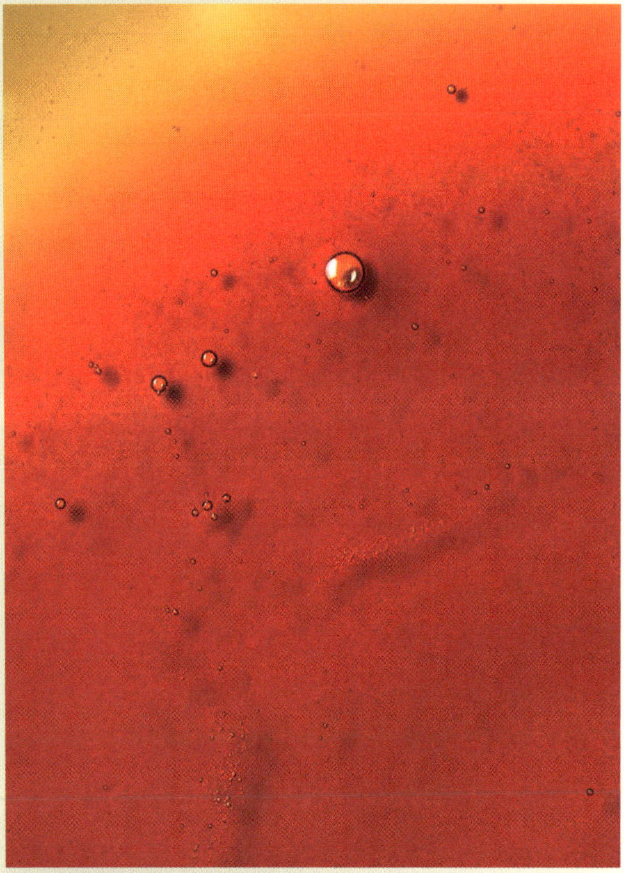

Soy maple glaze

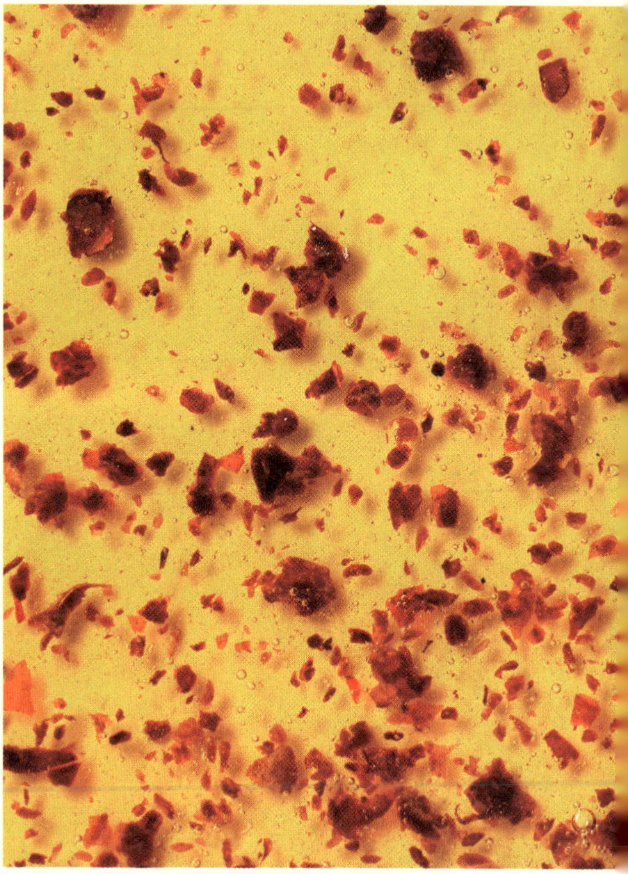

Hot honey

Mushroom XO → page 220

Chilli crisp oil → page 221

Soy Maple Glaze

Makes → 1 CUP (250 ML)

Takes → 30 MINUTES

½ cup (125 ml) light soy sauce
½ cup (125 ml) maple syrup
½ cup (125 ml) mirin
½ cup (125 ml) sake

This glaze is a terrific way of seasoning anything you would use soy sauce for – but with more complexity. Brush onto veg/protein on the grill, when marinating and roasting, or through your stir-fry sauces, adding just a teaspoon at a time, as you would salt. If you don't have maple syrup, use the same amount of honey, or dissolve in some sugar (preferably soft brown for extra oomph). Use it for the cauli steaks on page 192, the butternut dengaku on page 30, or even as a dressing base for the cucumber whack salad on page 91.

Combine all the ingredients in a small saucepan and bring to the boil. Reduce the heat to low and allow to gently concentrate, swirling occasionally, for 30 minutes, or until syrupy and reduced by half. (Don't be tempted to crank the temperature up to speed things along, or it will become bitter.)

The liquid will thicken as it cools; test by dipping a metal spoon into the mixture, then letting the liquid run down the tip of the spoon – if it's glossy and glazed to your liking, it's ready.

Remove from the heat and allow to cool. Transfer to a sterilised jar.

Storage + shelf life → The glaze will keep in the fridge for up to 2 months – possibly longer, as long as it smells and looks okay.

Riffs → For more of a glazed, honey-like viscosity, gently reduce the mixture for an extra 10 minutes. Double the quantities for a never-ending jar in the fridge.

Hot Honey

Makes → ¼ CUP (90 G)

Takes → 35 MINUTES

¼ cup (90 g) mild-flavoured honey
1 teaspoon mild dried chilli (I like Aleppo or Sichuan)

Give dishes and platters some extra punch and polish with a drizzle of hot honey (pictured left), which, despite its name, can be served warm, or at room temp too. The heat comes from chilli flakes, which you can dial up or down. Use it on a panzanella tray bake (page 49), hand pies (page 126), or anything that could use more sweetness and heat – from bruschetta and roasted potatoes to cheeseboards and anything fried.

Place the ingredients, along with a good pinch of salt flakes, in a small saucepan over very low heat. Cook gently for a few minutes until the honey is warmed through and runny.

Switch the heat off and leave the chilli to infuse into the honey for at least half an hour. Decant into a very clean, dry jar.

Storage + shelf life → Store your hot honey in a cool dark place like the pantry if you're in temperate climes, or in the fridge for the tropics. It will be at its best for 3–6 months.

Riffs → For extra aroma and flavour, add bruised garlic, hard spices like cinnamon quills and/or star anise, or hard herbs like rosemary, oregano and/or thyme.

Mushroom XO

Makes → 1½ CUPS (375 ML)

Takes → 50 MINUTES

- 40 g (1½ oz) dried shiitake mushrooms
- ½ cup (125 ml) neutral oil
- 4 banana shallots, finely chopped
- 5 garlic cloves (30 g/1 oz), peeled and finely grated
- 1 large thumb ginger (50 g/1¾ oz), peeled and finely grated
- 2 tablespoons cognac or brandy
- ¼ cup (60 ml) light soy sauce
- 2 tablespoons vegetarian mushroom sauce (Megachef brand is my pick)
- 2 tablespoons soft brown sugar
- 1 teaspoon gochujang (optional but excellent)
- ½ teaspoon smoked paprika
- ½ teaspoon Chinese five-spice
- ¼ teaspoon ground white pepper
- 1 star anise and/or cinnamon quill (optional but excellent)
- 1 tablespoon rice wine vinegar
- 1 tablespoon toasted sesame oil

XO sauce (pictured on page 218) is the shoulder-padded, gilded bathroom decadence of '80s Hong Kong, in condiment form. Though the 'XO' refers to 'extra old' cognac, this is more of a reference to the luxury of such a liquor rather than its inclusion in a sauce that is typically packed full of premium seafood, like dried scallops. But why not try adding actual cognac or brandy to the mix, instead of the traditional shaoxing rice wine? And why not sub the scallops out for vego-funk-bombs like a shiitake-load of shiitake, some gochujang and mushroom sauce, to make this a more inclusive XO, while we're at it? XOXO like a chef's kiss for flavour (and a nod to another iconic time: the Gossip Girl *years).*

Mushroom XO is perfect for tossing through steamed greens, drizzling on proteins such as silken tofu, fried eggs and omelettes, along with stir-fries and noodle dishes. Try it on the five-spice ET on page 92, or the steamed chicken drummies on page 91.

Soak the mushrooms in 2 cups (500 ml) of just-boiled water for about 20 minutes, until soft enough to squeeze. Use this time to get the rest of the ingredients ready.

Once soft, drain the shrooms, reserving the soaking liquor. Squeeze dry and mince with a sharp knife and a cross-chop motion, or place in a small food processor and whiz into a chunky mince.

Heat the neutral oil in a wide heavy-based frying pan over medium–high heat. Stir in the minced mushrooms and shallot. Cook for 10–12 minutes, stirring often, until the shallot has softened down, then frizzled and turned golden.

Scoop in the minced garlic and ginger and swish about the pan for a few minutes, until the liquid from these evaporates and the fragrance comes through.

Deglaze the pan with the cognac or brandy – or try a flambé, if you dare, by pouring in the booze, then carefully tipping the pan towards the gas flame (if using a gas hob) or using a safety lighter, until the alcohol ignites, standing well away until the flame subsides.

Splash in the soy sauce and mushroom sauce, and stir in the sugar, gochujang and spices. Splash in all of the reserved strained mushroom soaking liquor, along with the vinegar and sesame oil.

Bring to the boil swiftly, then drop the heat down to an enthusiastic burble for 20–25 minutes, until the water-based liquids have mostly evaporated, the consistency is jammy and juicy, and the oil has floated up to the top like a curry.

Tasting for seasoning. Allow to cool, then transfer into sterilised jar/s and cover with a thin layer of oil for longer storage.

Storage + shelf life → Your XO sauce keeps for 3 months in the fridge.

Chilli Crisp Oil

Makes → 2 CUPS (500 ML)

Takes → 30 MINUTES

- 2 cups (500 ml) neutral oil (I like grapeseed, peanut or rice bran here)
- 2 cm (¾ in) thumb of ginger, peeled and grated
- 20 g (¾ oz) Sichuan peppercorns
- 20 g (¾ oz) chilli flakes
- 100 g (3½ oz) crispy fried shallots (shop-bought, or MYO page 225)
- 1 tablespoon grated fresh garlic
- 1–2 spring onions (scallions), finely chopped
- 1–2 star anise
- 1 teaspoon Chinese five-spice
- ¼ cup (60 ml) sesame oil
- 2 tablespoons sesame seeds, toasted
- 1 tablespoon tomato paste (concentrated purée)
- 1–2 tablespoons light soy sauce
- 1 tablespoon black vinegar or rice wine vinegar

Reading through the ingredients, you'll notice I add tomato paste to my chilli oil (pictured on page 218). It may seem wild at first glance, but once you try it with this decidedly inauthentic umami-rich addition, you won't go back. You can add more heat with extra chilli flakes, or even fresh chilli bits. These days, chilli oil goes on just about EVERYTHING (including desserts!) – so, basically, for any dish that could use a kick of heat and umami, this should be by its side. For best effect, make the chilli oil at least the night before.

In a small saucepan, bring the neutral oil and grated ginger to 170°C (350°F). This takes about 10 minutes over low heat; the oil will be shimmering but not smoking.

In a large heatproof bowl, mix together the peppercorns, chilli flakes, fried shallots, garlic, spring onion, star anise, five-spice, sesame oil, sesame seeds and tomato paste. Set a fine-mesh sieve over the top. Being careful of spitting, pour the hot oil over the lot.

Add the soy sauce and vinegar to taste, then leave to infuse and cool for at least half an hour. Once cooled, pull out the star anise and pour into a clean jar.

The longer the oil stands, the more intense the heat and flavour will become.

Storage + shelf life → The oil will keep in the fridge at its best for up to 6 months ... though you'll probably use it up within a few months.

Spring Onion & Ginger Chunky Oil

Makes → ABOUT 3½ CUPS (875 ML)

Takes → 15 MINUTES

- 6 spring onions (scallions), trimmed
- 170 g (6 oz) ginger, peeled
- 2 teaspoons fine sea salt
- 2 teaspoons caster (superfine) sugar
- 2 tablespoons toasted sesame oil
- 2 cups (500 ml) neutral oil

You can use this versatile verdant condiment in so many ways. It's wonderful served with poached chicken or fish, dumplings, noodles, stir-fries, rice and congee, eggs and vegetables. It also makes a great gift and is perfect to pack with you for camping or holiday cooking. Have some on the table for adding to everything – especially dishes like the shiitake chicken drummies on page 91, Jenny Lee's macaroni soup on page 171, and the undone dimmies on page 165.

Slice the spring onions in half lengthways and finely chop, then finely grate the ginger. (If you'd prefer not to faff around with slicing, you could pulse the spring onion and ginger to a mince in your food processor instead!)

Put the spring onion and ginger in a heatproof bowl or jug. Scatter in the salt and sugar, then pour the sesame oil over the top.

In a small saucepan, heat the neutral oil over medium–low heat for about 4 minutes to 180°C (350°F), or until shimmering. (To test the temperature, add some of the frizzle trim of the spring onion to the oil – it should sizzle straight away. Or, pop a wooden chopstick in the oil and watch for bubbles up the sides of the stick.)

Pour the hot oil over the spring onion mix and watch the sizzle.

Leave to cool before decanting into scrupulously clean jars.

Storage + shelf life → The oil will keep in the fridge for up to a month but will lose its colour.

Crispy Fried Shallots

Makes → 2 CUPS (800 G)

Takes → 40 MINUTES + 1 HOUR COOLING

6 shallots (any type will do!), about 250 g (9 oz), to yield 2 cups when sliced
1 teaspoon salt flakes, plus extra to finish
1½ cups (375 ml) neutral oil, for frying

These shallots are like savoury hundreds and thousands, full of caramelised shallot splendour to lift a dreary salad or noodle dish with pops of sweet, salty crunch. Chuck some of these into your chilli crisp oil on page 221, or sprinkle over dishes like the choy-ful omelette on page 102. You can also make a super speedy microwave version by popping the salted shallots and oil in a heatproof bowl and zapping them for 3 minutes, then at 20-second intervals until sufficiently golden.

Peel your shallots, top and tail them, then slice about 5 mm (¼ in) thick against the grain. You don't want the slices paper thin, or they'll burn too quickly. Place in a non-reactive bowl and sprinkle with the salt. Mix about to coat the slices in the salt, then leave to sit for 20 minutes, to help flavour them inside and out, and to draw out moisture so that they fry up extra crispy.

Spread your salted shallots across either a tea towel (dish towel) or paper towel. Lay another tea towel or paper towel over the top and press out the excess moisture (a tea towel works best, if you can spare it).

Put the shallots in a small saucepan, pour in the oil and place over a low heat. Gently cook for 40 minutes, until they're a shade deeper than golden brown but not burnt.

Capturing the oil in a bowl, drain the mixture through a strainer. Label this infused oil and save for dressings or more frying, as it's packed full of flavour.

Line a tray with paper towel, then gently tip the fried shallots over the tray, to help soak up the excess oil. Sprinkle with a pinch more salt and leave to cool for an hour.

Transfer to a clean airtight jar or container.

Storage + shelf life → They'll last for a month or two in the pantry if you're in a cool climate, or in the fridge if it's humid. (If they go a little lank, pop them in the oven next time you're preheating to bring them back to life.)

Yoghurt Flatbreads

Makes → 4

Takes → 30 MINUTES

1 cup (260 g) Greek-style (or natural) yoghurt
1 teaspoon salt flakes (or ¼ teaspoon fine salt)
2 cups (300 g) self-raising flour, plus extra for dusting
2 tablespoons olive oil
1 tablespoon butter, for pan-frying

These soft, chewy flatbreads (pictured on page 84) are perfect for wrapping around veg and proteins like gyros, or for topping with spices and oil and baking for a super quick 'pizza'. This dough is also the basis of my pan pies on page 126, so if you're a small household, it may be worth making only a couple of pan pies and using the rest of the dough for flatbreads. The yoghurt activates the leavening agent in the self-raising flour to give it fun bubbles that trap steam and release the most delish aroma when you bite in.

In a bowl, combine the yoghurt and salt, mixing to dissolve the salt.

Dump in the flour and mix with a wooden spoon until it forms a shaggy mess. Now get your hands in there to form a ball of dough, then turn it out onto a clean, floured surface.

Start kneading for about 5 minutes, pushing the dough away from you, then back over itself. You'll want some extra flour on hand to stop things sticking. The dough's ready when it's smooth and springs back when you pop a finger pad into it.

Sprinkle some flour on a rolling pin (or wine bottle) and your bench. Cut the ball of dough into quarters, then roll out into four 10 cm (4 in) rounds. (You can either roll them all out in one go and keep them under a clean cloth if prepping ahead, or roll each one on the fly as you're starting to fry.)

Warm a pan over medium heat. Add a drizzle of the oil and a teaspoon of butter and wait for it to foam and melt. Pop one flatbread into the pan and cook over medium–low heat for 2–3 minutes on each side. You want a deep golden colour and edges that are creamy white, rather than opaque, which tells you that the dough hasn't fully cooked through yet.

Remove from the pan and cook the remaining flatbreads in the same way. To keep your cooked ones warm, stack them in a tea towel (dish towel) in a warm spot, or put them in an oven set to 80°C (175°F).

Storage + shelf life → The cooked flatbreads will happily sit in the fridge overnight. You might like to splash them with water and reheat in the oven, the toaster, or using a sandwich press.

Riffs → Brush the warm flatbreads with PG paste (page 214) when they come out of the pan.

Infuse the flatbreads with spice – foam some butter or ghee in a pan, sprinkle in some curry leaves or whole spices (cumin seeds would be lovely), then whack the cooked flatbreads on top until fragrant.

Sprinkle the flatbreads with sesame seeds before frying.

Basmati Rice

Makes → 4 CUPS (740 G) COOKED

Takes → 20 MINUTES

1½ cups (300 g) raw basmati rice
3 cups (750 ml) cold water

Basmati (pictured overleaf) is a great grain of choice for those who prefer a lighter, less sticky but still fluffy rice, compared to jasmine or calrose rice (the latter being often used for sticky rice). Basmati rice has a lower glycaemic index than other types of white rice, meaning that it is digested more slowly, so you stay fuller for longer, making basmati the preferred choice among many dietitians. It's also the rice I reach for when making South Asian and Middle Eastern dishes, as the long, fragrant granules soak up rich sauces and sumptuous spices stupendously. If you can, find an 'aged' basmati rice (which you'll find labelled as such), as it offers a richer, more intense flavour and aroma.

In a fine-mesh sieve, rinse the rice under cold running water, agitating until the water runs clear.

Tip the washed rice into your rice cooker or a medium saucepan with a tight-fitting lid. Add the 3 cups (750 ml) cold water and stir. If using a rice cooker, switch it on, put the lid on, then walk away and live your life (see page 9 for why this is one gadget worth investing in).

If using a pan and the absorption method, bring the water to the boil over medium–high heat, stirring occasionally. Once the water boils, turn the heat right down low, put the lid on and cook for 15 minutes, then turn off the heat and leave to rest for 5 minutes more.

Just before serving, fluff the rice with a fork, or deploy your rice paddle if you've used a rice cooker.

Storage + shelf life → Raw rice will keep well for around 2 years if stored in an airtight container free of light and moisture. Cooked rice is best used within the first 24 hours, but ask any grandma and she'll tell you it'll keep in the fridge for 2–3 days. You can also freeze individual portions in small containers or snaplock bags for up to 3 months; these will reheat well in the microwave with a little splash of water to help re-steam the rice.

Riffs → Add a tablespoon of toasted panch phoron (Indian five-spice) or cumin seeds when the water goes in. You can also add a teaspoon of ground turmeric, and/or a handful of curry leaves. (Try the carb-on-carb triumph of the rice and potatoes on page 174!)

Adding some dried fruit such as currants or apricots will turn this into more of a pilaf; you'll find my midweek riff on a pilaf/plov on page 188, and are welcome to chuck some dried fruit in there too.

Stir some ghee and toasted cashews through once the rice is cooked.

Some fresh dill, mint and/or coriander (cilantro) will take you towards the Caucasus and/or Middle East, and you're only a few veg away from a rice salad.

Jasmine Rice

Makes → 4 CUPS (740 G) COOKED

Takes → 20 MINUTES

1½ cups (300 g) raw jasmine rice
2 cups (500ml) cold water
½ teaspoon salt flakes

Popular throughout Asia, jasmine rice is prized for its subtle floral fragrance and slightly sticky texture – perfect for eating with delicately sauced dishes and ingredients. A good rule of thumb is that rice expands threefold, so 1 cup raw rice makes 3 cups cooked rice, and each serve of rice is around 1 cup cooked rice – so 1½ cups rice will typically serve around four people.

Although many people prefer using a knuckle to measure the water quantity to cook their rice with, a more precise water measure will ensure more consistent results with my method below.

Don't forget to use up any leftovers in dishes such as the fried rice on page 184 and omurice on page 64.

In a fine-mesh sieve, rinse the rice under cold running water until the water runs clear, agitating with your fingers to shake off any extra starch.

Tip the washed rice into your rice cooker or a medium saucepan with a tight-fitting lid. Add the salt and 2 cups (500 ml) cold water. If using a rice cooker, switch it on, close the lid and walk away (see page 9 for why this is one gadget worth investing in).

If using a pan and the absorption method, bring the water to the boil over medium–high heat, stirring occasionally. Turn the heat right down low, put the lid on and cook for 15 minutes, then turn off the heat and leave to rest for 5 minutes more.

Just before serving, fluff the rice with a fork, or deploy your rice paddle if you've used a rice cooker.

Storage + shelf life → Raw rice will keep well for around 2 years if stored in an airtight container free of light and moisture. Cooked rice is best used within the first 24 hours, but ask any grandma and she'll tell you it'll keep in the fridge for 2–3 days. You can also freeze individual portions in small containers or snaplock bags for up to 3 months; these will reheat well in the microwave with a little splash of water to help re-steam the rice.

Riffs → Pop some fresh pandan leaves in with the water and salt. Some fried garlic or crispy fried shallots (page 225) can go in at this point, too – delish.

Use a teaspoon of stock powder instead of the salt.

Check out page 192 for the sunshine rice method. Or indulge in simple pleasures with the soy butter rice on page 30.

Fry off some aromatics, such as finely minced ginger, spring onion (scallion) or a tablespoon or so of curry paste in oil, then add to the washed and drained rice before cooking.

A tablespoon of chilli crisp oil (page 221) through the rice is a kicker too – either as it's cooking or drizzled on top. You could use the chunky spring onion oil from page 222 here too.

Sprinkle over some rice seasoning, or even just some butter.

Amp up the veg by adding ½ cup mixed frozen peas, corn and carrot when cooking the rice.

Basmati rice → page 227

Jasmine rice

Thank you

First and foremost, thank YOU for giving this book enough of your attention to get to the bit I love to read (and write!?) the most: the acknowledgements! And thank you also for continuing to pick up what I put down! We're five books in together already, and I've no intention of slowing down. Thanks, especially, to all of my wonderfully responsive listeners, viewers and readers, whose emails and DMs inspire so many of the tips and tricks I know to include, along with the general direction of the recipes and vegspo that keep you happiest.

I'm able to commit my time to cooking, writing, talking and responding to your excellent questions because of the tireless work of my husband, Nick, who keeps our weekdays, weeknights and weekends wonderful! That's why this book is dedicated to him. We all cook on weeknights: me, him, my parents, The Nut ... I even receive weeknight updates from my brother and his family. It's our love language: when we can't feed each other, we fill each other's camera feeds with food. For that, I'm forever thankful.

To my publishing family at Murdoch Books – what a time! To Jane Morrow, who continues to believe in me and keep my creative wheels turning. Thanks to the broader *Weeknights* team: editorial manager Loran McDougall, design manager Sarah Odgers, designer Susan Le, editor Katri Hilden, indexer Helena Holmgren and proofreader Ariana Klepac, to the sales team (lookin' at you, Matt Hoy!) and to the publicity powerhouses Sarah Hatton and Lorraine Woodcheke. Globally, to the teams across my international publishing houses, I thank you in advance for taking this little Aussie book on a journey in your country.

I'm super grateful to our shoot squad: photographer Rochelle Eagle, stylist Kirsten Jenkins, videographer Wes Mitton, home eco Christine Knight, and photo chefs Lisa Parker and Michelle Geddes, who were also invaluable in the telly kitchens. To my right-hander, Jane 'Grylltown' Grylls and left-hander Madeleine 'Dobby' Dobbins, I love being on this crazy ride with you both – red dirt, red carpet all the way.

To my peers, to my pals, to the people who raise me up, to my people and my ancestors. To Pickles past and present. I am grateful every day.

Index

A

B

C

D

E

F

G

H

I

J

N

O

P

Q

R

S

T

Published in 2026 by Murdoch Books,
an imprint of Allen & Unwin

Murdoch Books Australia
Cammeraygal Country
83 Alexander Street
Crows Nest NSW 2065
Phone: +61 (0)2 8425 0100
murdochbooks.com.au
info@murdochbooks.com.au

Murdoch Books UK
Ormond House
26–27 Boswell Street
London WC1N 3JZ
Phone: +44 (0) 20 8785 5995
murdochbooks.co.uk
info@murdochbooks.co.uk

For corporate orders and custom publishing,
contact our business development team
at salesenquiries@murdochbooks.com.au

Publisher: Jane Morrow
Editorial manager: Loran McDougall
Design manager: Sarah Odgers
Designer: Susan Le
Editor: Katri Hilden
Photographer: Rochelle Eagle
Stylist: Kirsten Jenkins
Photo chefs: Lisa Parker, Michelle Geddes
Home economists: Jane Grylls, Madeleine Dobbins,
Christine Knight
Production manager: Natalie Crouch

Alice Zaslavsky and Murdoch Books acknowledge the Traditional Owners of the Country on which we live and work. We pay our respects to all Aboriginal and Torres Strait Islander Elders, past and present.

Our authorised representative in the EU for product safety is Easy Access System Europe, Mustamäe tee 50, 10621 Tallinn, Estonia, gpsr.requests@easproject.com

ISBN 978 1 76150 142 5

NATIONAL LIBRARY OF AUSTRALIA
A catalogue record for this book is available from the National Library of Australia

A catalogue record for this book is available from the British Library

Colour reproduction by Megan Ellis

Printed in China by 1010 Printing International Limited

Oven Guide → You may find cooking times vary depending on the oven and oven setting you are using. These recipes have been tested using fan-forced ovens. For conventional ovens, as a general rule, set the oven temperature to 20°C (25–50°F) higher than indicated in the recipe.

Tablespoon Measures → We have used 20 ml (4 teaspoon) tablespoon measures. If you are using a 15 ml (3 teaspoon) tablespoon add an extra teaspoon of the ingredient for each tablespoon specified.

10 9 8 7 6 5 4 3 2 1

FSC www.fsc.org MIX Paper | Supporting responsible forestry FSC® C016973